Yasmin Hai has been .... producer/director working for the BBC's N............... her awar................ inning programmes. She lives in North London with her husband and two children.

Praise for *The Making of Mr Hai's Daughter*

'Searing. funny, both demuring of ourselves and uplifting . . . d........... What a remarkable and telling totem of transition . . . Yasmi............ nt a time as no one else has . . . utterly beautiful and extraordinarily informing' Jon Snow

'Her story perfectly catches some of the small, daily dilemmas of an immigrant's life . . . The book is a gem, from a Briton who needs no lessons on Britishness' *Mail on Sunday*

'Had Mr Hai succeeded in turning his daughter into an Englishwoman? I'm not sure it really matters any more, but his kindly influence obviously enabled his little Yasmin to write this unbelievably funny, passionate autobiography' *Spectator*

'A thoughtful, funny memoir on the realities of immigration' *Guardian*

'This is a witty, charming book about being British . . . A very personal story filled with family tales, social history and politics, and making an important contribution to the debate about life in modern multicultural Britain' *Waterstone's Books Quarterly*

'Affectionate, sometimes sad . . . but always funny portrait of growing up in Wembley convinces me that it is entirely possible to be Muslim and British. It is a book I cannot recommend too strongly. Since hers is a tale told with such sharp observation and good humour . . . I found I could take it all in as though somebody had served me a plate of *gulab jamun* . . . Just as Ayub Khan-Din gave us an insight into 1970s Salford in *East is East* . . . so also Yasmin has, equally deftly, offered a sympathetic account of what it was like for a young Muslim girl to grow up in 1980s Britain. Her best quality is her light touch' *Eastern Eye*

Withdrawn

THE MAKING OF MR. HAI'S DAUGHTER

YASMIN HAI

virago

VIRAGO

First published in Great Britain in 2008 by Virago Press
This paperback edition published in 2009 by Virago Press

Copyright © Yasmin Hai 2008

The moral right of the author has been asserted.

A CIP catalogue record for this book
is available from the British Library.

ISBN 978-1-84408-270-4

Typeset in Perpetua by M Rules
Printed and bound in Great Britain by
Clays Ltd, St Ives plc

Papers used by Virago are natural, renewable and recyclable
products sourced from well-managed forests and certified
in accordance with the rules of the Forest Stewardship Council.

Mixed Sources
Product group from well-managed
forests and other controlled sources
www.fsc.org Cert no. SGS-COC-004081
© 1996 Forest Stewardship Council
FSC

Virago Press
An imprint of
Little, Brown Book Group
100 Victoria Embankment
London EC4Y 0DY

An Hachette UK Company
www.hachette.co.uk

www.virago.co.uk

To my father and Paul

THE MAKING OF MR. HAI'S DAUGHTER

Contents

PART TWO

Acknowledgements

I am enormously fortunate to have lived alongside and crossed paths with people who have not only been the inspiration for writing this book, but have enriched my life with colour, drama and humanity. I thank you for allowing me into your lives.

I also give thanks to my sister Farah Lavin, the Bhajis (they know who they are), Nadera Latif-Shaikh, Sohel Shaikh, Naomi Cole and Finn McGough for revisiting the past with me and helping to rouse memory. Similarly to my mother, Noorjehan Hai, who – aside from having been a constant source of strength throughout my life – supplied me with endless 'culues' on stories I should pursue. She is a natural story-teller in her own right.

I am also indebted to Ian Katz for critical advice in the early stages of writing this book. And, of course, to my agent, Pat Kavanagh, whose wise counsel and support have been invaluable.

My thanks to the wonderful team at Virago who expertly turned my manuscript into a book – in particular, I couldn't have done it without my editor, the indomitable Lennie Goodings, whose gentle yet steely guidance was vital in helping me unravel years of memory.

To Nico and Allia for sharing me with the book in the first few years of their precious lives.

But, most of all, I am indebted to my husband, Paul. Not only have you been a constant source of encouragement, support and inspiration. Not only has your intellect, passion and rigorous attention to detail ensured that no lazy thinking or writing wormed its way into this book – but you gave me courage to voice my story. For that I am truly grateful.

Author's Note

Out of consideration for the privacy of the people in my past, I have changed names and completely disguised identities. No one, other than my family and university friends, have their real names. But every story I tell is based on first-hand experience or rooted in testimonies related to me by witnesses. Every event I write about happened.

Our parents might have ordered us not to leave the house, but we still found a way to sneak out. Giggling, we scrambled through the kitchen window, clambered over the garden fence and into the side alley. With the racket we were making, our mother soon appeared at the window. Battling through huge swathes of white net curtains, which kept on getting caught in her sari, she shouted at us to come back. And did we listen? Well, usually we would have, but not today – today was different.

Dressed in our best tracksuit outfits and each clutching our new Kevin Keegan 10p scrapbook, we had no time to waste. We were on a mission. As we turned into our road from the alleyway, a quiet buzzing sound drifted over us. We knew we were on our way.

We ran and ran, serenaded by bursts of excited TV commentary wafting out of the houses on our road. When we turned the last bend, the full spectacle, what we had been waiting months to see, finally revealed itself.

Our mouths dropped in awe. We didn't know the word then, but now we knew the feeling. A sea of coloured banners, waves of red and white crashing into shores of blue and white, was rolling off the motorway, driving right past us. Yes, right past us.

The noise was deafening, a cacophony of car horns, drumbeats and sirens; men whistling, chanting, shouting . . . it was like Disneyland (not that we had ever been there) and the Queen's Silver Jubilee celebrations all rolled into one. Except this ecstatic parade was making its way to Wembley Stadium.

Wembley, the great Wembley. That's where we lived. Well, not in the stadium, but near it. Really near it.

'ARRRRRSSSSSENAL!' a spotty faced guy with long side-burns suddenly cried out drunkenly at us from his car, as his friend exposed his big hairy bottom from the window.

'Did you see that – did you see it?' my brother cried. Of course we had, it was the rudest thing we had ever seen.

On those big days, the big world came to us. They came from all over England – mysterious faraway places with strange names like Huddersfield, Liverpool, Sheffield and Cardiff City – to celebrate their team. It looked like really good fun to belong and care for something, even if it was just a football team.

But that was as far as it went. My brother, my sister and I watching from the corner of our road, as the parade made its way – right past us – in the direction of the great Wembley Stadium. Never for one minute did we dream of joining in any further, for we knew it wasn't our party to join. Football was an English people's game. And we were not English.

Part One

1

Operation Immigrant

We were sitting in the dark, courtesy of a power cut, thanks to another standoff between Prime Minister Callaghan and the trade unions. To distract us, our father was telling us one of his stories. Not any old story, but a real story of his past in Pakistan, something that he rarely spoke to us about, unless it was in jest.

Maybe he was finding it easier to talk in the dark. His face did look more animated than usual. But that could have been the flickers from the candlelight, which danced about on his face and gave his eyes a hypnotic energy. The three of us – tucked up under a blanket on our living room sofa – were mesmerised. While the rest of young Wembley sat in the dark, twiddling their thumbs, we were getting to hear real-life action stories with our father starring as the hero.

My father told us how, disguised as a Sindhi peasant, he had been forced to go underground. I wanted to ask him what a Sindhi peasant was, because it sounded like quite a clever disguise, but my father had already moved on to the next dramatic stage in the story. The Pakistani Secret Service had finally discovered his secret hideout and now – dead in the middle of the night – they had come looking for him.

Bang, bang, bang! My father thudded his fist on the coffee table to demonstrate the police's loud knocking. We shrieked. My mother grunted. She hated it when my father told us these stories, in case it gave us ideas. Well, what was wrong with that? My father had been a real-life hero, back in Pakistan. Uncle Aslam once described him as being a 'Stalinist revolutionary', which sounded equally impressive to me, especially once I found out that a 'revolutionary' was someone who fought on behalf of poor workers. But the Pakistani government obviously didn't agree. They wanted people like my father out, which is why they were now knocking on his door.

'But where was Ahmed?' I cried.

My father leant back, disappearing into the shadows.

'Where was Ahmed?' I heard my father repeat slowly to himself.

Ahmed was the nice medical student who had been given the job of go-between between my father and 'the network'. Every day for nearly six months he had loyally brought my father food and the latest news of the struggle. To show his gratitude, my father had happily shared his reflections on subjects ranging from labour rights in rural Bengal to voting patterns in Britain. Ahmed always listened intently and sometimes even took notes.

'It was Ahmed who betrayed me,' my father whispered through the dark. 'You couldn't trust anyone. He was a spy all along.'

'A spy?' all three of us cried out.

'Like the Russians in James Bond?' my sister asked.

My father didn't answer.

'Mr Hai!' my mother called out. That is what my mother called my father in front of us. Maybe that is what she called him in private, too.

'And when I wouldn't answer the door,' my father continued, his voice suddenly losing all caution, 'they started breaking it down. Bam, bam, bam! They were shouting: "Come out, Mr Hai, come out!"'

'What did you do?' my brother cried in alarm, as if the troops were outside our own door.

Annoyingly, the street lamps outside began to flicker. Orange–silver–orange–silver, throwing erratic light on the terraced houses across the road. I hoped they wouldn't come on until my father finished, because I so wanted to hear the end while we were still in the dark. I knew it wouldn't be the same in the light.

'What happened, Dad?' I begged. 'Tell us, quick.'

My father leaned forward. I could see he was grinning, enjoying the effect he was having on us. 'Well, as they tried to break in, I went to the kitchen, opened the window . . .' My father played out the action, his raised arms throwing long, frightening shadows onto the wall. 'Opened it wide and then I shouted out, "Long live the Revolution!" And then . . .'

'You escaped,' I cut in.

'No,' my father said quietly, his voice trailing off. My heart sank. I crossed my fingers, willing him not to turn this story into one of his jokes. Why did he always do that about his past? But it was too late – for he was already starting to chuckle.

'No, I didn't escape. Guess what I did?' his laugh ringing between his words. 'I hid under the bed. Isn't that funny?'

We forced out a laugh, but then went silent.

'Mr Hai, *ek aur dafa bolyai* [explain again],' came my mother's exasperated voice through the dark.

'Don't you understand?' my father said, his voice more playful this time round. 'I hid under the bed, so when they came in and saw the window open, they thought I had escaped – and went out to look for me. The silly fools didn't even search under the bed.'

This time we did laugh. The ending sounded plausible. Our father had often told us how stupid the Pakistani Secret Service was.

'And when they left, I made a quick getaway. The End.'

We giggled and clapped enthusiastically. It confirmed to us – once and for all – that our father was a real-life James Bond. Well, a Pakistani version of him anyway.

'You don't know how lucky you are to have me here today. Because, I tell you, if they had caught me that night . . .'

I flinched. I didn't want to hear this. My mother quickly recited a prayer.

'So, will you ever go back?' I asked, changing the subject and lowering my voice to suit my father's anticipated reply. I already knew the answer, but I still liked to hear my father say it over and over again.

'No – that is all behind me,' I heard my father reply. 'Our life is here now.'

My father, Syed Samsamul Hai, arrived in London in 1964. I think it must have been hard for him, as he was soon to be hitting his fifties – a bit late, really, to be starting up a new life. But he was travelling light. He wasn't married and didn't have any children yet.

I would have thought that giving up such an illustrious and dangerous political career back home for a mundane life in cold and damp England would have been upsetting. And though, for the sake of a good story, my father liked to pretend to us that that was the case, it wasn't true. He was very happy to come here. Very happy indeed.

While the likes of our neighbour, Mrs Campbell, always

moaned about England going down the drain – pointing out people such as us to her friends, people like my parents never lost their excitement when talking about British citizenship. Being Commonwealth citizens, many immigrants like my parents had grown up with an incredibly romantic idea of what England was all about.

There are a few facts about my now deceased father's past that I have gleaned over the years. I know that his childhood was pretty miserable and that he was brought up in a mosque orphanage.

But how can that be? Wasn't I always told that my father's family was one of the richest in all of India? Ah yes, once upon a time. That is until the elders squandered all their money on dancing girls. Prostitutes!

'Mum, how can you lose all your money like that?' I ask her sceptically. To my commonsense English head, it sounds too silly for words. My mother does not know the answer either. It's just the story she's always been told.

'His life was hard,' she says, veering back to the facts. 'No welfare state like here.'

My father did the only thing he could: study.

'Under street night lamps,' my mother adds.

My father studied so hard that he eventually won a scholarship to the prestigious Aligarh University in Uttar Pradesh. The college was established in 1875 and was the first of its kind to offer Western-inspired education to Muslims without compromising on Islamic ideals. The founder, Sir Syed Ahmad Khan, believed that if Muslims were to preserve their political and social clout under British rule, then they must become proficient in English and Western ways. He elaborated a set of strict rules fundamental to his vision for the college. They included:

All students shall be required to put on a pair of socks
  and shoes of Western style.
It will be mandatory on boys in residence to join the
  congregational prayers (*namaz*) at all the five times.
They will have food either on tables of European style or
  on *chaukis* in the manner of the Arabs. This will be
  decided by the students themselves, by a majority of
  votes.
Bad and abusive words which boys generally pick up . . .
  will be strictly prohibited. Even such a word as 'liar.'

My father and his radical friends came to believe that only
through Communism could the Indian people truly free themselves from both the shackles of the British Empire and the
dark forces of religion, poverty and feudalism. In his view,
Communism allowed them to be modern as well as fervently
anti-Imperialist.

My father became so committed to the cause of the Left that,
during the tumultuous years leading up to partition in 1947,
along with other stalwarts of the Communist Party of India,
he moved to the other side of the subcontinent – Pakistan.
Opposed to the concept of a Muslim nation, they optimistically
believed the place was ripe for revolution.

In Pakistan, my father became Professor of English at the
prestigious S. M. Law College in Karachi, while continuing to
agitate for the revolution. In the early fifties he was appointed
Chairman of the Pakistan Peace Committee, and was summoned
to China for talks with Mao Tse Tung and Chou En-lai.

But the Communist Party of India was banned in 1954 and
some of my father's peers were imprisoned, others tortured or
murdered. My father managed to go underground, but being
forced to live in hiding for years took its toll on him. He decided

to escape to England and arrived here courtesy of an immigration policy fuelled by a British labour shortage.

Flicking through an album of his photos – snapshots of a lost world – I can feel his excitement about finally being in London, England.

Here is my father casually leaning against a railing. He's positioned himself so that right behind him Buckingham Palace can be seen in its full splendour. My father is wearing a dapper cream suit, which shimmers in the bright summer light. He looks the picture of a model English gentleman. Or is it more like the picture of a foreigner playing at being English – dressing more English than the English? A pen casually juts out of my father's left breast pocket, a signal to the world that he is also a man of books.

The life of sixties London spins on around him. Schoolboys dart across the road, a woman dressed in an Audrey Hepburn-style floral frock swishes by and blurred faces peer curiously out of an Austin Minor in the direction of the brown-faced man leaning against the railing. But none of this distracts Syed Samsamul Hai. He looks content, a man at ease with the world around him.

Here he is again. This time he is with his friend, the man we called Uncle Aslam, in Trafalgar Square. Nelson's Column shoots up out of their heads. They are both wearing woollen overcoats with black trilby hats perched on their heads, smiling in that grey winter world.

Mr Hai is now British.

My father's first home in England was just off the Holloway Road in north London, not the most salubrious of locations. The house, with its Victorian façade, must have looked very grand from the outside, but it wasn't really.

11

I know the Holloway house with its musty, dark hallway and a solitary, naked lightbulb dangling from a fraying wire, because when I was eight years old, my father took me to see the place. Faded and poor as it was, he was proud to show it off. 'My first English home,' he said nostalgically, raising his arms as if to embrace it. But I didn't like the house on Holloway Road and felt terribly sorry that my father had been forced to live there.

The rooms had been partitioned off into much smaller units to create tiny bedsits. Some didn't even have windows. Each room had a gas stove and sink. And there was a shared bathroom on each landing. His landlord was a Polish refugee who knew what newly arrived immigrants would accept when they first came to live in England: very little, because they knew no better.

But my father and his friends, Asian men like himself – some from India's elite class – seemed to settle in well, despite their impoverished conditions. My father knew some of the men from back home. But others were friends of friends who had connected up with each other through contacts back in India.

There was Dr Hasan, retraining to be an eye surgeon. Mr Ali, a leading Bengali journalist and comrade in the struggle. Dr Patel, a heart specialist, whose family was somehow related to Mr Ali's. Mr Shyam Sidiqui, a trainee accountant from Pakistan. And, finally, there was an honorary visitor, the very senior Uncle Aslam, an ex-colleague of my father from back home. My father felt relieved that he had found such congenial company in England.

My father's Holloway friends were all Muslim. I once mentioned this to him when he was telling us stories about his early years here. Instead of commending me on my astute observation – I was just seven years old – my father instantly rejected it. He reeled off a list of the Hindu and Sikh friends he had back in

India and Pakistan. 'All Socialists,' he added. Politics first, religion second.

While my father and his Holloway friends might have passed the time reciting the works of Urdu poets to each other or talking about the great Islamic accomplishments of the past, when it came to practising Islam, the consensus was that religion should be kept a private matter. And more so because they were now living in England.

As far as my father and many of his peers were concerned, Indians had allowed themselves to be colonised in the first place because they had clung onto old, regressive ideas. This kept them weak. Well, this should never be allowed to happen again. Indians must modernise; Indians must become progressive. Wasn't that what the English were like? My father often recounted cheeky stories to us, to show off his secular modern politics.

This ideology was immediately tested when, a few days after his arrival from Pakistan, Dr Hasan sheepishly disclosed that one of his favourite English pastimes was popping out to the Local for, 'a . . . umm, yes . . . a drink'.

My father, realising that he was being asked to comment on an activity that would seriously test how 'modern', how 'English' and how 'progressive' he was, just laughed Dr Hasan off, saying, 'What's the problem? Of course a Muslim can have a drink.'

Apparently Dr Hasan was terribly relieved. But then, as my father would later tell me, religious edicts were just another one of those historical constraints that had kept men like them weak.

The best role model of all was Uncle Aslam. For a start, Uncle Aslam did not live in the Holloway house but in 'fancy' Hampstead with his wife. Secondly, having been in his past life a distinguished professor, renowned writer, plus an Indian diplomat in the Soviet Union during the Stalinist period, here in England Uncle Aslam was teaching science at one of the London universities. He wasn't a professor as before but, unlike almost every other Indian man who came here, he had not had to make huge professional compromises.

But there was something else that made Uncle Aslam the most special of all the men in the group: his new wife was an Englishwoman, Hilda Hulme. Aunt Hilda, like Uncle Aslam, was in her mid-fifties. Perhaps, before she got married to Uncle Aslam, she had resigned herself to living out life on her own, for in my father's photos she always looks rather uncomfortable around company. Her head is always tilted down, her watery blue eyes never quite meeting the camera lens. But still my father and friends gaze at her — or more precisely, at the top of her head — with respectful admiration.

Aunt Hilda wasn't an ordinary Englishwoman, like the kind you saw at the Local. Aunt Hilda was highly educated, with a Ph.D. in English. Apart from being a lecturer at London University, she was also one of England's leading authorities on Shakespeare, her most famous work being *Explorations in Shakespeare's English: Some problems of the lexical meaning in the dramatic text*, published in 1962.

Whenever Aunt Hilda visited the Holloway house — which, to be truthful, wasn't often — my father and friends would go to great lengths to make her feel welcome and treat her like the revered academic that she was. My father would tell us how they would rearrange the living room so that Aunt Hilda could sit on the comfortable chair by the window. How they would go and buy up all the English cakes and pastries they could find. And, most considerately of all, how they would bring down all their best books from their rooms and place them on the coffee table, so that Aunt Hilda could browse through them if she grew

14

bored with their conversation. Of course all this fuss probably embarrassed Aunt Hilda, but she was prepared to put up with it all to keep Uncle Aslam happy. For she adored him.

And my father and his friends had another reason to look forward to Aunt Hilda's visits. For them it was a great opportunity to find out, straight from an actual English person, what being English was all about. This was something that was starting to confuse them. For while becoming British, vis-à-vis a passport, had been relatively easy, becoming English was proving to be much harder.

Like many newly arrived foreigners, my father came to England loaded with English facts and figures to help him adjust to his new country. He knew all the words of the English national anthem, he could reel off all the English national holidays (and give the historical reasons as to why they came about) and, more importantly, he knew, inside out and back to front, English sayings such as 'fair play' or 'an Englishman's home is his castle'.

'Oi, give it a rest, you stupid Paki!' a small weaselly man from the next table at the Local had shouted once, having overheard my father drop some of his phrases into conversation with Mr Ali.

'YEEEEEssssSpppppppeeeeeaaaaaaakkkkk English!' his friend imitated, this time going right up to Mr Ali and spitting the words into his face. Neither my father nor Mr Ali knew what to say or do. They were gobsmacked. (Another word my father would learn later on.)

'Fools,' Aunt Hilda had remarked when she heard the story. 'Working-class yobs. Plenty of them around, Mr Hai. I tell Aslam that all the time.'

Apparently, Aunt Hilda's comments on the matter had been a revelation to them all. Until then, they hadn't realised that the men, in fact all of those people at the Local, weren't necessarily genteel Englishmen. They were your average working-class men, a type they knew well from home. The different context of England had prevented them from seeing that.

My father and his friends laughed heartily. They felt relieved. It felt good to make sense of the incident. To discover that it was not your fault, but the fault of ignorance and cultural misunderstanding.

Later on, once Aunt Hilda had gone, my father and his friends would discuss the whole matter again, and whenever my father recounted the story to me in later years, his conclusion rarely put him and his friends in a positive light. Maybe they were feeling guilty for betraying the international working classes or maybe it was because their immigrant complexes had begun to kick in.

Yes, he would say, there were some ignoramuses out there. But perhaps he and his friends had also been to blame for the incident at the Local. After all, what did they really know about the art of English small talk and banter? Did they know who Mick Jagger was until Aunt Hilda mentioned him? No. And who at the time had realised that the mince pies they had offered Aunt Hilda were not a savoury dish but a sweet cake? No one. My father and his friends concluded that it was up to them to try harder to fit in.

Life in those early days couldn't have been easy; trudging around the cold, wet streets looking for work made all the more demoralising after being told that your professional qualifications from back home counted for so little. Suddenly evening courses have to be signed up for to improve your employment chances, menial jobs have to be accepted to fund your dreams and money has to be borrowed to keep afloat. And still the English turn their noses up at you and metaphorically shove 'No Wogs' signs in your face.

16

The grim Holloway house became a sanctuary for my father and his friends. 'Home away from home,' they'd say, rolling out another one of their glib English sayings. In Holloway they could talk and laugh away the problems they had encountered during the day. One of them might even attempt to cook some Indian food, though this did prove to be challenging, given the lack of spices in the local shops. They could be themselves – Indian. How ironic that they felt more Indian in England than they had ever felt back home.

My father would often tell us how he and his friends would huddle together in one of their cramped rooms and, sipping endless cups of sweet tea, talk the night away – half in Urdu, half in English – about the most urgent political and social issues of the day. I can just imagine how their conversations might have unravelled. All from the perspective of the Left, of course.

'Mr Hai, what do you think, will [Zulfikar Ali] Bhutto last?'

'Mr Ali, he's our only chance. You'll see, the working classes will rally right behind him.'

My father was still holding out for a Socialist revolution in Pakistan, even though he must have worked out by now that there were no working classes to mobilise – plenty of peasants, but no working classes. A bit tricky, given Marx's top ten rules for revolution. But still he lived in hope.

'Mr Hai, you idealise them far too much. There is only one thing they care about and that is . . .' Mr Ali rolled up his M&S 65 per cent woollen pullover and patted his rather immense stomach, 'this.'

The others laughed.

Occasionally there were lighter issues up for discussion in the Holloway household. After all, this was the sixties. When the hippy trail wound its way to India in the wake of the Beatles and other pop groups, my father and his friends did not know

17

whether to be flattered, repelled or just plain bemused by the fad that seemed to be gripping England. In the end they settled on bemusement.

'It must be something to do with being young,' Mr Ali reckoned.

When Shyam, the youngest, nodded, the others decided to agree too.

But years of the same conversations with the same people night after night was enough to tire out even the great debaters. Attention in the Holloway house began to turn to less worldly matters – women.

2

Operation Wife

It was Mr Ali and Dr Hasan who were responsible for bringing women into the men's lives. Their recent arranged marriages had brought them wives from Pakistan and Bangladesh respectively.

Each would have arrived wearing her finest clothes to impress her husband and to kindle desire. The other men would affectionately tease her, play at being brothers, to make her feel at home. Her husband would sit by – protective and proud. She would hold her head low, feeling terribly shy. It would feel like her wedding day all over again. And before long she, too, would grow to love the Holloway house, a haven from the alien outside world.

I'm not sure why my father hadn't married before, given how prized marriage is in the Asian culture. But as he often said to us, with enduring bitterness, 'The Pakistani government stole my best years.'

Many years later, Mr Ali told me that it was he who brought the subject of marriage up with my father.

'What kind of life is this?' he had said to my father, who was about to turn fifty. 'This living on your own. No one to talk to, no one to cook for you . . .'

The arrival of Mrs Hasan had revolutionised the Holloway diet beyond recognition. Where she managed to find all the spices no one knew, but every day (and no one ever asked her to) Mrs Hasan would conjure up unimaginable treats for them to eat. One day *biryani*, another day *aloo buri roti* and one day even *shish kebabs*. Proper Indian food. All this made marriage look even more attractive to my father.

'And, Mr Hai, think about this,' Uncle Ali had resumed. Mr Ali wasn't related to us but in Asian culture any man is called an uncle and any woman, an aunt. 'Do you want to die on your own with no family, like the English?'

Maybe, my father concluded, it was time to move onto the next stage of his life, especially now that he had found a decent paying job as a schoolteacher at a Roman Catholic comprehensive in Hackney.

'English wife or Indian wife?' Uncle Ali had asked him.

'English wife?' I cried out to my uncle when I heard this. How had that been an option?

And I guess it never was, because my father had replied, '*Apne*, one of ours.'

As Mr Ali was about to return to Pakistan, he was more than happy to put out the word: Mr Hai was finally looking for a bride. Were there any specific qualities he was looking for in his new bride?

'She has to be able to speak English because she will have to live here and . . .' My father had stopped, trying to envisage what other qualities his perfect future wife should possess. 'And, well, she has to love politics,' he finally said, looking up at Mr Ali, 'otherwise, what will we talk about?'

Mr Ali had agreed.

So off he went to Pakistan to see if anyone suitable could be found for my father. And eventually – after a long line of whispers between eager in-laws and matchmakers, along with some mullahs and merchants – my mother, Noorjehan Begum, was found. She sounded ideal: a young woman, twenty years my father's junior, with an MA in political science from Karachi University.

Now, as far as my mother is concerned, one can never be too careful with personal information. 'The world is full of bad people,' she often tells me. But there are a few facts she grudgingly allows me to have. She was born in Bihar, India on 31 December 1941. I am not convinced that is her correct birthday, as such events were rarely recorded back then. But my mother, ever fearful that any inaccuracies in our paperwork might still mean an instant one-way ticket back to Pakistan, insists it is true. My mother's father was once a successful tradesman, but he lost his business when India was partitioned in 1947 and the family decided to move to Pakistan, settling in Karachi.

Her father soon established himself in the perfume trade. They were relatively well off and my mother led a pretty conventional middle-class life. Translation: dull and uneventful. Yes, she was educated to university level, but that's what was expected of girls from her background. The rest of her time, it seems, was spent at home honing her domestic skills.

'We were told: learn how to cook and clean or our mothers-in-law will throw us out of house,' my mother tells me, still shivering at the thought.

'That's nice!' I reply, sarcastically. 'So what else, Mum? What was life like before you got married?'

'OK. We stayed at home. Not like you, with all your freedom.'

My mother was told that she was marrying my father only a couple of weeks before her wedding.

'Wow, how did you feel?'

'Nothing.'

'But you must have felt something,' I say to her. 'I mean, didn't you wonder what kind of man you were marrying? And what about the fact that you would be moving to London, the first one from your family to travel abroad?'

'I felt nothing,' my mother replies. 'We don't ask questions.'

Despite having no opinion on her own marriage, the match to my father was considered by everyone else to be ideal. And so in the summer of 1969, my father, now a British citizen and no longer fearful of the Pakistani authorities, took three weeks leave from work and travelled to Karachi to marry my mother. Two days later, he was back in London.

My mother arrived at Heathrow Airport, Terminal Three, in the cold winter of 1969.

'Mum, what was that like?' I ask, as she rinses lentil grains under the tap.

'Cold.'

'Yes, I know that, but what else?'

'Well, nothing.'

I prompt her. 'Mum, think. I can't write that. Tell me: how did you feel when you came here? You'd never been out of Karachi, had you? So it must have been a shock. Right?'

'I just came here.'

'Come on, Mum – what else, is that it?'

'Really, what silly questions you have. Just like your father. Now out of my way, I have to finish cooking.'

And that's all my mother has to offer on the subject. She has no time for musings on the past.

But there was one problem with the match. Or more like two – each discovered only after the marriage.

1. My mother had little command of proper English.
2. Despite having an MA in political science, she had very little interest in politics. As my father would later discover, much to his horror, the examined life held no attraction for my mother. Intellectual inquiry or cerebral discussions of any sort only bored her. No, the only thing that mattered to her was the practical. In fact, her whole purpose in life would turn out to be the family, a cause she would devote herself to with her signature no-nonsense pragmatism.

Was my father disappointed?

My mother turns away from the sink and looks at me as if I am insane. 'Why should he have been?' she says, furrowing her eyebrows.

I pause, unsure on how to proceed on this rather sensitive matter. 'Umm, because didn't Dad say he, umm, wanted a wife who liked politics . . . and umm, you weren't exactly interested in that?'

At this point, my mother's face softens as she recollects my father's efforts to engage her in the bitter struggles that had torn the Soviet-led union of international Communism.

'Your poor dad,' she giggles. 'Oh, how he tried to teach me . . .'

But my mother was right; he wasn't disappointed. No, after years of leading a 'bachelor' life, he often told me how life took on a new purpose once my mother arrived. I think he felt inspired again. Recharged, even. And more so because, now that there was no longer a political mission in Pakistan to distract

23

him, he could embark on his next project. A radical project to make my mother English. Operation Wife.

My mother says she had hardly recovered from jet lag, homesickness and disorientation when my father's crash course began. Desperate to be a good wife and never one to question male authority, my mother would prove to be a very good pupil, as evidenced by what my father often referred to as the Scarf Incident, infamous in the Hai family mythology.

My mother always wanted to look her best. For these were the honeymoon days, that special time when – according to Asian wedding custom – husband and wife start to bond. Being an attractive woman, not much effort would have been required. Though she felt herself to be a bit on the dark side, her big eyes made up for it.

When my father told me this story he said it was because Mrs Hai's scarves had been annoying him ever since she had arrived. Being the modern man he was, they must have mocked everything he stood for. Maybe he thought my mother would do away with them once she met Aunt Hilda and saw how other Englishwomen walked around with their heads uncovered.

But that's not what happened. My mother kept wearing the scarves.

After much reflection, my father thought he had come up with the reason why. His wife didn't dare take her scarf off in front of him because she thought he was a traditional Indian man who would disapprove of such bold behaviour. Mr Hai laughed to himself. How sweet she was. But it was time for Operation Wife to commence.

'Sit down,' he said, patting the bed. It was the only place to sit in their room – well, that is if you didn't count the chair with the broken back. Mrs Hai promptly sat down.

'Wasn't it Ataturk who said that scarves were a sign of ignorance?' said Mr Hai.

Mrs Hai nodded, sensing that she had just been asked a rhetorical question. But, in truth, she had no idea exactly what she was nodding about. This was because Mr Hai was speaking in English and using all those big political words that she never understood.

She was still trying to work it out when Mr Hai suddenly rose to his feet and gathered up her scarves and the black burqua that she had travelled from Pakistan in. 'There is only one place for these,' he said.

And to her horror, Mr Hai – her husband in sickness and health – marched over to the fireplace and threw all her scarves in. Little would she have known that this was Mr Hai's symbolic version of bra burning. Being synthetic, the scarves and burqua immediately went up in flames. It was a frightening sight. She jumped up in shock and ran over to the fireplace.

'What have you done?' she cried. Suddenly all the good advice that her aunts had given her, on patience and exercising self-control, flew right out of the window. She turned to Mr Hai, angry. It all came out, a torrent of emotion mixed up with the tension and stress from the last few days. How could he? Was he mad? She had been told he was a gentleman – a civilised gentleman.

Mr Hai didn't know what had hit him. He'd never seen Mrs Hai behave like this. It was slowly occurring to him that maybe he had pushed things just a bit too far, too fast. But now Mrs Hai had flung herself on the bed and was bawling her eyes out. Mr Hai had never seen a woman screaming and crying before. What were you meant to do? He put a consoling hand on her shoulder. She shrugged him off and howled some more.

'I am sorry. I am sorry. I thought it was for the best,' he tried to explain. Nervously. As if his new wife was some sort of sensitive explosive. 'You don't want to wear those scarves – do you? Do you?'

Through her tears Mrs Hai could hear him talking in the background – something about how covering one's head stripped away a woman's dignity.

What did he know? she reflected angrily. She was the one who had now lost her dignity. Did he – her husband – understand that? And suddenly she stopped. Her husband! What was she doing? Was this any way to behave in front of him? He would divorce her now, for sure. She would be cast out of the house and made homeless. She would have to beg outside Buckingham Palace for money. She would die in the streets, penniless, so far from home. She suddenly felt weak and tired. All she wanted to do now was sleep.

Mrs Hai closed her eyes. Mr Hai watched her as she slept. He felt bad – very bad indeed. He had failed to be a good husband. He vowed to himself that he would never bring up the scarf issue again.

But the next time they went out – to Regent's Park, actually – my mother showed herself to be the good, obedient wife. Mr Hai was surprised and pleased when she came down the stairs with her head uncovered. What had happened to the pretty new scarf he had bought her as an apology for the 'episode', as he now called it? He was about to ask her, but, remembering his vow, decided not to. Privately he was pleased, very pleased indeed. What a good modern wife Mrs Hai would eventually make.

'What are you talking about?' my mother remarks when I recall this story. 'That never happened.'

I look at her, stunned.

'But Dad always talked about having burnt your scarves.'

'He didn't burn them,' Farah, my sister, says on entering the room and overhearing our conversation. 'I remember him telling me, he threw them all in the bin. And he thought it was really funny.'

'Funny?' I exclaim, wondering how my father could have found humour in the situation. But then he always did adopt a comical tone when recounting stories to my sister. With me, he preferred to take a more serious note.

'I am telling you,' my mother says, over us, 'it didn't happen.'

My mother is so forceful in her statement that I now begin to doubt my memory. Did my father embellish the story to paint himself as some sort of crusading hero against religion?

But then I hear my mother pipe up: 'Your dad very good Muslim.'

My sister and I snigger. Is my mother's denial of the story an attempt to preserve my father's Islamic credentials in the community? After all, one can't be too careful these days.

There is no way to know the truth any more.

'But Mum, what about the bus story?' I ask. This is a less contentious incident from the family mythology.

My mother sighs. But from the way her face dissolves into a smile, I can see that the memory still amuses her.

Apparently, the idea had come to my father during their visit to Oxford Street. How exciting that trip had been for my mother. Again she dressed up in her best sari, carefully applied her make-up and sprayed on her best perfume.

'Did Dad notice, Mum? Did he?' I ask dreamily.

'How do I know? It was a long time ago,' she replies, pulling out some Tupperware boxes from the cupboard to clean.

They boarded the number 29 outside the Holloway Odeon and climbed to the top. My father suggested they take the front seats, so that my mother could watch – or study – London as it went by.

My mother was mesmerised. England was so different from back home. She noted to my father how clean and ordered the streets were. 'Civic sense,' my father proudly said. My mother noticed that many English people liked walking around with dogs on chains. 'The English say, A man's best friend is his dog!' Mr Hai explained to her. Back home, dogs were seen as scavengers.

But what fascinated my mother most during her journey were the women of England. Whether they were big, small, young, old, fat, thin, they triggered a million questions in my mother's head. How did they feel, walking around with their heads uncovered – didn't they feel exposed? And what about those women who wore mini-skirts, weren't they scared about what could happen to them? Or were they just shameless, as Mrs Sidiqui had said the other day? And where were their husbands? Didn't they mind their wives walking around alone? Did they visit their parents often or had they forgotten all about them? With these questions running through my mother's mind, the bus soon arrived at the corner of Tottenham Court Road. They walked the rest of the way to Oxford Street.

My parents spent the day wandering around the department stores. My mother had never seen such grand shops in her entire life: the lofty ceilings, the moving staircases, the lift attendants, the revolving doors, the mannequins and so on. As they browsed around the shops, my father translated terms into English that might come in handy if Mrs Hai ever went out shopping in the future, such as 'loose change', 'receipt', or 'How much please?' My father bought my mother a small present. As he handed it over, he cited the English word.

'Gloves,' he said.

'Gloves,' my mother obediently repeated back.

They ended their trip by having fish and chips with mushy peas at Woolworths.

'It was so cheap,' my mother says.

At the end of the week, my father took my mother back to Oxford Street. They were standing outside Woolworths again, having just finished their meal, when my father handed my mother a set of doorkeys. A feeling of dread descended on my mother. She sensed that something 'unexpected' was about to come her way.

'Today, I want you to find your own way home,' my father explained.

My mother, who had never been anywhere on her own, let alone in a strange country whose language she didn't speak – and without a scarf – was petrified. It was only a short bus trip, but for her it was the equivalent of going to the moon. She would have protested, but she was on strict self-orders to behave – as a good wife should.

'You have to learn,' my father said. My mother reluctantly took the keys. She was on her own. My father allowed her one concession. He took her to the bus stop.

My mother climbed on to the Routemaster, clutching tightly to the shilling fare my father had given her. But much to her shame, as the bus began to move she burst out crying. And, much to her embarrassment, she sobbed all the way home. The bus conductor, not knowing what to do, decided not to trouble her for the fare. Unknown to my mother, my father was following her on the next bus.

'He says he saw me crying. But he couldn't change buses. It was far too late.'

But my mother soon recovered from her bus-trip ordeal. In fact, after that she started making her own small trips to the shops.

'Mum, why do you think Dad was so desperate to make you independent like Englishwomen?' I ask.

My mother smiles, sadly. 'He knew he would die early. He was much older than me,' she replies. 'He was preparing me for life in England.'

Slowly my mother grew to like England. My father was doing a good job of showing it off to her, as if it were his own home. Shuffling through pictures, I see my mother in her red sari, posing shyly in front of some of England's major sites: Windsor Castle, the Tower of London, Brighton Pier, Oxford University, Canterbury Cathedral, London Zoo, and the list goes on. Sometimes a passer-by has taken a photo of the happy new couple. Sometimes Uncle Aslam and Aunt Hilda join them on their excursions, bringing a picnic basket along. More snapshots of everyone eating sandwiches and English cakes. There is often a tasteful rose bush behind them. Copies of these pictures will be sent back to Pakistan for my mother's family to excitedly examine at great length.

'Ahh, so she's there in Queen Victoria's England,' they would enviously say to each other, not bothered by the fact that Queen Victoria had long ago passed away.

'And look, who is that Englishwoman?' They will point at Aunt Hilda – an actual white woman. This will have impressed them. They will study her carefully and take in how comfortably she sits next to my mother. 'Ahhh!' they would then say to each other. 'Our sister has moved on in the world.'

But despite my mother's progress on many fronts, my father never managed to get her excited about politics. A few months into the marriage, while my father was still trying hard to guide my mother through the important details of Stalin's first Five Year Plan, he learnt that he was going to become a father. He was overjoyed – finally a father at fifty-one.

*

I was born in 1970 at London Hospital. 'You were apple of eye,' my mother says, showing her command of British expressions.

A year later, my brother, Yasir, was born and then the following year my mother became pregnant again. Mr Hai now had a family to boast of. He could proudly assure Mr Ali that he wouldn't die alone.

Now that there were four of us in the family and another on the way, the Holloway bedsit was getting cramped. Others in the house were feeling the same way, too.

'Do we want to spend all our lives here living in Little Karachi?' Mr Ali once said.

One by one, the families were deciding it was time to break away into smaller, English-style nuclear units, 'an Englishman's home is his castle' becoming the latest saying to do the rounds in the Holloway house. It was high time to move out of the inner city and into the green-belt suburbs. The 'fashionable' locations sought by the Holloway housemates were Dollis Hill, Forest Gate, Bounds Green, Harrow, Northolt, Norwood and Woodford. The more nondescript and pedestrian the area, the more romantic they sounded to my father and his friends. Once again the men were starting to dream about a mythical England.

However, it didn't take long for my father and the other men to become overwhelmed by the house-buying process. No amount of Shakespeare, Hardy, Tawney or Russell had prepared them for this most confusing and frustrating of English experiences.

There were all the house features to contend with, good local schools, the wrong sort of neighbours and, more importantly, the big bogey word: *damp* – the soggy, yellow–brown water patches that menacingly crept over tired-looking ceilings and walls. My parents from the sunny subcontinent concluded that, even more than mice and bad local schools, damp was something to be feared.

Finally, they enlisted the help of one of Shyam's pluckier friends from his young Asian network, a sharp dresser named Waseem. Uncle Waseem, twenty years junior to my father, was not the least bit misty eyed about England. Brought up in England and having attended a local comprehensive in Kilburn, he could talk for hours about real English things like working-class Brits, racism and Arsenal FC. Uncle Waseem had acquired a lot of street savvy and nous, much prized skills amongst wide-eyed immigrants like my father. In no time at all, he found a suitable terraced house for us on the outskirts of Wembley.

Wembley was a great location. With its just-about-affordable terraced houses and pretty postage-stamp front lawns, the area had become a much sought-after location for aspirational immigrants. Moving to Wembley said: 'Hello, I've arrived.'

And the suburban two up, two down with plenty of bay windows (for the all-important net curtains) that Uncle Wassem had found certainly looked ideal for our needs. Yes, the upstairs would have to be rented out to lodgers to help support mortgage payments. My father might have secured work as a teacher, but his contracts were still erratic and much of what he did earn was usually sent back to India and Pakistan to support family. The two rooms plus kitchen and bathroom on the lower floor would do us fine. But my mother was not convinced – yet.

While they were looking around for houses, my father had discovered that his wife had plenty of good old common sense. 'No estate agent can pull the wool over her eyes,' he told the others, using another apposite English expression.

'It's one minute walk from the Tube,' said Uncle Waseem.

'Hmm,' replied my mother.

'And there is a paraffin heater system.'

'Hmm.'

'And it has been damp-proofed . . .'

He had said the magic word. My mother looked over at my father and nodded. Yes, Wembley would do – it would do very well.

Goodbye to Holloway and Little Karachi. They could now look forward to real English living. Just what my father needed to kick-start his next project: Operation Children.

3

Jean Wali

Our convoy consisted of three cars: the first car carried us; the second car our clothes, and the third car, our furniture – just two baby cots, a load of my father's books and my mother's pots and pans.

As my parents began unloading with the help of Uncle Waseem's two friends, they glanced around at their new neighbours, who were emerging from their houses to run their Saturday-morning errands. First impressions were promising. There were enough white people in the area to make my parents feel they were living in England. And yet there were just enough brown faces to stop them from feeling like outsiders.

Knowing Mrs Khan as I do now, I can just imagine her excitement when she saw us – another Asian family moving in. In fact, we had only pulled up the car hatch when we spotted her small, agile frame scurrying towards us. Dressed in a pink silk sari, her face glistening with Pond's Face Cream to give her complexion that whiter sheen that so many Asian women craved, Mrs Khan appeared nice and smartly dressed. Her husband, Mr Khan, a burly man about six-and-a-half-feet tall, wearing a flat cap, lagged behind.

'*Apne log. Apne log*,' Uncle Waseem whispered excitedly to my father.

'*Apne log*' (one of ours) was fast becoming a common refrain amongst us Asians living in Britain. 'Asians' was the way we described ourselves back then. Not Muslims, Sikhs and Hindus. When filling in a form you were asked to tick your geographical background. So officially we became Asians, in the same way that our neighbours, the Jobsons (who we would meet soon), became Afro-Caribbeans.

Apne log was a phrase that brought all of us together – Sikh, Hindu and Muslim alike – anyone who originated from the Asian subcontinent. Sometimes the words were used disparagingly. For example, when an Asian employer paid his Asian employee badly, then one would say, sneeringly: 'What do you expect from *apne log*? Much better to work for the English.' But more often than not the words were used inclusively – as it was being applied now to the approaching Mr Khan.

Mr Khan lowered his head, instantly feeling everyone's eyes on him. Despite his huge presence, he was rather a shy man. My father extended his hand in friendship. Mr Khan clumsily grabbed it.

'*Hai Sahib*,' my father said, introducing himself. (In Urdu the name comes first and the title *Sahib*, or 'mister', comes second.)

Mr Khan lifted his head with interest, revealing big, grey, puppy eyes.

'*Muselman?*' he asked, as he registered my father's name.

My father nodded blankly. But my mother and Uncle Waseem grinned broadly. They were not interested in religion, but they knew the pleasure such information could bring fellow Muslims. Being a Muslim was just like being part of some big tribal family.

'I help you?' Mr Khan mumbled enthusiastically, his shoulders rolling back to reveal his gigantic stature. In fact – as the story goes – Mr Khan had gone one step further than just 'help'. He single-handedly lifted and carried the two cots into the house.

'He's a *Pathan*!' Mrs Khan proudly revealed to my parents.

'Ahh,' they replied respectfully. For only Pathans built men like Mr Khan.

'*Pathan, qua he?*' [What is a Pathan?], I asked. Back then, I only spoke in Urdu to my parents.

The adults laughed and Mrs Khan congratulated me on my perfect Urdu accent. I smiled shyly. Close up, I didn't think Mrs Khan was that pretty. She looked like a gerbil. Every time she sniffed, which was pretty often, her nose and mouth would fold into each other to form a perfect snout.

'One day Ali, my son, be like his father,' Mrs Khan said, deliberately in English, to impress upon my father her 'modern' credentials. She had guessed that my father might be an educated man. Maybe this was because he was wearing a tie. My father always made sure he was respectfully turned out, even when he was moving house. Mrs Khan was obviously a very optimistic woman because little Ali, with his tiny frame, looked as if he was more likely to take after his mother than his father. Unlike his well-built sister, Afshan, who was currently dictating to a group of young girls how to chalk out the perfect hopscotch on the pavement.

A classic Asian exchange was now transpiring between the adults. 'Which part of Pakistan do you come from?' 'When did you come to England?'

They were interrupted by the noise of the people from no. 7 and no. 15 approaching from the other side of the road, a motley crew of Asian women, dressed in gaudy synthetic *salwar kameezes*, shrieking and screaming in Punjabi patois. Some were pushing prams, others dragging children. Some of them laughed and revealed their red *paan*-stained (betel-nut juice) teeth. When the women saw us, their voices began to level off.

'Village people!' Mrs Khan sneered disdainfully. 'Live like they are in Jalalabad, fifteen to a house. *Maloom nahee he, yeah England he?* [Don't they know this is England?]'

'Keep away from them,' I heard Mrs Khan say. 'They are *jahil* [illiterate].'

My father nodded. He hadn't come to Wembley for that. He had moved here to become something better.

I soon cottoned on to the idea that, as one grew older, there was something that one had to 'become'. We – meaning my family, and those like us, for example, the Khans and Uncle Waseem – were not there yet. But it was understood that, by working hard, we could get there. I later learnt a word for 'this' thing that you had to become, 'this' place you had to get to. It was called 'English'.

'Ahh!' my father and his friends would say admiringly to each other whenever English manners, English clothes, English education, English toys, etc., were mentioned. English, it seemed, was something good, something to be proud of. In fact 'English' sounded so nice that when I imagined what it could look like, I would see a bright, white light and I would hear the comforting sounds of children laughing and playing. I once told my mother my description of 'English'. She looked at me slightly bemused, before returning her attention to Farah, my newly born baby sister.

The discovery that the neighbours on both sides of our house were white delighted me. Perhaps, if I observed them carefully, I might learn what 'being English' exactly meant.

Mrs Campbell lived in the next house over to the left. From

37

first impressions, Mrs Campbell demonstrated all the signs of being a real English person. She had grey hair like everyone white in my area. She had a little brown dog named Wilbur whom she loved. And she had a beautiful garden full of flowers. This was very unlike our own garden, which was soon shaping up perfectly as model Asian garden of the year: unkempt, scattered with discarded furniture and strewn with sad roots, a recent legacy of my mother's attempt to grow some tomatoes. But the most important single thing that firmly established Mrs Campbell in my mind as English was her piano.

Every Sunday morning, our house would be flooded with notes wafting through the adjoining walls. Sometimes Mrs Campbell would put on the record player to accompany her piano playing. The music was often so loud that you couldn't think or talk – you could only listen. I remember how Beethoven or Mozart filled our living room as bright sunlight pierced the net curtains, catching specks of floating dust in the air, transforming the very Asian chaos of our home into something ethereal. In those moments, I would dance around our living room, imagining I was a fairy. I would dart from one side of the room to the other, spring from one sofa to the next in pursuit of the floating 'magic' dust that always eluded me. That is, until the music reached its crescendo. Then I would freeze. The music would come to an abrupt halt and the room would go quiet. But my arms would remain suspended in mid-air, in perfect pirouette pose. And just when I couldn't hold them up any longer, a sly note or two would drift through the walls to bring me much-needed respite. For now Mrs Campbell had slowly taken the lead again on her piano. I would metamorphose myself into a ballerina and tiptoe quietly around the room as if I was in *Swan Lake*.

Mrs Campbell was not really English. She was Scottish. Every now and then her husband, William, wore a skirt when he went out.

'Hello Jazmine,' he'd cry whenever he saw me. I'd wave back. For some reason I never bothered to correct him about the pronunciation of my name. Mr Campbell was really nice. But Mrs Campbell quite clearly did not like us. She often told us that we were an example of how the neighbourhood was going downhill, pointing to our garden as prima-facie evidence.

Observing closely, I realised that Mrs Campbell was not as perfect as she thought herself. I had been told that nice English people were very polite and quiet, but Mrs Campbell never was. I would often hear her shrieking out, 'Biillliiieee!' or clattering her pots loudly around the kitchen. As we grew older and more spirited we increasingly became the focus of Mrs Campbell's wrath. This would often end with her having a full-scale argument with my mother over the garden fence or banging on our common walls with a stick to show her displeasure at our existence so close to hers.

My father told us to just ignore her. But my mother would not let matters lie. We would often find her, sari pillow falling off her shoulder, her hair bun starting to unravel, smashing her biggest cooking spoon against the wall, in response to Mrs Campbell's banging. My brother, my sister and I would stand in a row watching her in silence, not daring to distract her. Only when the banging from the other side finished would my mother stop. And then, 'cool as a cucumber', she would walk away and resume her housework. We would carry on playing.

Mrs Campbell knew everyone in the neighbourhood. That is, everyone English. They would stop outside her house for a chat on their way to the shops. They would often talk about the war, which I knew was important to English (and, apparently, even Scottish) people. And if we happened to stumble out of our

39

house, they would all turn round and stare at us – before turning away to mumble something to each other.

But Mrs Sherman was never like that. She would always smile whenever she saw us. She was the mother of a very pretty little girl, whose shiny blonde hair always made my mother and Mrs Khan go weak at the knees.

'Like gold thread,' they would say dreamily to each other. The girl's name was Britt, after Britt Ekland. Whenever Britt and I would cross paths we would stare at each other. My mother and Mrs Khan named Mrs Sherman, '*Jean Wali*'. The Jeans One.

Jeans, for them, as for many other Asians, were synonymous with being rebellious, modern, sexually permissive and risqué. They were something only rebels and teenagers wore – bad people. Asian girls were banned from wearing them. But here was Mrs Sherman, a responsible mother who always smiled at them, wearing jeans. Perhaps all those people who wore jeans were not such bad people after all? It was a revelation to my mother and Mrs Khan.

Then one day Mrs Campbell suddenly dropped her implacable hostility and began talking to us. Her topic of conversation: the McGuinness family. The McGuinnesses lived on the other side of us and, according to Mrs Campbell, they had a worse garden than we did.

'Have you seen it?' Mrs Campbell cried out to my father in horror. 'They're paving over it.'

I had been carefully observing the McGuinnesses for some time and had figured out that they weren't English either. No, apparently they were Irish. And, as Mrs Campbell now assured my father, they were very typical of the Irish, too.

'There's six of them, for a start,' she would point out.

It was true; there were six of them and all to be avoided at any cost – for they were rough. Through our thin walls we would often hear them screaming and shouting at each other: 'bloody, this' and 'bloody that' followed by the sounds of doors banging, a dog barking and girls wailing.

Gary McGuinness, who was roughly the same age as my brother, often came to our house to play. This was something that united Mrs Khan and Mrs Campbell in utter incomprehension. 'Are you mad?' Mrs Khan would cry at my mother. Maybe they were right, because Gary always left our house in a state of absolute devastation. He was forever scribbling on our walls, smashing our glasses, turning furniture upside down, pulling our hair and laughing at the food we were eating.

'Smelly, smelly,' he would cry, before gobbling up the plate of food my mother had given him.

But my father said we had to be patient with him because he came from a 'broken home'. This really interested me. I vaguely understood that 'broken home' was a bad word like 'divorce', 'drunk' and 'single mother': words that my parents always pronounced in a hushed tone. I also knew that these words were associated somehow with being English and we, being Asian people, were not like this. Which apparently was a good thing, because my mother would always say a quick thankful prayer to Allah whenever the topic came up.

'I am telling you,' Mrs Khan would cry at my mother (though only when my father was out of earshot, for she had figured out that he would not always share all her opinions), 'English people are dirty. All they think is sex filth! Sex filth, sex filth!'

My mother would nod uneasily at Mrs Khan. Sex was one of those things that she never discussed in public. Who talked about sex so openly, anyway? Well, the English did, according to Mrs Khan, and all the time.

'And they bathe in their own dirty water,' Mrs Khan would say with contempt. 'English, dirty people.'

Mrs Khan's comments about the English never failed to shock me. She was the first person I had ever come across who had anything bad to say about them. And while I felt uneasy listening to her, part of me was intrigued by what she had to say. Like Mrs Khan, I, too, had been astonished to learn that the English didn't bathe like us. We had bucket baths, which basically meant standing a plastic bucket in a bath tub and then filling it up with water. You stood in the bath and after you finished soaping and shampooing, you washed away the grime with clean water from the bucket, using a plastic jug. The dirty water would then disappear down the plughole, preventing one from having any further contact with it. If one desired a more luxurious bath, one could always drop a blob of Matey bubble bath into the bucket.

'Oh yes, I saw it on TV. Yes, sitting in bathtub in dirty water. Have you ever heard of anything so disgusting?' she continued, her body writhing in disgust. 'I made Ali stand in front of the TV.'

'Standing in front of the TV' was something I had often seen Ali do whenever I was over at the Khans' watching television. Whenever a lewd scene came on the screen – and this encompassed everything from a mild kiss to a woman having a baby – three-year-old Ali would be instructed to jump up and dance in front of the screen, his arms flapping madly to ensure our vision was truly obstructed. Why no one ever thought of just changing channels, I don't know.

'*Shaabaash* [well done],' Mrs Khan would say to Ali when he sat down again.

That was the strange thing about Mrs Khan. While she desperately wanted to be modern and even emulate the English, she couldn't help getting all worked up whenever discussion of Western hygiene or morality came up.

So you can just imagine the heart attack Mrs Khan nearly had when she saw Fiona McGuinness lean against her front-garden fence and snog her boyfriend. I happened to be playing hopscotch with Afshan at the time.

But now, confronted with Fiona and her boyfriend, we could not stop staring. I'd never seen anything like it before. It was tongues and everything. But Afshan said she had seen it loads, most recently on a car ride to Huddersfield, where her relatives lived. The nearest I had ever got to seeing a real snog was on TV, never in actual life. Until then.

It was completely fascinating. Mrs Khan's net curtains were quivering with rage. In fact, once Fiona and her paramour had moved on, Mrs Khan had gone out and even inspected the spot where they had done 'it'.

I suppose, looking back, we didn't have the best English role models in Wembley. But our family was lucky. We always had Uncle Aslam and Aunt Hilda to fall back on.

4

Operation Children

By now, Aunt Hilda and Uncle Aslam had moved to a big house in Highgate, overlooking the cemetery where Karl Marx was buried. From all accounts their new house sounded really nice. But my siblings and I weren't allowed to visit. The house was very posh, with white walls, and there were concerns that we might leave grubby handprints on the wall. Better to leave our visits for when we were older. However, to compensate, Aunt Hilda and Uncle Aslam now took to visiting us every fortnight on Sunday.

It didn't take long for my brother, my sister and I to work out that our parents considered Aunt Hilda and Uncle Aslam to be VIP guests. They might have been expected for lunch time, but on those special days we would wake in the morning to the sound of a Hoover whirring somewhere in the background and the musty smell of ghee frying.

My mother would be in the kitchen cooking away. There would be pakoras sizzling in the frying pan, kebabs spluttering under the grill and the fish (marinated overnight) would be slowly baking in the oven. All this while my mother prepared the main course, maybe stewed lamb with fenugreek leaves or chicken cooked in an onion-based sauce or perhaps prawns fried in mustard seeds. (Though in fact it usually ended up being all three.)

Meanwhile, a separate batch of each dish would have to be made for Aunt Hilda, this time omitting the hot chillies and spices. Once all that had been accomplished, there would be the fresh coriander to be chopped, the pilau rice to be cooked, the naan breads to be baked and finally the sweet dish to be chilled.

My mother's culinary skills must surely have impressed Aunt Hilda, especially as I often heard my parents say: '*Bachari* [poor woman], she doesn't know how to cook.' (When I finally did get to stay with Aunt Hilda and Uncle Aslam a couple of years later, aged seven and three-quarters, Aunt Hilda gave me a cheese and onion roll with some ready-salted crisps for supper.)

While my mother prepared the feast, my father busied himself cleaning the house. That was my father for you – the modern man. He felt strongly that with no servants or family support in England, as one would have had in India or Pakistan, all chores should be shared between them.

'Oh, but he have no idea,' my mother now says. 'One time, he wash dishes with baby bib on. And next time, he feed your sister, he put my apron on her.'

Like most Asian homes of the time, or in fact any immigrant abode at any given time, there was not much to show off in our house. Interior design had not yet entered our vocabulary, let alone our consciousness, though to be fair, my parents tried. Our living room was papered in yellow-green flock and my mother hung yellow nylon curtains to match, but our furniture was all second-hand – and filled the room.

On one side was a tired-looking red nylon-upholstered sofa-bed that Uncle Waseem had found for us. When guests came to visit, we kids had been well trained to hastily direct them to sit instead on the mustard-coloured fake leather three-piece suite. To get to there, one had to negotiate the brown Formica coffee table, which was just a bit too large for our room. Still, once seated, one could admire from the settee my father's much-cherished book collection; works by Shakespeare, Dickens, Milton, Russell and R. H. Tawney jostling for space on the shelf, alongside more practical books like the Urdu–English dictionary, or the 150-page hardback guide on *How to Write an English Letter!*

The centrepiece of the living room was the *almarhi* – an enormous wardrobe, a must-have for all Asian houses. Inside, one would find all the family's belongings: clothes, sheets, pillowcases, an ironing board, books, paperwork, matches, sacks of spare coal and more. And if you still needed space to store away your possessions, then you could always put your belongings into any one of the suitcases, that permanently resided on top of the *almarhi*.

After hoovering, my father would arrange the plastic flowers, dust the bookshelves, puff up the cushions, hammer in the red sofa's springs – all before throwing us into the bath so that we were nice and clean for when the honoured guests arrived.

With all the activity around the house, it felt like Christmas. Not that I knew what Christmas felt like, but I had read about it in Louisa May Alcott's *Little Women* and thought it to be a fitting description of those frantic mornings. And more so because when Uncle Aslam and Aunt Hilda did eventually arrive, they always brought us loads of presents. Not the normal box of Quality Street that your usual Asian aunt and uncle would buy you. Real presents. Real English toys: wooden jigsaw puzzles, toy soldiers, quaint dolls' houses, pencil cases, old train sets, model fighter planes and much, much more. Thanks to Uncle Aslam and Aunt Hilda, our imagination was well stocked with Edwardian images and stories. I think they found pleasure in spoiling us because they didn't have any children of their own.

They were obviously very much in love. I knew this because whenever they spoke to each other, they always called each other 'darling': 'Darling, what do you think?' 'Will you pass the salt, darling?' 'I agree, darling.'

I didn't know any Asian adult who spoke to their spouse in such a manner. Well, not in public, anyway. I mean, one could be affectionate with young children, but with fellow adults, no. I must admit that whenever I heard them say the 'D' word, I would go red with embarrassment. But then that was the thing about Uncle Aslam and Aunt Hilda: whenever they came, they brought the 'English world' with them.

No one looked forward to Uncle Aslam and Aunt Hilda's visits more than my father. He was now working as a supply teacher at a local comprehensive in Brent. I don't think he ever felt disappointed by his career path because, compared to our Asian neighbours – who were all doing night-shift work at the McVitie's Biscuit Factory in Willesden – he was doing relatively well. But his specialised work – teaching immigrant children the three Rs – did often drive him to despair. He would regularly return home bemoaning the lack of discipline amongst the Afro-Caribbean children and the poor level of literacy amongst the Asian children.

Uncle Aslam and Aunt Hilda's visits offered my father an opportunity to offload his despair. Subsequently though, he depended on them for sound advice on how he should prepare me for starting school in the coming autumn.

My father was worried. We children might be able to speak

English, but Urdu still remained our first language. And somwhere, my father feared that not only would our Asian background lower our teachers' expectations of us, but also that being bilingual might hamper us from fully grasping the rudiments of the English language. His own experience of teaching Asian children had taught him that this was not a matter to be taken lightly.

'No matter how much you try and teach them about nouns and adverbs, they struggle to understand,' he once said to Aunt Hilda and Uncle Aslam. 'No wonder some of them leave school without even knowing how to speak English properly.'

We were in the living room and my father, Aunt Hilda and Uncle Aslam were settling into one of their postprandial discussions, which normally lasted all afternoon. While they talked, we would play with our new toys. My mother would spend the time catching up on some mending.

'It's the girls I used to worry about,' Uncle Aslam replied, recalling his own days teaching at an Islington comprehensive when he first arrived in England. 'They would just stand around in the playground in their *salwar kameezes*, only speaking Bengali or Punjabi. No English.'

I – always half listening in – knew the kind of girls my uncle was talking about. The girls from no. 7 were like that. Samira and Munira, with their long plaits, always wore *kameezes* over trousers and only spoke to each other in Punjabi. Once they had tried speaking to Afshan Khan and me in Punjabi. When we didn't understand, they giggled and ran away.

'But what can you expect when their only ambition is to become a housewife?' my father interjected.

Aunt Hilda looked appalled at the concept. My mother just nodded, as always. That's how she liked to participate in those conversations – quietly listening in. Not because her opinions would not have been welcomed. The few times my mother had offered up her views, she brought an earthiness to the conversations that the others relished. But such occasions were rare. As far as she was concerned, she didn't have anything useful to contribute. She was still in learning mode.

'I blame the parents,' my father said. 'They don't care that their children are always at the bottom of the class, unable to read and write.'

'Well, that's because these parents think that as long as their children are getting a British education, everything will work out,' my uncle said.

'Yes, that is it,' my father said, nodding in agreement.

One thing was for sure: he wasn't going to allow his children to go the same way. We were going to become English.

Aunt Hilda and Uncle Aslam were people who understood the importance of education and people who could unravel the mysteries of being English. And, even more importantly, they were more than happy to help my father out – they didn't want us to become loser Asian children either.

So, on top of the toys and books, my uncle and aunt now began to give us subtle lessons in being English. This was great, for English lessons revolved around fun activities like being taken to the pantomime at the Old Vic, visiting Windsor Castle during summer holidays, watching Punch and Judy on Brighton beach, making daisy chains in Hyde Park, tossing pancakes on Shrove Tuesday and so on. I remember how privileged I felt to have an Uncle Aslam and an Aunt Hilda to help us out. I mean, who did no. 15, no. 7 or even Afshan Khan (even though she was meant to be modern) have to show them the finer details of being English? No one. Who was going to teach them about Christmas stockings, Enid Blyton, tea and cakes, tiddlywinks, poppy day, table manners? No one.

49

One Sunday, my sister and I carefully laid the table out. Not the way my mother did it – self-service, Asian style – but in the English way that Aunt Hilda had taught us. Knives on the right, forks on the left, spoons on top and napkins by the side. I did the knives and forks. My sister did the spoons and napkins. We even laid out a set for my mother who, usually, ate with her hands. The table looked proper; to my mind our small kitchen had an air of grace that it had never enjoyed before.

'The table looks so nice, girls,' Aunt Hilda said as she entered the kitchen. 'Oh, and what lovely flowers,' looking at our centrepiece.

'I got the idea from the Snow White book,' I said proudly.

My uncle and aunt laughed heartily at this, which made me blush. Still, maybe I did allow myself to get overexcited that afternoon. For I dropped my guard.

Once everyone was seated, we took our cue from Aunt Hilda and put our napkins on our laps. My uncle tucked his into his neckline, so that it looked like a bib. But we'd been told that this was fine, too. Then my uncle and father began their customary exchange. 'You start.' 'No, you start.' 'Oh Hilda, why don't you start?'

So my aunt started first, though not before the usual hoohah that involved the search for – on the table crowded with serving plates – the chilli-free dishes that had been specially prepared for her. For some reason this was never an easy job and often required my uncle to sample different dishes before the right ones were located. Aunt Hilda was very apologetic for all the trouble she was causing. But we didn't mind – better trouble than one of those painful coughing fits she underwent whenever she mistakenly ate a chilli.

Once Aunt Hilda's dishes had been identified, my mother then served us three children.

Instead of picking up the knife and fork that I have so carefully arranged on either side of my plate, I plunge with my right hand straight into my food. My fingers nimbly cut into a piece of chicken, which I then mix into a bit of rice – just how my mother and uncle often do. I dip my morsel into the minted raita before shoving it into my mouth. The yoghurt and spices from the chicken have melded into the rice to give it a deeper and more intense taste.

'Yasmin, what exactly do you think you are doing?' I suddenly hear Aunt Hilda say, shattering the food bliss I am in.

The room has gone silent. I don't need to look up to realise what I have just done. I can see that my fingers are coated in bits of rice and chicken. My first thought is: how has this happened? I look at my mother, who is watching me, slightly perplexed. I then quickly look over at Aunt Hilda, who is carefully picking the bones out of her fish – with a fork. Time stops.

'You know, only Pakis eat with their hands,' Aunt Hilda says, very calmly, without looking up.

The world has turned upside down. I don't want my Aunt Hilda to think that I am a Paki. 'Paki' is a bad word, a very upsetting word and, when you hear it, you feel very scared – not least because your parents are dragging you away from the offending yobs, looking completely terrified.

But I know that on this occasion Aunt Hilda is not trying to upset me or scare my parents. I might only be young, but I already know that the word 'Paki' has come to take on another meaning. It has become synonymous with being uncivilised, primitive, savage, ignorant, backwards, uneducated, illiterate and uncultured. In other words, not English.

The room is quiet. No one has yet spoken. Maybe everyone is reeling with shock at the utterance of that dreaded word at the dinner table. I feel deeply ashamed. It is all my fault. My brother is grinning at me, his blue-velvet bow tie speckled with splashes of yoghurt. But Aunt Hilda hasn't finished.

'Are you a Paki?' she asks me again. This time she does look up. Her watery blue eyes lock into mine.

I shake my head. My face is burning, and my head starting to swirl.

From the corner of my eyes, I can see my father shaking his head in despair. The word doesn't offend him one bit. I can see he even agrees with her.

'Only Pakis eat with their hands, don't they?' my aunt continues. She then looks at Uncle Aslam. 'Darling, pass me some yoghurt please.'

The table moves fast to get the yoghurt to Aunt Hilda.

'I think, madam, that you should go and wash your hands,' I hear Aunt Hilda say.

I nod, gratefully. I quickly get up and go to the kitchen sink. I don't look at anyone. I turn on the taps and the warm water washes over my hands. It is comforting.

When I return to the table, the adults are busy discussing Idi Amin. I look over at my brother, who kindly gestures at me to use my cutlery, in case I have forgotten. Slowly I pick up my knife and fork to eat. But before I do, I sneak a glance over at Aunt Hilda. She smiles encouragingly at me. I smile back and warmth floods through me. Aunt Hilda is so kind – all she really wants is the best for me. When I next look up again from my food, I notice that my uncle and mother are using their cutlery too.

Despite my little lapse at the kitchen table, I was soon growing into the perfect little English child. 'It's a case of when in Rome do as the Romans do,' my father now took to saying to us. And

I began to see things that way too. What use were Indian ways in England, anyway?

Soon I was even trying to look English. My sister and I stopped wearing Asian clothes – unless it was a special occasion. As we could not afford to buy new clothes, every summer my mother would make four English dresses each for Farah and me on her little Singer sewing machine. The dresses, complete with frills, laces and bows, would see us through the year; the inspiration for patterns coming from *Little House on the Prairie*, my favourite show.

But to perfect our English look, my father also began to encourage my mother to keep our hair short. My mother had agreed. No, she didn't want her daughters to look as if they had been plucked out of some Indian village. So one Saturday morning, off went my hair.

My mother placed me on the kitchen table, wrapped a bath towel around my neck and then carefully began to snip off my long, wiry curls. My brother and sister watched attentively, ready to scream out if my mother neared my ears. '*Chup karo!* [Be quiet!]' she cried at them, though at the same time trying to stifle a giggle as my siblings immediately sat down, petrified. My mother was tackling my hair as if it was a complicated surgical operation. I frowned indignantly at my siblings for distracting her, for which I received a cuff on my back. '*Sar neechai karo* [keep your head down]!' my mother cried.

I sat there for nearly an hour as my mother slowly snipped away at my hair. I couldn't help being alarmed by the sight of my dark curls gradually piling up on the floor. What was this new 'me' going to look like, I wondered? Would people laugh? I suddenly wanted the old 'me' back.

Stepping back, she took stock of her work.

'Stay there.' She ran out of the room to fetch a mirror for me to admire her work. 'It's really nice, really nice,' my siblings cried out enthusiastically, as I waited anxiously for my mother to return.

When my mother held the mirror up, I saw a perfect little bob, just like Milly-Molly-Mandy, the English heroine of the book I was reading. I looked like a proper English girl.

That Saturday, I followed my mother to the shops, desperate to show off my new hairstyle. Mr Campbell said that it looked really nice. Afshan asked her mother if she could have her hair cut too, and Gary McGuinness burped in my face – which meant he had also noticed.

'What have you done to her hair?' Mrs Jobson cried at my mother in her soft Jamaican lilt. Mrs Jobson lived next door to the Khans. 'All those wavy curls, where they all gone?' Mrs Jobson, dressed in her Caribbean Saturday best, a huge canary-yellow hat on her head, like an ungainly bird struggling to take off, was on her way to church. Her three sons, Joe, Danny and Sam, strolled wearily behind. Today, they were all looking very smart in their sharply creased beige suits and big black bow ties. Their Afros were also perfectly combed up, so nice and bouncy looking that I wanted to reach out and pat their heads. I wondered if they felt the same about my hair. Did they think I looked 'English'?

My mother was squeezing my hand very hard. She was staring at Mrs Jobson strangely, struggling with what to say back to her. No black person had ever spoken to my mother before. Somewhere she had heard that Jamaican people were aggressive and lost their temper easily.

I suddenly felt sorry for Mrs Jobson, waiting there for my mother to answer. I squeezed my mother's hand, urging her to reply.

'Well, it will always grow back,' Mrs Jobson finally said.

My mother could only smile politely at Mrs Jobson before hurrying us away.

Someone else seemed to have noticed my transformation. One day, Mrs Sherman, *Jean Wali*, invited my mother and me to her house for tea. Of course, I was thrilled because I had been watching Britt from afar and believed her to be the most English girl I had ever seen.

Not only did she boast a great collection of clothes: Rupert the Bear socks, Minnie Mouse T-shirts, flowery skirts with matching ribbons, all bought from proper shops like Woolworths. She also had a mother who always wore jeans; a father who sported sideburns and did English things like go to the pub; a granny and granddad with white hair who took her for walks; an older brother who wore football shirts and looked like Richie Cunningham from *Happy Days*; a puppy called Trevor who licked her face and a nice set of English girlfriends who would visit her house every Saturday to play.

Unlike me, who always played out on the street with Gary McGuinness, the Jobson boys, Afshan and Ali plus some of the younger members from no. 7 and no. 15 (that is, when my father wasn't looking).

Britt's English life had always felt like a world away from my existence.

The next day my mother, all dressed up in her best red sari and carrying a box of Quality Street Gold, took me to Mrs Sherman's house.

'Come in, come in,' Mrs Sherman cried, ushering us through the door. She greeted my mother as if she were a long-lost best friend.

'Your mother looks like a queen,' Britt whispered to me in

the hallway, when my mother took off her coat. I giggled. What a funny thing to say!

Her mother looked like a film star. Blonde hair all puffed up, wearing orange lipstick, which I suppose complemented her red–orange hippy top.

As we entered Britt's hallway, with its sweet vanilla aroma, it suddenly occurred to me that this was the first time that I had ever been inside an English home. Britt's living room was perfect. There was no creaky sofa-bed for Mrs Sherman to quickly guide us away from. There was no clashing colour scheme to give you an instant headache. And, most notably, there was no wardrobe dominating the centre of the room. Instead the whole place was tastefully done up in primrose and maroon, with soft furniture that had been bought new.

My mother couldn't stop looking around, especially at the porcelain figurines that lined the mantelpiece, the nest of tables in the corner, the spider plants on the window sills, the family photos in the glass cabinet and a million other details that made up this dream life. I think this was also the first time my mother had ever set foot in an English house.

'Please, sit down,' Mrs Sherman said, pointing vaguely into the room, so that my mother could make her own choice about where she wanted to sit. My mother glanced around the room and finally chose the mock-Georgian paisley armchair. But then, suddenly realising that she had forgotten to give *Jean Wali* the chocolates, she quickly got up again.

'Mrs Sherman,' she announced, presenting her with the box of chocolates as if participating in an elaborate ceremonial ritual. Mrs Sherman looked at my mother as if she was the sweetest little thing she had ever seen. 'Oh, thank you. But please, call me Faye.'

My mother smiled shyly back, and sat back down on the arm-chair.

'So what shall I call you, Mrs Hai?' Faye said.

My mother looked at her, puzzled. 'Mrs Hai,' she said abruptly.

'Oh,' Faye replied, quickly sitting up, as if she had just been caught off guard.

'So, Mrs Hai,' I heard Mrs Sherman chirp to my mother, in an attempt to jolly things up a bit, 'where are you from? India?'

'Pakistan,' my mother replied, just a bit too fast. I could feel that she knew that she had just made a blunder, but wasn't sure what it was.

'Oh, sounds lovely,' Faye enthused. 'My top is Indian,' she said, pointing to it.

My mother nodded, unsure of what to say next. Those tops were one a penny back in Pakistan. An awkward silence followed.

'Do you have any other family here?' Mrs Sherman asked enthusiastically.

I could feel my mother looking at me. It was my cue to give a translation. I often had to do this. It wasn't that my mother didn't understand English. It was just that sometimes the English accent confused her – especially when she got nervous. So I repeated what Mrs Sherman had just asked. And before I had a chance to finish, Mrs Sherman was oohing and ahhing at my Urdu language skills. And then my mother suddenly burst out laughing.

'Oh, silly me,' she now piped up, laughing, having finally figured out her earlier mistake. 'My name is Noor.'

My mother's laugh was so infectious that soon Faye was laughing too, which made Britt and I fall about as well. I suddenly felt very proud of my mother's ability to entertain.

I'm not really sure how Mrs Sherman and my mother got on after that because Britt dragged me upstairs to play dolls in her room. She had her very own room: pink wallpaper, pink lampshade, pink rug, pink pillowcases and pink bedsheets.

That evening, my mother and I returned home full of inspiration.

'Mr Hai, you should have seen their kitchen. It was beautiful like TV,' my mother chirped. 'We could do that to ours.'

I couldn't wait for next Sunday to arrive. Aunt Hilda and Uncle Aslam were coming over for lunch and I was dying to tell them about my visit to Britt's house. I knew they would be interested in hearing about Britt and Mrs Sherman – after all, they were real English people, too.

Over lunch, as we made our way through my mother's ten courses, I eagerly recounted details of our visit: Mrs Sherman's nice living room, Britt's teddy-bear collection, the pink wallpaper, how my mother had made us all laugh.

'Slow down, slow down,' they would cry out, as I raced through the high points of our visit. 'And don't eat with your mouth open!'

My parents narrowed their eyes at me. I slowed down, but soon I was rambling again. This time I was telling them about the spider plants, the doorbell, Mrs Sherman's orange top and on and on.

Later on that afternoon, when we were in the living room, I overheard my uncle mention Britt's name, followed soon afterwards by the words 'mother tongue'.

I instantly sat up. Mother tongue was a thing that I often heard my father and his friends talk about – it always seemed to get them very worked up. Through my father and his friends, I had come to understand that mother tongue wasn't a proper language as such; it was something that Asian people spoke, especially Asian mothers, because they didn't know how to speak English. Anyway, something about the phrase 'mother tongue' had obviously upset my father again because he had gone rather quiet and was staring at my uncle and aunt, deep in thought. I put my head down; I could sense that the conversation was not really for my ears.

I am sitting with my brother and sister pretending to busy myself with the picture I am painting, a flying Mary Poppins, coloured in a flourish of bright colours.

'Remember Milan?' I hear Uncle Aslam say. Who can forget Milan? I certainly can't. Milan is our ex-lodger's nephew, a mixed-race Welsh-Indian boy who always gets dragged up in conversations to illustrate what can go wrong if you bring up someone to be 'half-half'.

'What's happened to him now?' Aunt Hilda asks, in a tone that suggests that there might be some 'answer' in Milan's story.

'Parents divorced,' my father says, sighing, as if to say: 'No point looking to Milan for answers.'

My mother comes in with some tea and an assorted mix of halwa. Everyone coos with pleasure. My father asks my mother to sit down. He has something to ask her.

My ears strain to make out what the elders are talking about. I miss something and then I hear my mother say in English: 'This isn't my country. I not know.'

Aunt Hilda says that she knows where she stands on this issue. But, she quickly adds, it's not her opinion that counts, it's my mother's that matters. Everyone protests at this – of course Aunt Hilda's opinion matters.

My mother explains in her broken English mixed with Urdu – which is translated to Aunt Hilda via my father and Uncle Aslam – that she doesn't want her children to be 'half-half' like Milan.

'The children could always pick Urdu up later — that is, if they are still interested in speaking it,' Aunt Hilda says, consolingly. 'Just think about Mrs Sherman. What must she have thought when Yasmin started speaking in Urdu and then English and then back in Urdu again?'

My mother is now explaining how much Mrs Sherman really liked my Urdu. But Aunt Hilda interrupts her.

'The problem is not now. It will be later,' she says. 'They won't speak English. They won't speak Urdu. What will they speak?'

'Yasmin starts school next autumn — we can't allow her to be confused,' Uncle Aslam adds.

My mother nods understandingly. Uncle Aslam did have a good point. But my father suddenly sits up. He sounds excited. He says he has a solution. My mother carries on speaking to us in Urdu, but we children only speak to her in English. By doing this, he explains, my mother can still communicate with her children, but our English — and also her English — will improve.

My mother says she likes this idea. Everyone begins to relax and halwa is passed around. It is settled. Urdu has to go. Conversation now turns to Edward Heath. My mother picks up some mending. What a hullabaloo for nothing, I think, returning to my picture. And what did any of their conversation have to do with Britt?

Over the next few months we did gradually stop speaking Urdu. It wasn't hard — I didn't even miss it. If we ever did slip up, my father was always on hand.

'Ahh uh, not in Urdu, in English please,' he would say. We would quickly correct ourselves.

My father was right — our English did improve. My mother's English got better too. She was very pleased with her progress. And so were we. But something else changed once we dropped

Urdu, something quite fundamental. It just became too frustrating trying to explain complex matters of the head and heart to my mother in English. After dropping Urdu, she became lost to me for ever.

5

Paki Land

'Hop over it!' the big girl screamed at me again. Her pigtails were shaking, her glasses slipping down her nose.

Afshan Khan nervously tugged at my jumper, her usual confident self vanished.

'Let's go,' she whispered. The last thing Afshan wanted was to become embroiled in any unpleasantness with one of the big girls at school.

'Hop! Or it's gonna be too late!'

I stared at the big girl. There was an urgency in her voice that seven-year-old me could not safely ignore. I slowly turned around. And thank goodness I did. I might have sailed through nursery and infant school but I was just about to make the biggest mistake of my entire junior-school life and I hadn't even begun the first day yet.

'Don't you see it?' the girl yelled.

Afshan and I looked at each other. We were standing at the edge of a patch of Tarmac, about the size of a tennis court, just outside our new school's entrance.

'It's, it's . . . Paki Land,' the girl said to us, her eyes bulging in horror at our ignorance. 'You can't walk over it. You have to hop.'

I looked at the black patch of land in front of us. It seemed so innocent. But it wasn't. We had even been warned about it back in infant school. Paki Land was a place where you never wanted to be caught with both your feet on the ground. Rumour had it that if you were ever seen doing the unimaginable thing of actually walking on the patch, then you had better be prepared . . .

'Prepared for what?' we would ask each other anxiously, clustered together, gazing over at the building across the street from our infant playground. It was Big School. And it loomed darkly in all our febrile imaginations.

But no one ever knew the answer.

Thank goodness the big girl, Sarah Booster, self-appointed guardian to us younger ones, had been on hand to protect us from our ignorance. Afshan and I were ever so grateful.

Just then, Perveen Shah, the big girl who lived a few doors down from us, whizzed past on one leg.

'Hop!' she waved, her high ponytail bobbing playfully behind her.

'Wait for me,' screamed Sarah Booster, hopping right after her.

At the other end of Paki Land they linked arms and ran off giggling towards the main junior playground. As I watched them disappear into a crowd of schoolchildren, I felt a wisp of envy. How nice it would be to be as assured as them.

My old infant school might only have been in the adjacent building, but walking through the junior playground was like entering another world. This was not the friendly and cosy world of my infant school where, with my elementary skills in Englishness, I had thrived.

Here in the junior playground, the air vibrated with restlessness. Everywhere I looked pupils were charging about, knocking into each other. The girls, dressed in T-shirts emblazoned with pictures of the Bay City Rollers or Legs & Co., with their arms territorially linked, were ready to crush anything that got into their way. The boys stampeded around in herds chasing footballs or playing British bulldog. Many of them had shaved heads. They didn't look like the sort of boys you would want to mess with.

Scanning the playground, I didn't see anyone playing nice games like happy families or doctors and nurses, which we used to play at infant school. I was terrified. How was I going to survive this place? Here were new rules and sub-codes about Englishness, ones that I suspected my parents, Uncle Aslam and Aunt Hilda knew nothing about.

Just then I heard a familiar voice yell out my name. It was Britt waving at me furiously as she deftly hopped across Paki Land. I was very happy to see her.

Sudbury Junior was a pretty ordinary mix of Victorian red brick and sixties' modern surrounded by concrete playground. The school had produced one celebrity it could boast of: the legendary Green Cross Code Man who, through government-sponsored poster campaigns, had been teaching children up and down the country how to cross the road. I suppose one could describe him as some sort of hero. Anyway, the school was proud of him.

Even though nearly all the Asian children in the vicinity went to Sudbury Junior, the school still ended up having a predominantly white English intake. And while the school worked hard to accommodate its ethnic minorities, the policy towards us was pretty clear: fit in and be English. And, as I was soon to find out, the school's concept of being English was different in a million ways from what I had ever been taught.

This became apparent to me that very first morning during school assembly. Assembly took place in a large hall that over-looked Paki Land. As the hall also doubled up as the school's gym, the strong smell of sweat, rubber plimsolls and stale dis-infectant hung in the air. That morning the proud pupils of Sudbury Junior filed into the hall in orderly lines before sitting down on the gym floor in neat, long rows, arms and legs crossed with precision. Mrs Griffiths, the music teacher, played a suit-ably formal tune on her piano to accompany us walking in. Being the new pupils, we were seated right up front. I was next to Britt.

Unfortunately, Afshan wasn't with us. Despite Mrs Khan's aspirations for her daughter, Afshan had been placed in Class Two. Class Two wasn't the dunce class, but it wasn't Class One, the top class, which I had been placed in. Afshan begged the teacher to let her stay with me, but it wasn't to be.

I didn't want to be separated from Afshan either, especially when I met my new teacher, Ms Smith. She wasn't exactly the smiley type. And as for my classmates, I didn't know anyone other than Britt. Britt knew some of the girls from Brownies. As I was now Britt's new best friend, I was hoping it wouldn't take long before I also got to know the Vickys, the Sarahs, the Traceys and the Sharons in my class. Glancing over at Afshan a few rows back, I was happy to see that she was settling in too. She was sitting with Danny Jobson, the youngest of the Jobson boys who lived at no. 14.

Once the whole school was seated, Mrs Griffiths put her index finger to her lips. When we were suitably quiet, a rather solemn-looking man entered the hall. We all craned our necks to look as Mrs Griffiths started playing a more sombre tune on her piano. This was Mr Morris, the headmaster. Mr Morris slowly made his way down the centre aisle of the hall and onto

65

the stage. Then, without saying a word, he lifted his right hand to indicate that we stand. Also without saying a word, Mr Morris closed his eyes and lowered his head.

'Our Father . . .' he bellowed.

What a strange thing to say, I thought. I was just about to nudge Britt to share a giggle when I saw her lower her head, too. I was glad she didn't see my startled face. By now all my other classmates down the row had also lowered their heads. And the hall was beginning to echo with chanting. The same words that Mr Morris was chanting. It sounded like a song, but there was no melody. The pupils were behaving as if they were in a trance, monotonously reciting words that didn't make much sense to me. The spectacle was so strange, and made doubly bizarre by some pupil I could see outside through the tall windows of the hall, late for school, hopping furiously across Paki Land. I felt myself shrinking.

When Mr Morris said, 'Amen,' I suddenly realised 'Our Father' was a prayer. I was stunned. Wasn't being non-religious synonymous with being modern, which was synonymous with being English?

'They made you say prayers, Christian prayers?' my father asked, later that evening. He seemed surprised. We had just finished supper and my father was settling down to listen to the BBC World Service news.

I nodded, looking terribly aggrieved.

'Umm,' my father said, thinking hard. Usually he would have consulted Uncle Aslam and Aunt Hilda about the matter, but unfortunately they were away in India. My father sat up, and then his face dissolved into a smile. 'Don't worry, all your prayer problems will soon be solved.'

When he came home from work the next evening he passed

66

me a little package from his briefcase. The package was wrapped up in brown paper and string, just like a gift Milly-Molly-Mandy would have received. My brother and sister looked on with envy as I tore the wrapping off. Inside I found a little red book. It looked very important.

'Let me see, let me see!' my sister cried, trying to grab the book.

'No,' I said, hugging it closer to my chest.

'Open it,' my father said, encouragingly. He was obviously pleased with his present.

I carefully opened the tightly bound book as if it were a fragile ornament. Underneath the hard cover, I found hundreds of thin, flimsy pages, like tracing paper, full of small black text. But there were no pictures.

'It's a prayer book,' my father said, taking it from me. 'There's even hymns at the back.'

He flicked to the back of the book until he found 'All Things Bright and Beautiful', the hymn the school had sung after prayers. 'See,' he said, passing the book back to me, 'now you will never get stuck.'

I should have been more grateful. But I wasn't. What kind of answer was this to my prayer question? My brother and my sister had already wandered off, bored.

'Christianity is very important to English people,' my father said, seeing my face fall. 'It is everywhere.'

I couldn't help thinking he was terribly wrong. Christianity wasn't everywhere.

'One day you might even try reading the Bible,' my father continued. 'It's an interesting story. Think of all those Christmas plays that Uncle Aslam and Aunt Hilda have taken you to. Mary and Joseph, Noah's Ark, Joseph and his dreamcoat . . .'

'Jacob's ladder,' I added.

'Yes!' he exclaimed, pleased that I was finally responding with interest. 'Well, all those stories come from the Bible.'

For a few minutes I allowed my mind to drift over these stories. I hadn't realised they came from the Bible. Maybe Christianity wasn't that bad after all. For a moment I let my imagination roam over the gifts that the three wise men had brought Jesus, the rush basket that Moses was carried down the river in, the size of the stone that David had thrown at Goliath, the thickness of Samson's jet-black hair . . .

'Just remember though,' I heard my father say, his face turning serious. 'There is no God. Education is number-one weapon.'

A strange thing happened after my father's little sermon on religion: he turned out to be right, Christianity really was everywhere. Britt and my other English girlfriends – Emma, Lisa, Vicky – all wore gold crosses around their necks. Britt never came out to play on Sunday mornings. And now I guessed the reason why my father would never let me join the Brownies, no matter how much I pleaded and pleaded; because it was closely tied up with the Church.

My father might have tried to educate me about Christianity to stop me from feeling alienated, but the more I became acquainted with Christian England, the more I began to realise that there were some things about England and the way that the English lived that I would never be part of. And it was all because I wasn't a Christian. It was as if I lived in a parallel world.

With time, I got over my shock about prayers and even began to enjoy assembly time, especially the hymn-singing part. Now I could happily sing along to the hymns, courtesy of the red book my father had given me. Unlike the other Asian kids in my year, who sat three rows in front of me, looking rather restless at assembly time, much to Mr Morris's utter frustration.

They were exactly the kind of children my father and Uncle Aslam often spoke about so disparagingly. The girls wore synthetic Indian tunics over trousers, while the boys wore mismatched clothes. Their hair was always thickly coated with olive oil – a sign of vitality in Asian culture – which their mothers would have lovingly massaged into their heads that morning, oblivious to the fact that in England, oily hair was seen as dirty.

Some of the Asian kids I knew from down my road, like Samira and Munira or the Quereshi three, Amir, Shazia and Tanveer. (There used to be five of them but the two eldest daughters had run off with their boyfriends.) I didn't exactly know the Quereshi children, as one tended to steer clear of them. They had a reputation for being rather rough, especially Amir, the eldest.

Yet Amir, along with Samira and the others, always waved at me as I filed out of the hall at assembly time. And though I would smile back, I secretly felt sorry for them all. They just weren't English in the way the school demanded and definitely not English in the way the playground demanded.

I was soon doing so well at school that Mrs Griffiths had no hesitation about putting me forward to represent Sudbury Junior in the Brent Primary Schools Country Dancing Championships. This was a first for an Asian girl.

On the big day, my mother, dressed in her best sari, proudly watched her little Yasmin do-si-do, jig and skip a figure of eight to Mrs Griffiths' repertoire of best English country-dancing hits, hammered out on her piano. My mother beamed with pride when the teachers came up to her and congratulated her on my fine dancing, though she was probably more interested in hearing what they had to say about the dress that she had so painstakingly sewed for me. Though I wanted a simple frock from Woolworths or C&A like the other girls wore, my mother was not having any of it. As far as she was concerned, the more bows and ribbons on a dress, the more affluent the Hai family would appear to the outside world.

'But Mum, everyone will laugh when they see me in that,' I cried in frustration when I saw the dress she was making for me.

'Laugh, *kyoon* [why]?' she replied.

'Because I'll look like a meringue!'

'Meringue? *Kya hai* [what is that]?' she asked, tying a stray ribbon on the collar into a pretty bow.

'You know, a meringue,' I answered, exasperated. 'Like cake.'

My mother looked at me as if I were insane. How could a dress be a cake?

I took a deep breath. Why did all my conversations with my mother take this route? I attempted a different tack. 'Mum, if I wear that,' I said, pointing to the dress, 'I will look like Samira and Munira.' I pointed dramatically out of the window, in the direction of their house across the street. 'Do you want that?'

My mother put her needle down. Her eyebrows creased in contemplation of what I had said. After a few seconds she shook her head. No, she couldn't see what was wrong with Samira and Munira's clothes. She thought they looked quite nice, especially given that they didn't have that much money.

'Mum!' I cried, stamping my feet. My mother shook her head and returned her attention to the dress. I racked my brain trying to find the words that could simply explain to my mother the concept of English fashion, not immigrant Asian fashion. But it was to no avail.

'Mum, do you know what fashion is?' I asked.

'*Feshon*?' my mother said. She repeated the word slowly to herself.

'No, fffffaaaasshion,' I said.

'*Feshon*,' my mother said again, perplexed.

70

I gave up. The next morning I had no choice but to leave the house wearing my mother's meringue-like dress. As I waddled out of the house, tears of joy welled up in my mother's eyes. Maybe that is why she always beamed with such pride during the dances. Not only did I always dance the best but also, compared to the other girls, in their dowdy frocks, she was convinced that I looked the prettiest, if not the classiest.

The class register was one of those school rituals that always reminded me that maybe I didn't fit in as well as I thought. For some reason, many of the teachers always pronounced my name as Jasmin.

'No, Yasmin,' I'd pipe back.

'Oh,' Ms Smith would say, glancing back at the register. Then she would look at me. 'Really, how odd.'

How I dreaded words like odd. But I had learnt how to get round this irritation.

'My name is Yasmin,' I would say. 'But Jasmin is my Christian name.'

The teacher would nod knowingly. For every non-English person was expected to have a Christian name. The way it worked was that you had your real name, which had been lovingly given to you by your family but which no one in England could ever pronounce. And then you had your other name, which meant nothing to you or your family but which everyone in England could pronounce. And this was the name you often ended up using. Calling it your 'Christian name' gave it more legitimacy.

Once the little problem of my first name had been resolved, act two of the excruciatingly embarrassing play would follow.

'OK, well, YYYYaaaasmin Hayyyyyy!' Ms Smith would continue.

'No, Hai as in "high",' I would reply.

'Hi, Yasmin,' some clever twat would now interject.

'Yeah, hi, hi, Yasmin,' others would join in, rolling about with laughter.

To jolly things along, I would sometimes play up. For by now I understood that one of the keys to thriving in big school was to be as rowdy and funny as possible in class. The rowdier you were, the more popular you became with your classmates. This was not like infant school. One didn't aspire to be the best student in the class, one tried to be the naughtiest, if not the hardest nut of all.

My father had deeply imprinted into me his belief that academic success was all that mattered. But on the other hand, how was I going to succeed as the eternal butt of the class joke? This was especially imperative because the next name on the register was Jayesh Gangamata-Bhatiya. Jayesh might have giggled along with the rest of the class, but all the time his gaze had remained low, painfully aware that everyone's attention would soon be turning upon him.

On cue, after having struggled with both of our names, Ms Smith would now inevitably quip: 'Oh why can't you lot be like everyone else and just have English names!'

I knew that she wouldn't dare say anything similar to any of the black kids in the class. I was convinced she was scared of them. Or to be more exact, she was scared of their parents. Mrs Jobson had come marching down to school because Ms Smith had apparently made some unpleasant remark to Danny Jobson. The whole first year had gathered to watch the showdown.

'You think you better than us?' Mrs Jobson had berated her. 'The dark ages are long gone, you know.'

Everyone had clapped furiously at Mrs Jobson's reference to the 'dark ages', though no one could have understood what she meant. Still, for me the moment was magical. A feeling of pure euphoria that I had never experienced before rushed through me. For a short moment, Mrs Jobson's victory felt like mine.

I dreamt of my father marching down to school, appearing outside the window of my classroom, ready to put Ms Smith masterfully in her place! But I quickly put that fantasy out of my mind. For what would everyone say when they saw my father charging through the playground? My father didn't wear casual leisure clothes like other normal seventies' parents. He and Uncle Aslam preferred formal attire all the way: 1930s-style suit and tie with a trilby hat, like they wore in black-and-white films.

I did manage to put a smile on Ms Smith's face eventually, courtesy of my father. We had been learning the Green Cross Code on fireworks safety for Bonfire Night.

'Guy Fawkes was a Catholic,' I said, unable to resist giving the class a bit of background information on Christianity, gleaned during my night-time educational sessions with my father. 'He was hanged because he wanted freedom for Irish people and . . .'

'Well done, Jasmin,' Ms Smith said, 'excellent knowledge of English history. How did you know that?'

I shrugged shyly, slightly taken aback by Ms Smith's praise. But for a brief moment, I had a glimpse into what my father meant about education being a weapon. Maybe there was some mileage in his advice.

To prevent the white teachers labelling us failures, my father had decided to give my brother, my sister and I extra lessons at home, so that we always remained one step ahead. In fact, he even went and designed a curriculum of English, maths and reading for each of us, which we had to adhere to strictly. We were rewarded with gold stars for good work and punished by occasional stick beatings on our palms if we did not do well. In

73

addition, every fortnight we would be asked to look up the meaning of twenty long words, which my father had carefully selected from his reading of the *Guardian*. We would then have to write the words down with their meanings beside them, and then pin the list up by our beds and memorise the words. Woe betide any one of us who failed this task.

School holidays were the worst. I dreaded them. In fact, all three of us did. For us, school breaks were not about play or sleeping in: they were about more boring maths and grammar. The holidays just couldn't go fast enough. My father would occasionally organise a 'fun' visit to the Tower of London or the Natural History Museum – but when we got back home we would have to write an essay about our trip, which my father would then mark with gold or silver stars.

Maybe that is why, despite Paki Land and Ms Smith, I began to love school. In comparison to lessons with my father at home, it felt like a holiday.

Meanwhile, I was learning lessons at school that I could never have been taught at home. It was mid-morning break, and Britt and I had been cornered by Perveen Shah and Sarah Booster. They were painstakingly trying to educate us about the facts of life which, as far as Britt and I were concerned, was the daftest thing we had ever heard of.

'That's silly,' screamed Britt, as Sarah demonstrated with her fingers.

'No, it's true,' giggled Perveen from behind her hands. 'That is what happens and once it goes in . . .'

She was about to expand further when we were interrupted by a high-pitched scream behind us. Turning around, we saw Gary McGuinness running after the remedial kids, who were about to board their bus. The 'remedial' class – the ones suffering from learning difficulties – consisted almost entirely of the school's Asian kids who were struggling with English. Twice a week they would be taken to another location on the school bus to learn their second language. It was similar to the school bus that ferried the local disabled children around.

Gary McGuinness had run in front of Samira and Jelal and was jumping up and down as if in fits of spasms. It was his impersonation of Quasimodo, a cruel put-down currently very popular in the playground if you wanted someone to know that you thought they were a moron.

'Go on, Gary! Do it again. Go on!' a boy named Mick Turton shouted, hurtling across the playground, followed closely by his scruffy gang. Soon Samira, Munira, the Quereshi three and the other Asian kids were surrounded and being taunted with Quasimodo impersonations and chants of 'Joey'. 'Joey' was another stinging put-down for someone who you considered a dunce.

It was all getting too much. Amir Quereshi suddenly turned round and then ran towards Mick Turton and threw him to the ground. For a second everyone stood back, shocked that someone had dared to take on Mick Turton. But then Mick's friends piled in, laying into Amir, whooping wildly with unashamed pleasure. I turned away, unable to watch.

Finally, Mr Morris came striding across the playground, Perveen leading him. The boys saw him, too. They pulled themselves off Amir and turned . . . to me! I suddenly saw Mick and his stupid gang charging at me, hooting and screaming. I froze. I stood there alone, unable to move. They were buffaloes on a rampage, unstoppable.

I closed my eyes and started to pray, 'Our Father, who art in heaven . . .' I could hear them getting closer. And then everything went silent. The gang ran right past, not laying a finger upon me.

'Are you OK? Are you?' I heard Britt asking me.

I nodded, but in truth I felt sick. Deep down I knew that it wasn't God who had saved me. No. Mick Turton and his friends hadn't touched me because they saw me as one of them.

At times like that, I didn't know whether to be happy or sad about how English I was. But wasn't that why no one gave me a hard time at school? I was seen as being part of the elite crowd of Asians who were considered English. Or at least English enough. There weren't many of us in the school – just me and a few others. We were the kind of Asians Mick Turton would never dream of raising his fist to.

We were the sort of Asians considered acceptable enough to get invited to our English friends' homes for tea. We were the kind of Asians that teachers felt confident enough about to give leading parts – OK, secondary leading parts – in the school play. And, more importantly, we were the type of Asians the school could confidently put forward in national competitions. I should have been happy about how far I had come. But after the Mick Turton–Amir affair, my achievements were starting to feel rather sour. It seemed that for every so-called winner like me, there were plenty of losers like Samira and Jelal.

And then my father's attitude towards Englishness took an unexpected turn, threatening to undo all the progress I was making.

6

Curry Lover

'Western low-brow rubbish!' my father angrily cried out. He was standing in front of the TV, as Britain's number-one, never-to-be-missed programme, *Top of the Pops*, was nearing its climax.

It was Thursday evening, and the new chart number one was just about to be announced. I got up to turn the TV off. But it was agony.

'Come on, hurry up,' he said, annoyed at my dawdling. I toyed with the idea of arguing back.

'But Dad,' I wanted to say, 'all my friends watch it.' But what was the point of objecting? He would never be convinced. Still, my father's attitude baffled me. Hadn't he always taught us that being *modern* was good? But apparently *modern* wasn't good when it was tied up with this thing called *westernisation*.

It was was a tricky concept, this difference between being English and modern and being 'Western'. Though, I was coming to suspect that being 'westernised' had to do with being American and therefore connected with that naughty word 'sex' – a word we were not allowed to mention in the house. 'English', on the other hand, was to do with being intellectual.

'Look at all those playboys and discos in Tehran,' I once overheard my father saying to Uncle Aslam in disgust. 'That's westernisation for you!'

But then we watched a documentary about the Saudi princess who was stoned to death for having a boyfriend. Apparently, the princess was very westernised. I thought my father would have disapproved of her, but instead he got on the phone to Uncle Aslam and ranted on about how the girl's murderers were 'barbarians'.

At some point my father had started discouraging – or more like banning – us from engaging in a whole range of so-called Western activities. These included: rollerskating, chewing bubblegum, listening to pop music and watching *Top of the Pops*.

The older I grew, the more impatient I began to feel about his diktats, especially as a lot of his dos and don't's seemed to contradict each other. For a start, I was constantly being reminded how good the English were. But, at other times, not only was I warned off from doing archetypal English things (like eating fish and chips on the street), I was told to despise the British for keeping us down. Similarly, we were banned from watching Richard Attenborough's film *Gandhi*, because my father concluded it was a piece of British propaganda. But we regularly sat together on Friday nights to watch the latest episode of *Mind Your Language*. And while we were encouraged to play sport, especially football, we were discouraged from taking an interest in cricket because my father said it was an 'upper-class English' game.

And now, instead of finding out who was number one this week in the charts, I was faced once again with the fallout from one of my father's paradoxical principles. Did my father not realise that by stopping me from watching the crucial moment in that night's *TOTP*, he was putting his dream of turning me into a typical English girl in jeopardy? In fact, he was putting my entire future popularity in the playground under threat. For rumour had it that Britain's new number one, to be announced that night, would be none other than 'Summer Loving', from the film *Grease*.

While missing out on a whole decade of pop music was painful enough, being banned from seeing *Grease* was one of the most unforgivable things my father ever did to me. No matter how much I pleaded with him to take us to see the film, he wouldn't give in. I even deployed my dependable wild card, informing my father that even all the Asian children down the road had been 'modern' enough to have seen it. But he would not be swayed, which subjected me to months of slow torture in the playground. For these days the only game my friends and I would play at break time was *Grease*.

'No, like this,' Britt cried at Emma, who was playing Sandy, AKA Olivia Newton-John. Britt, who was playing Danny / John Travolta (it was an all-girl show), momentarily stepped out of her role to pick up a stick lying beside her feet. Britt turned into Sandy, tossing her shoulders back and affecting a petulant pout as she threw the stick – her make-believe cigarette butt – onto the ground and sexily stubbed it out with her heel.

Britt looked up at the rest of us. 'And then you wait a few seconds before saying: Tell me about it, stud.'

'That's not how it goes,' Emma protested, looking dubiously at Britt. 'Sandy doesn't wait a few seconds before she speaks. She says it as she stubs the cigarette out.'

'No, she doesn't,' Britt cried back, stamping her foot so hard that her left sock slid down her calf.

Britt shook her head at me in exasperation. 'Yasmin, tell Emma.'

'No, Britt's right,' I said firmly to Emma. 'And then, after that, John Travolta falls to the ground in shock.'

During the whole time we played *Grease* at school, I never let on to anyone that I had never seen the film. In fact, I told the others that I'd seen it four times. The only reason I had got away with it, up to now, was because I listened hard and had picked up the storyline.

But maybe I hadn't been working hard enough, because now Emma was shaking her head at me, looking puzzled. 'That's not what John Travolta does.'

I felt my face go red. 'Yes, he does,' I said, trying to look her directly in the eye, without much success.

'Emma is right,' Lulu suddenly said from behind me.

I flinched. Trust Lubna Hussain to butt in. I slowly turned towards her, trying to look contemptuous of what she had to say. But inside, I was starting to panic.

At first appearances Lubna – who insisted that we call her 'Lulu' – was the sort of girl who should have become my close friend. Not only did she come from the kind of Asian family that my father would have approved of, she was also neat and tidy, spoke very good English and always said her pleases and thank yous. She went on proper family summer holidays to places like Butlins, unlike our educational day trips. And, most impressive of all, she had seen *Grease* more than ten times. No wonder she was so popular with Britt and the others.

But I didn't like Lulu. There was something about her that didn't feel quite right. Not that I ever let on to anyone: she was far too popular to bitch about. And Lulu wasn't too keen on me, either. Not that *she* ever let on to anyone. I knew this because whenever we played British bulldog she never held my hand tightly and whenever we played *Grease* she always ensured that I was cast as one of the background characters.

'No, Yasmin can't be one of the Pink Ladies or one of the T Birds,' she would cry. 'She is not wearing a Rupert the Bear dress, like the rest of us. We have to look like a gang, right?'

The others, glancing at my homemade dress, would reluctantly agree. And I would quickly give in; keen to deflect any attention away from myself before it gave others ideas.

But at that moment, I wasn't in the mood to give into Lulu. Having dreamt the night before that John Travolta and I had walked arm in arm down my road, I was feeling rather emboldened.

'He does fall down in shock,' I cried, turning to look straight at her.

My forcefulness made an impact.

'Yes, maybe Yasmin's right,' I heard Emma concede.

'Course, she is,' said Britt loyally, grinning at me.

Aware that everyone was awaiting her response, Lulu reluctantly gave in. 'OK, maybe,' she said, shrugging nonchalantly.

I smiled graciously, but I was pleased to see her cheeks had gone slightly red.

One day, Jayesh whispered to me that his mother said that Lulu's family were *chumchas*. I didn't quite understand what the word meant, but I soon figured it out.

The Asian Mothers' Mafia, for whom school pick-up time was always a bit of a social occasion, would turn up at the gates dressed in their best *salwar kameezes*. As they eyed up each other's clothes, they would exchange gossip, swap recipes and Hindi music tapes before wandering back home with their children to cook dinner for their husbands.

The first time I saw Mrs Hussain, I couldn't stop staring and neither could the Asian mothers.

'*Behenji, dekho* [Look at her, sister, look at her],' the women whispered excitedly to each other. 'Look at her, look, sister, look.'

She was wearing a short blue skirt and matching jacket with a white scarf tied at the neck and a blue leather handbag with white straps over her shoulders. While most Asian women wore their long black hair in either a plait or a bun, Mrs Hussain wore her hair shoulder length in a seventies flicked style, like Diana Rigg from *The Avengers*. I had never before seen an Asian woman wear English clothes. Asian women only wore Indian clothes. It would have seemed more normal if Mr Morris had turned up wearing a dress.

My mother had to prod me twice before I stopped staring . . . and still I turned around to have a quick peek. And so did she and the rest of the Asian Mothers' Mafia. What would their husbands say if they came home one day with their hair cut off or their legs bare? Shame, shame!

'Who is she?' Mrs Khan squealed.

'Christian, *ho gi* [must be Christian],' Aunt Farida said, knowingly.

'*Han* [yes]. Goan?' Aunt Feroz suggested. For Goan Christians were the only Indians who wore Western clothes. But that didn't seem to be the case here, because little Samira had just told her mother, Mrs Rehman, that the woman's name was Mrs Hussain.

'Hussain? Muslim name? Like us!' Mrs Khan cried. 'What village does she come from?'

'Must be Bombay,' my mother said, handing me a packet of ready-salted crisps.

'*Nahin, Karachi se ho gi* [no, must be Karachi],' Aunt Feroz said, before adding in English: 'My cousin's sisters dress like that.'

The women didn't get a chance to satisfy their curiosity. No matter how much they smiled at her, Mrs Hussain simply wasn't interested in them. In fact, she didn't acknowledge them at all. No, she walked right past and stood at the other end of the school gates along with the English mothers. This didn't go down too well with the Asian mothers. 'Pahh, she thinks she's *modon!*' they whispered to each other, their usual put-down for anyone who thought herself to be above the others.

The mothers watched as Lulu, dressed in a denim pinafore, came bounding out of the school, hopped over Paki Land, and ran over to her mother, who planted a kiss on her cheek.

'*Pata hai, ghar se bhaagi ho gi* [you know, she might be run away from home],' Aunt Farida reflected. Aunty Salma and Aunt Hasna agreed. They said they had heard about those types before. There had even been a piece about an Asian girl on the six o'clock news the other night. She had run off with her white boyfriend. The women whispered quick prayers.

'Ohh, yes, I saw that,' said Mrs Khan. 'I make Ali stand in front of the TV.'

Mrs Hussain was now handing crisp packets to Lulu and her brother. And they were not ready-salted flavour – so old fashioned! – but packets of Monster Munch. I wondered dreamily what it would be like to have a mother who handed out fancy packets of crisps. A mother who wore English clothes and knew about fashion, not *feshon*.

'She's probably married to a *gora* [white person],' Aunt Bilquis said.

'No, her girl is far too dark,' Mrs Khan tut-tutted.

'Sometimes, they come like that,' Aunt Hasna said. 'My granddad was so white that everyone thought he was English . . .'

That evening, as my mother cooked dinner, I couldn't help thinking about Mrs Hussain. My mind began to wander as I imagined what life would be like if Mrs Hussain were my mother. The fun times we could have . . . and how there would be no confusion between us because Mrs Hussain understood

English perfectly. Suddenly, out of nowhere, images of my mother floated across my mind, dressed in her best sari, beaming away at me while I danced the figure of eight at the Country Dancing Championships.

I felt my stomach turn with guilt. My mother was smiling at me apologetically as if she knew what I was thinking. At least, that's how it seemed to me. I wanted to kiss my mother and tell her that I loved her and would never leave her behind, no matter how English I became. But how would I explain that to her?

After seeing Mrs Hussain, I couldn't help feeling slightly in awe of Lulu. I had to admit that she was properly English in ways I could never be. And maybe I would have continued grudgingly looking up to Lulu if she hadn't gone and upset me that lunch time.

I was one of those rare, strange cases who loved school dinners. Every morning I would hassle Lisa and Vicky to find out from their mothers – who were the school's dinner ladies – what was on the menu. If it was roast, I would be ecstatic. My morning lessons would be broken up with daydreams of crispy roast potatoes and gravy. I had been given the option of bringing a packed lunch, but once my father had discovered that the table was full of Asian kids who brought leftover curry from home to eat, he decided that sitting on the packed-lunch table wouldn't be the best for me.

One lunch time, Lulu and I were sitting amongst our English friends, eating fish and chips, when I picked up the pepper shaker and sprayed pepper all over my food.

'Uhh, that's disgusting,' Lulu cried out, wrinkling her nose.

I instantly put down the pepper pot. But it was too late. Everyone on the table was looking at my plate.

'The cap slipped,' I found myself saying apologetically, though not entirely sure why I was saying that.

'No it didn't,' Lulu cried out, leaning forward to inspect my plate. 'Face it, you like spicy food.'

'Curry lover, curry lover, Yasmin is a curry lover,' Lulu began chanting.

'I don't eat curry. You do, like Jayesh!' I petulantly cried back, hastily putting my fork down.

'I don't eat curry,' she replied, dramatically flinging herself back in her seat as if to illustrate how far off the mark I was. 'You do, your mum cooks it every day.'

'No, she doesn't,' I replied. 'She only cooks fish and chips.'

'You are such a liar,' Lulu screamed, breaking into howls of fake laughter, though she did dart a nervous glance at the others.

Britt, Lisa and Vicky were staring at us, slightly amused and yet bewildered. But this didn't stop Lulu and me. We were oblivious. I proudly claimed that I ate fish and chips every day except Sundays, when my mother cooked roast lamb. For a second Lulu looked stumped. But she quickly collected herself.

'Fish and chips on Mondays,' she said, counting the first day on her finger. 'Sausages and mash on Tuesdays, shepherd's pie on Wednesdays, steak and kidney pie on Thursdays,' Lulu paused, registering the look of dismay on my face. 'And then liver on Fridays and burger and chips on the weekends.'

Lulu sat up, looking very pleased with herself. But she wasn't finished yet. 'And during the summer, we eat salad and . . .' she paused, trying to find her killer line, 'and . . . and prawn cocktail.'

What was prawn cocktail? I wondered.

'And for breakfast we have bacon and . . .' Lulu suddenly gasped and put her hands to her mouth. Her face went pale. 'And, and,' she stuttered. Her voice dipped. '. . . And we have toast and jam . . .'

I was staring straight at her.

Lulu raised her chin sheepishly, daring me to say something. I had never met a Muslim who ate pork and, from the look of horror that had passed over Lulu's face, I guess she hadn't either.

Lulu was now looking down at her plate, feebly prodding the fish. She would have loved to retract her words, but knew it was too late. But she also knew that if I made a fuss about her family eating bacon, then I would reveal how un-English I was. It was a case of mutual checkmate.

'You know, I'm only joking,' she purred, after a few seconds of quiet. 'Nothing wrong with being a curry lover.'

Before I knew it, my glass of orange juice was all over Lulu's stupid face.

Everyone in the dining hall stopped to watch. But I didn't care. I was glad I did it. And I didn't regret what I had done, even when Lulu began to scream. Britt was looking at me, horrified. The dinner ladies were calling me a savage. Other pupils were jumping about excitedly, pointing at Lulu's dripping head. Mr Morris appeared and led me out of the hall by my ear. I felt proud of what I had done. It was like when Mrs Jobson fought back against Ms Smith. I suddenly began to fancy myself as a bit of an outlaw, a rebel – maybe like Robin Hood. Maybe I would wear red to school tomorrow. I felt invincible.

That is, until I got home.

The school had rung my father while he was at work. Mr Morris had recounted the gory details.

'A savage. That is what they called you. Is that what my daughter is?' my father kept crying at me. Each time I shook my head. My father seemed more agitated by the word savage than by what I had done to Lulu. I tried to tell him my side of the story, but he wasn't interested. In fact, the only time my father showed any sympathy was when he discovered that Lulu was Asian. This unexpected detail temporarily seemed to change matters.

'Asian, like us?' he asked.

'*Modon* Asian,' I replied, trying to fully convey the kind of person I had been dealing with in Lulu.

But as I opened my mouth to explain further I found myself stumped for words. I suddenly felt silly saying that the reason why Lulu and I had fallen out was because neither of us wanted to admit that we ate Indian food. Had we really argued over that?

In the end, feeling totally deflated, I said that I would apologise to Lulu. My father nodded approvingly. But I knew I had let him down.

I didn't wear red to school the next day and, given my reception, maybe I should have worn black. When I went up to my friends in the playground, they all turned their back on me – even Britt. She put a protective arm around Lulu. Fine, I thought to myself, as they divided themselves into groups to play British bulldog. I will find new friends. No one stopped me from walking off.

Samira and some of her Asian girlfriends were ever so thrilled to have me play with them. They went out of their way to make me feel welcome. When they played baddies, they let me be the heroine. When they played weddings, they let me be the bride. And when they played *kapadia* (the Indian version of British bulldog), they let me choose sides. But despite all their kindness, I didn't really enjoy myself. Maybe it was because Samira and her friends only spoke in Punjabi to each other, which I didn't really understand. Or maybe it was because their games involved play-acting some Indian film star that I had never heard of.

By the time it came to afternoon break and I could hear the lyrics from 'Summer Loving' starting up, I was aching with loneliness. All my grand ideas of being the romantic outlaw were losing their appeal. Maybe Britt noticed that my revolutionary zeal was slackening, because she finally came over to talk to me, just as I was leaving the school entrance.

'Please say sorry to her, she's really upset,' pleaded Britt.

I didn't reply.

'She was crying all last night,' continued Britt, as if this small detail might sway me. 'In fact, my mum had to speak to hers.'

'What!' I said, surprised. This was news to me. 'Speak to her mum? When?'

'On the phone, last night,' Britt replied.

'They spoke on the phone?' I said, amazed.

'Yes, Lulu rang us all last night. She was really upset.'

I didn't know whether to be outraged that Lulu had the cheek to phone everyone or to be surprised that she was allowed to use the telephone. Lulu really must come from a modern family.

'Can't you say sorry?' begged Britt. 'We all miss you.'

That made me perk up a bit. 'But she's the one who started it,' I said, not ready to give in. 'Didn't you hear what she said?' I struggled to say the words 'curry lover'.

'But you threw your drink over her,' Britt pointed out, reasonably.

I knew that whatever I said to Britt, none of it would make any sense to her. But then it didn't really make sense to me.

'Please say sorry,' pleaded Britt.

I turned away, pretending that I wasn't interested. Just then Samira walked past with Munira.

'Bye, Yasmin, see you tomorrow,' she cried, just a bit too shrilly for my ears.

'Yes, see you tomorrow,' I replied, waving back at her.

It was while watching Samira hop across Paki Land with her plaits, lunch box and odd terrycloth socks tucked into her *salwar kameez* that I knew that I was going to have to apologise to

Lulu. The prospect of spending another day playing happy Indian families with Samira and her friends was already filling me with dread.

Lulu loved my grovelling apology. A big, inauthentic tear ran down her face to show how much she really appreciated it. Of course, on cue everyone then went, 'Aahhh.' I felt sick, especially as I caught Samira watching me from the other end of the playground. She smiled at me but I knew I had let her down.

School life soon returned to normal. I should have been happy, but I wasn't. Something had changed. It wasn't that I had been exposed for being less English than Lulu. For some reason I didn't care about that any more. It was just that from then on, whatever I did or wherever I went, I knew how out of place I was. It wasn't that I hadn't noticed it before. But before I'd believed that with a bit of knowledge and a bit of wiliness I could make myself belong anywhere. Now, I no longer believed that.

7

My uncle, the mullah

Interestingly, even though my father did not have much in common with our Asian neighbours or the wider Asian community – the *mahalla* – he thought it important that we keep in contact.

'Who else have we got here?' I once heard him say to my mother. 'This is our lot. These are the people who will celebrate our future joys and these will be the people who will bury us, too.'

'Allah!' my mother exclaimed. 'Don't talk like that.'

We would often meet up with the *mahalla* at the Asian gatherings. My father didn't care much for these occasions, but my mother loved them, especially when we played host. And once I got over the embarrassment of our English neighbours watching in horror as hundreds of Asians descended upon our house, I enjoyed them too.

As soon as the front door closed behind me, I would allow the festive mood of the gathering to carry me away. The adults would be in particularly carefree spirits, highly aware of how precious the next few hours were; a rare moment to put the outside English world behind them.

'*Urreh*. Is that you Sahib, how long has it been?' uncles would exclaim, greeting each other with exuberant bear hugs.

'Oh, first class,' the women would sing as another aunty took off her heavy English woollen overcoat to reveal the Banarasi silk sari worn underneath.

'Oi, over here,' my brother, my sister and I would cry from the stairway, as another child walked through the door, tightly clutching the obligatory boxes of Quality Street chocolates – a present for us. With so many children to play with, we were dizzy with excitement. We could be as boisterous as we wished, and for once no adult would tell us off.

'Just like home,' the parents would say wistfully, watching us run around without a care.

As we played, the women would huddle into the kitchen to help my mother with the food that she had been preparing all week. They had the option of sitting in the living room with the men, but for some reason they never did. One aunty would start chopping the salad, another would start rolling out flour for the chapattis, another would sift the rice, another would prepare the garnishes, all the time laughing and chatting. 'Too many cooks spoil the broth' was obviously not a proverb that any of the aunties were familiar with.

Meanwhile the men would commandeer our small living room. How they all fitted in, I don't know. But they found space. And once settled, the discussions began, often about politics and often with my father taking the opposing side to all of his guests. The few times I wandered into the living room, along with all the other aunties and children alarmed by the raised voices, I would see my uncles screaming at my father, hands in the air, imploring him to understand. Some would even be on their feet, stamping the floor with passionate frustration. All the while my father would sit back, shaking his head in despair. It was such a frightening sight to see the men arguing with my father that I often wished he would just give in. But he always stood firm. And just when I thought the argument couldn't get any worse, the men would collapse into laughter. The noise would be so loud that, again, all the children and women would rush into the living room to see what had happened. The men, including my father, would be doubled up in their seats, slapping each other's backs, tears rolling down their faces.

At some point, the delicious smells of kebabs, biriyani and stews would start floating through the house. That's when the teasing would start.

'*Ehh, bhache*, tell the ladies we are getting hungry,' the men would cry at us, as we darted around them.

'No,' we would retort, looking slightly cross.

Being British born, some of us couldn't help thinking that it was all a bit unfair.

'Why are the men sitting around talking while our mums do all the work?' we would ask, very indignant.

Our parents would laugh at us.

'*Urreh*, did you hear what Jelal just said?' our parents would cry.

'Go on, shoo!' they would chuckle before shaking their heads. 'British kids!'

For some reason, describing us as 'British kids', would make them laugh even more.

In fact, the only miserable-looking creatures at the party would be the teenage boys. They would either hang out in one of the bedrooms upstairs or loiter about in the garden enjoying a sneaky fag. They seemed to inhabit a dark, moody world. They traded ominous words like 'gangs' and 'beat-ups'. Hearing them talk, I was happy to run off and return to the warmer, more carefree world of our jovial parents.

One thing my Asian neighbours enjoyed almost as much as a party was a visit to Heathrow Airport, Terminal Three. They often did this even when they were not going there to meet anyone. It wasn't just that they loved watching the planes taking off and landing; visiting the airport also gave them a chance to reminisce about the past. The sight of families reuniting or waving goodbye always reduced them to tears, transporting them back to the time when they, too, had left loved ones behind to make their journey to England.

But today we were not going to the airport to watch planes take off or to ogle tearful passengers. Today was a special occasion. I knew this because Uncle Waseem had borrowed his best friend's car – a yellow Datsun – to drive us. We were going to pick up my uncle – my father's brother – who was arriving from Karachi, and I could hardly contain my excitement.

'Are we nearly there?' my brother, my sister and I cried out every time another plane roared over the motorway. The airport wasn't far from Wembley, but the journey felt endless.

'Keep still,' my father ordered Farah, who was sitting on his lap.

'Oh, Hai Sahib, don't be harsh, they're excited,' Mr Rehman said, tickling my brother, who was sitting next to him. Mr Rehman had offered to come and help carry my uncle's luggage. But we all knew the real reason he was coming was because he couldn't pass up an opportunity to visit the airport. 'Aren't you excited?' My brother nodded, resolutely refusing to face Mr Rehman, who had the wonkiest betel-juice-stained teeth in the world.

But Mr Rehman was right. We were excited. I had never

met my uncle. His name was Syed Islamul Hai. My mother had told me he was a famous poet, which thrilled me no end. How lucky we were to have such an illustrious person in our family. I had already taken the liberty of drawing up an itinerary of places we could visit while he was in England, making a special point of fitting in Keats's house in Hampstead. I hoped my father had told my uncle that I was thinking of becoming a writer too one day.

'Daddy, does he look like you?' I asked.

'I don't know, I haven't seen him for over ten years,' said my father, quietly. He had been very subdued throughout the car journey.

'Ten years!' I tried to imagine what it would be like not to see my brother and sister for such a long time.

'How will you recognise him then?' Farah asked, concerned.

'Don't you worry!' my father replied, now laughing. 'I will. You never forget your brother.'

The airport terminal was buzzing with activity when we arrived. Uncle Waseem led us to a huge board in the centre of the hall, which flickered with random numbers and names of exotic faraway places.

'Where's Karachi?' I heard my mother say. 'I can't see it.'

There was a good reason for that. As usual we had arrived too early for the flight to register on the board. In fact, we would have to wait a whole four hours more before the flight was announced. My parents didn't believe in taking chances. At least this gave us time to wander around the airport. Uncle Waseem even offered to take us over to salubrious Terminal One, where all the European and American flights came in. Terminal One was clean and orderly, unlike Terminal Three. My parents were grateful to Uncle Waseem. Little did they know that he was dying for a fag.

We returned just as the first Indian faces started walking out of customs. I climbed onto the metal barrier to get a better look. I wondered what my uncle would be like. I had over-heard my mother saying that uncle no longer lived with his wife.

'Does that mean he's divorced?' I asked, excited by the notion of a scandal in the family. My mother ordered me to watch my tongue. 'Never say bad word again. Understand?'

But later, realising that she might have been unnecessarily harsh on me, my mother explained that my uncle wasn't divorced. It was just that he was so busy with work that his wife had gone to live with her family.

'Is that him? Is that him?' we cried each time the door opened and a new Indian face appeared.

My father was watching too intently to reply. But as we waited, I couldn't help feeling slightly alarmed. Many of the arriving Asian passengers didn't look too healthy. In fact, many looked downright scrawny and malnourished. Some weren't even carrying proper suitcases. One rather emaciated-looking man was carrying a brown cardboard box tied up with string, while another carried a white bundle of cloth like Dick Whittington. Were Indians and Pakistanis from back home really that poor?

'*Aa gaye* [he's arrived],' I suddenly heard my father say.

'Where, where?' we said, craning our necks.

From behind a young Pakistani Burt Reynolds lookalike appeared an old man dressed in a traditional knee-length brown Nehru suit and a brown fez-like hat on his head. The man was scanning the hall, all the while stroking his big white beard. I went cold. The man didn't look like a poet; he looked like a tramp. But underneath the beard, there was no mistaking it: the man bore an uncanny resemblance to my father. He had the same angular face, high cheekbones and wide forehead. I looked up at my father, but he was no longer there.

To my utter surprise he was bending down in front of my uncle, touching his feet. I had never seen my father bend down to anyone. Tears welled up in my uncle's eyes as he patted my father's head. I turned away; something inside me resisted watching them. And then they were standing next to us and my mother had also bent down to touch my uncle's feet. My uncle patted the top of her head and sternly mumbled some prayers.

'Go on, go, go,' I heard Mr Rehman say, pushing me excitedly towards my uncle. But I found myself holding back. Up close my uncle looked even more disturbingly foreign. I think Yasir and Farah felt the same way, because they were standing back too.

'They're shy,' my father said to my uncle, apologetically.

I think there were tears in my uncle's eyes. But my uncle didn't seem to mind because before I knew it he had gathered us up in his arms. A musty odour of sandalwood oil and betelnut juice engulfed us. My uncle muttered something about, 'Allah . . .' splattering me with red spit. Things were going to be different with my uncle around. And I wasn't sure I was looking forward to it.

An inkling of what was to come revealed itself on our journey home. While no one had worried about *the issue* on the way to the airport, now that my uncle was here, Mr Rehman and Uncle Waseem suddenly got very flustered. Apparently *the issue* was my mother. According to cultural traditions, which I didn't think any of us cared about, no man was allowed to sit next to my mother unless it was my father. But my father was required to sit in the front of the car to help guide Uncle Waseem home.

'No, why don't you sit there,' said Uncle Waseem to Mr Rehman, pointing at the front seat.

'No, that won't work,' interjected a very anxious Mr Rehman. 'What if I sit there and . . .'

'No, no,' replied Uncle Waseem.

My father told them not to worry, but my mother elbowed him hard, gesturing him to behave now that my uncle was present.

'OK, what about if sister sits in front . . .' said Uncle Waseem.

'How will that work?' Mr Rehman cried, exasperated.

'Just listen to me . . .'

And on and on they went, standing in the middle of a car park, shouting loudly at each other in Urdu as the whole of Heathrow Airport looked on. All the while my uncle stood off to the side, mumbling prayers to himself.

The car problem was finally resolved. My father sat in the back between my mother and uncle, but just behind Uncle Waseem, to help guide him home. My brother sat on Mr Rehman's lap, my sister on my mother's and lucky me on my uncle's. Sitting in such close proximity to my uncle, breathing in the cloud of his pungent perfume, I considered what was so unsettling about him.

My uncle looked and behaved like someone from . . . well, Pakistan or India. And no one Asian that I knew was interested in being like that any more – with the possible exception of Samira and Munira's family.

In fact, the only Asian who could get away with his traditional look was Rajesh, who drove the 92 bus. He wasn't exactly a family friend, but my father often chatted to him while travelling. Rajesh, like Uncle Waseem, was young and had been brought up in Britain. When we first knew him, he was really cool; you could tell by the length of his sideburns and the fact that he always greeted us by putting his thumbs up like the Fonz in *Happy Days*.

Except one day when we got on Rajesh's bus, we were surprised to see that he no longer had sideburns. Instead he was wearing a blue turban, with a silver bracelet around his wrist and the beginnings of a beard on his chin. I couldn't help feeling rather disappointed by his appearance. Apparently his new look had something to do with Sikhs in India and Indira Gandhi's assassination. Of course, my father was soon examining the crisis with him while I stood there wondering how events in some faraway place could matter so much to people here, to the point that they would want to stop looking cool.

Over the next few months I got a clearer picture of the relationship between my father and uncle. They had been born into one of India's most prestigious Muslim families. Prestigious, that is, until all the family wealth had been squandered. Still, my uncle had followed the family tradition and gone on to become a cleric, while my father, distressed by the poverty around him, had become a Communist. Apparently, his decision embarrassed my uncle terribly, especially in later years when my uncle became a prominent religious figure in Pakistan. Tension between the two brothers had escalated until one day they fell out. They had only reconciled – many years later – when my father was about to escape to England. And now he had invited my uncle over to cement their peace.

'I thought you said Uncle was a poet,' I said to my mother when my uncle went upstairs to rest. 'He doesn't look like one.'

'What are you talking? He is religious poet. A mullah.'

'But how can he be a mullah? And Daddy be so different?'

'Your dad is Communist,' my mother replied proudly, stressing the word *Communist* as if it were some sort of honour from the Queen.

98

'Yeah, I know that,' I replied exasperatedly. 'But how come they are so different?'

'*Ho jata hai* [it happens],' my mother replied. And that was all that she had to offer on the matter.

Over the next few days I saw how keen my father was to put past tensions behind them. Whenever my uncle entered the room, my father made sure he had a comfortable chair to sit on. My uncle was consulted on what he would like to eat. And to stop my uncle from feeling homesick, my father even went all the way to Drummond Street in Euston to buy some betel-nut leaves. But my uncle didn't seem that grateful at all. He would just nod gruffly whenever my father did anything for him, which angered me.

My mother tried to calm me down by explaining that this was how elders were treated back home. 'Not like here,' she said.

My uncle might have been an elder and an important poet, but he did have some very strange habits. Every morning he would spend at least an hour in the bathroom – gargling, burping, blowing his nose and so on. My brother, my sister and I would stand outside giggling at all the noises he was making. And then there was the *lungi*, which he wore around the house. It made him look like he had just got out of bed and wrapped the sheet around him. My uncle was everything un-modern and un-English rolled into one *lungi*-wearing, betel-nut chewing foreigner. And while he would talk the night away with my father, with us it was a different matter.

'So what class are you in?' he would ask, beckoning us over. This was a typical question that Asian adults always asked, even though no possible reply could make any sense to them.

'Ms Smith's class,' I replied. 'Class One.'

'*Shaabaash* [very good],' my uncle said, looking less disapproving than usual.

'And what about you?' he asked my brother.

'Class Eight,' my brother replied.

'*Shaabaash*,' he said, even more pleased.

'And you?' he asked my sister.

'Class Twelve,' my sister said perkily.

'*Shaabaash*, very good.'

My uncle would then close his eyes and return to chewing his leaves. We would run out of the room, trying hard to control our giggles.

Coping with my uncle at home was just about possible. Outside the privacy of our home it was a different matter. I dreaded anyone seeing him. What would Mick Turton or Lubna say if they found out that this Asian Father Christmas lookalike was related to me? My carefully cultivated English image would surely fall apart.

But there were even more disturbing reasons behind why I was so desperate to keep my distance from my uncle. I always knew that there were people like Mrs Campbell out there who did not like us. But now I was old enough to understand that there were people who were actually prepared to harm us just because we were not English. I would often hear the adults talk about some uncle or aunty who had been harassed or even knifed on the streets. I already knew of one woman down the road who had been so bullied by her white work-mates that she had thrown herself off a railway bridge one day on the way home. Who were these people who hated us so much?

I came to know them as skinheads. Even the word triggered fear inside me.

'There's a skinhead over there,' my brother would whisper to me. We were permanently on the lookout for them every time we ventured out. The skinhead might have been a hundred yards away, but just seeing his shorn head was enough to unsettle us for the day.

Whenever skinheads came on TV, I would scrutinise their faces to see if I could identify what it was that made them hate us so much. My brother would be glued to the screen too. The strange thing was that as we watched the images, we never talked. I think we feared that any discussion of the skinheads would make them feel more real. It was easier not to talk – or think.

It was around this time that I began to have nightmares about the Holocaust. I don't know how I first came to hear about the Holocaust or of how Nazi Germany treated the Jews, but the subject came to fascinate me. For the first time, I began to take a real interest in the Second World War. I soon became aware of TV programmes about the concentration camps that my mother stayed up to watch. I wasn't allowed to watch these films. But as I lay in bed, I could hear the horrors being re-enacted on the TV in the room below.

In the Holocaust of my nightmares it wasn't Jews who were the victims, it was Asian and black people. I would often wake in the middle of the night numb with fear, having dreamt that all the black and Asian families on the street had been frogmarched to Sudbury Junior to be gassed. I would dread falling asleep again in case the nightmare returned.

Whenever the adults gathered, I would listen in on their conversations, hoping that they might shed some light on skinheads. But their exchanges only made me feel more alarmed.

'Avoid East End,' Dr Hasan would say.

'Isn't that where Mr Mansoor lives?' Mr Ali would reply.

Dr Hasan nodded.

'And avoid Dagenham too,' Dr Hasan would add.

These places found an indelible place in my imagination.

What did they look like? I found a Tube map, which I began to mark, circling the places that I knew were hot spots for National Front activity. In my head, I would repeat the names of those places over and over again – Mile End, Plaistow, Stepney, Dagenham East, Upton Park – hoping that it might reveal why they had become breeding grounds for race-haters. But the names always sounded so innocent.

'And avoid West Ham on match days. That's when they come out,' Mr Ali added. Meanwhile my father chuckled in the background. For him the skinheads were one big joke. But then I suppose he had lived through worse.

Still, laughing them off would have been fine, if we were just talking about a few skinheads. But given that there was a whole army of them out there, I felt a more in-depth explanation was required. Could it be that we – the immigrants – were in some way to blame for the situation? After all, if we didn't exist there would be no skinheads, I reasoned. That is how I came to conclude that the only sure way to avoid trouble was not to draw too much attention to ourselves.

So when my father announced that we were going to the Tower of London followed by a trip to the East End, alarm bells began to ring. I prayed that on the day of the excursion my uncle wouldn't come down all dressed up in his Nehru coat and Indian hat. But of course he did. Followed by my mother, dressed in the most garishly orange sari ever seen on these shores.

The journey started off fine but, the further the train travelled east, the more tense my brother and I became. Every time the train entered another station we peered out of the window to see if there were any skinheads loitering on the platform. Our eyes scanned the station walls for racist graffiti. Then we prayed for the train doors to close before any racists got on and had a chance to murder us all. All the time my father sat calmly read-ing the *Guardian* while my uncle played with his worry beads.

Luckily we managed to arrive in one piece. And, surprisingly, the East End wasn't half as bad as I had imagined it to be. Walking out of Dagenham East Tube station, I was relieved to see many Asians walking around, not one of them battered or bruised. Still, I wasn't going to take any chances, and I rushed my father to get to our destination as fast as we could. But my uncle was more than content to amble along, taking in his new English surroundings. Everything fascinated him; from the orderly queues at the bus stop to the garden gnomes in the small front gardens. Of course, my father couldn't have been more thrilled; he had finally found a receptive audience on the subject of England.

'This is pub,' my father said, stopping outside a rather decrepit Ox and Bull.

'Pub,' my uncle repeated to himself, as my brother and I hur-riedly searched the pub's walls for NF insignia. 'What happens in pub?'

I could see how they might be related. My uncle seemed to share my father's love for idle rumination.

'Have a look,' my father grinned, mischievously. To my horror, my uncle pressed his nose against the glass to peer in.

'*Sharaabi* [alcohol],' he said, giggling like a schoolboy. My father chuckled too.

How relieved I was when we finally arrived back in Wembley.

'Is that your granddad?' Danny Jobson asked, pointing at my uncle trailing behind us.

'Sort of,' I replied.

'He looks like Papa Smurf,' said Gary McGuinness.

Just then my uncle threw back his head, coughed up some phlegm and, then, with a quick professional flick of his head, spat it out on the roadside. I looked down; his phlegm was red.

'He's a weirdo!' screamed Danny and Gary, fleeing in mock fright.

My uncle looked up, startled, while I just slowly died.

My pious uncle from Pakistan was a kind of fantasy dinner guest for the aunties of the *mahalla*. But it wasn't until a month after his arrival, when it was determined that he had 'settled in', that my parents accepted an invitation to the Waseems for a party. I was thrilled. I had became convinced that if my uncle was exposed to the way other Asians lived, he might be inspired to renounce his old-fashioned ways. And there could be no better way to educate my uncle about England than to expose him to the supermodern Waseem.

Uncle Waseem was no longer the bachelor student. He was now a budding businessman, married with children and living in the most stylish house that I had ever seen. Not only did it have central heating, black leather sofas, a shower unit and a proper lawn, it also had a snazzy food trolley, which Aunty Waseem (the most glamorous Indian woman I knew) would wheel around whenever guests visited, like a hostess on *Play Your Cards Right*.

But for me, the most impressive feature of the Waseems' house was the cocktail bar recently installed in the living room. Though only soft drinks were kept in it, the bar still looked like something out of *Dallas*. A huge pineapple-shaped ice container took pride of place on the bar counter. How I wished my father could possess enough taste to consider installing a bar in our own house.

The Waseems' eldest child, Irfan, was our age. More importantly, he was our sworn best friend. Visiting Irfan was always fun. Irfan had real toys like Scalextric and Action Man. His current favourite was a pair of red boxing gloves.

'I'm the greatest, I dance like a butterfly,' Irfan would cry out as he glided around the garden punching the air and, sometimes, us. He was impersonating his hero, Muhammad Ali. I didn't know who Muhammad Ali was, but then I only knew about old-fashioned famous people like Charles Dickens or William Shakespeare. The Waseems even had modern heroes to revere.

Maybe I should have had a hunch of what might transpire when we entered the Waseems' house. I had imagined the other guests would have taken one look at my uncle and started to giggle. But nothing like that happened. Instead, as my uncle strode in, the hallway went quiet and everyone lowered their heads in deferential respect. Walking behind him, I was in prime position to witness it all.

'*Aslam-al-ekum*,' the guests whispered as my uncle walked past them. My uncle nodded back, occasionally muttering prayers of thanks.

'*Aslam-al-ekum*,' they whispered to me, trailing behind.

Disarmed by the excitement my uncle's arrival was generating, I momentarily forgot my hidden motives for visiting the Waseems and found myself nodding graciously back at the guests.

'Such an auspicious occasion,' Mr Rehman said to my uncle as they hugged. He was wearing a long silver *sherwani*, which rested awkwardly over his potbelly. A murmur of agreement rippled through the hallway. I couldn't resist grinning. Irfan, who had been whizzing around on his latest toy, a pair of rollerblades, was watching my uncle in awe.

'That's my uncle,' I mouthed to him.

As we entered the Waseems' living room, a sobbing Aunt Waseem darted in front of my uncle and bent down to touch his shoes.

'*Jeetai raho, jeetai raho* [long life, long life],' my uncle muttered to her, patting her scarf-clad head.

For some reason all the women, who wouldn't come beyond the kitchen doorway, had scarves loosely draped over their heads.

I was about to follow my uncle further into the living room when I saw Aunt Waseem scuttling back to the kitchen. Suddenly a feeling of panic, of being a girl, swept over me.

These weren't exactly new feelings. I noticed they often crept up on me when I was in the presence of tradition. I suppose I was becoming aware that very strict rules existed in the Asian culture on how women, or girls, should behave. I didn't know what the precise rules were, but I knew terrible penalties existed for breaking them.

'Shame, shame,' is what Mrs Khan always said when referring to women who broke those rules.

The words would burn in my ear, bringing up naughty images of topless girls that I had once seen in newspapers lying about in Britt Sherman's house.

And now here at the Waseems, with the sexes sitting apart, all those confused feelings of shame came flooding back. I suddenly wished I had worn a longer skirt, anything that would have covered my exposed calves.

'Come, come,' Uncle Waseem cried, eagerly beckoning my uncle to come and sit down, while I deliberated which way to go. I slowly edged back towards Irfan, who was waiting for an appropriate moment to show his Evel Knievel Man to my uncle.

As my uncle settled into the leather armchair a glass of Coca-Cola was instantly placed in front of him. And that was just the start.

'Boring,' whispered Irfan to me as the men began sombrely to discuss events back in Pakistan, which basically meant them asking my uncle very polite questions to which they already knew the answer. My uncle would reply by delivering long soliloquies in a monosyllabic drone, frequently punctuated with throaty grunts and references to Allah.

There was a glimmer of hope when Uncle Waseem finally moved onto the subject of what life was like in their new home called England. But that soon turned sour when the other uncles drifted on to the horror stories – the tales of sacrifices that one had to make living here. In the past this had always proved to be a good tactic, winning the empathy and admiration of foreign visitors, as well as making the guest feel less socially inferior to his/her British hosts. But I sensed that it wouldn't work with my uncle.

'And let me tell you about Mr Iqbal,' Mr Rehman was saying. He was citing examples of beautiful Indian names that had been debased by the English language.

'At work they called him Egg Ball. One of his colleagues even threw an egg at him!'

'Shame, shame these *angreze*!' said Mr Sidiqui, shaking his head.

My uncle grunted while smearing some white paste onto his betel-nut leaf. I could tell he didn't quite understand what the problem was. But then he was more interested in his betel-nut delicacy.

Noticing that my uncle's glass was empty, ever-vigilant host Uncle Waseem suddenly bounced up and cried:

'*Urreh*. Coke for Sahib. Quick, quick, get from bar.'

'Bar?' my uncle mumbled in surprise.

Uncle Waseem suddenly stiffened up as if he'd just been caught out. And Aunt Waseem, who had just come into the room to clear the snack trays away on her super-duper trolley . . . well, her face turned ashen. This was some feat, given how pale skinned she already was. Aunt Waseem was glaring at her husband; I felt sorry for her.

She had been passionately against the bar from the start, worried that people might come to associate her good name with alcohol. And she had been right. For even though Aunt Waseem only kept soft drinks in it, the aunties never stopped winding her up about the oceans of alcohol she was rumoured to keep in stock secretly. This line of humour did not amuse Aunt Waseem.

'It's not a proper bar,' Uncle Waseem stuttered, glancing shamefully in the direction of it. 'Umm, no *sharaabi* [alcohol].'

One could see the effort it had taken Uncle Waseem to utter the 'S' word in the presence of my uncle. Beads of sweat had appeared on his brow.

'Dad you're sweating,' cried Irfan.

'*Chup karo* [shut up right now]!' snapped Uncle Waseem.

'It's just a fancy fridge,' Aunt Waseem quickly interjected.

Uncle Waseem nodded enthusiastically, hoping the answer would protect him from my uncle's scorn, restore his good name, salvage his precious honour. But my uncle didn't look convinced. In fact, he looked downright disgusted. His lips were pursed tight.

'Umm,' he grunted, staring at the bar. The men standing in front of it dutifully stepped out of the way, so that my uncle could have a better view of it. I could see my uncle's eyes drifting over the giant pineapple ice bucket, the crystal tumblers, the fake bottles of vodka and whiskey, finally coming to rest on the mini cocktail umbrellas. His brows arched as he tried to work out what they were for. And I think he was just about to ask when Aunty Waseem strategically intervened: '*Khaana lagaaoon* [Shall I lay dinner]?' Her voice was strained.

My uncle sat up, patting his stomach in an automatic reaction. He didn't need to say anything, but the answer was clear.

'Yes, yes,' Uncle Waseem said.

'Oh yes,' the other guests said, glad of the diversion. The guests broke into polite chat and a very relieved Aunt Waseem rushed out of the room.

How disappointing, I thought, as I returned to play with Irfan. I was hoping the Waseems' party would inspire my uncle to change but, if anything, the opposite had happened. Still, at least I could take consolation in the fact that, we – the born and bred British children – would never have to live under the shadow of those dark rules. Or so I thought.

8

Umm, that's haraam!

Every school day, at exactly 4 p.m., Samira, Munira, Gary McGuinness, the Jobson boys, Michelle the Afro-Caribbean girl from no. 59, Mr Gurjit Patel's two children from 73, the Anglo-Indian Catholic twins from no. 123, Perveen and Shireen from a few doors down – to name just a few – would gather outside the Jobsons' house. If our parents had had reservations in the past about our playmates (meaning should Hindu Patel Jr be mixing with Muslim Khan Jr), they were now forced to give them up. The street was too alive with the sound of our laughter for any parent to keep their child locked up indoors.

Our favourite game was Knock down ginger, which basically involved knocking on Samira and Munira's door and running away, until their father – who worked nightshifts – woke up to answer the door. While he waved his fists madly, clutching tightly onto the strings of his cream *kurta* pyjamas, we would hide in the Jobsons' front garden and watch him, laughing. If we were in a bolder mood, it was time for more radical games like Chicken. The rules were simple. You lay down in the middle of the road, waited for a car to approach and then competed to see who would be the last one to chicken out and roll to the kerb.

One Friday afternoon, I noticed that Samira and Munira were missing from the group. I was walking up to their door when it opened to reveal them transformed: dressed up in smart *salwar kameez* and the fragrant perfume of Lux soap wafting off them. And then, to my surprise, none other than Afshan Khan appeared behind them, identically dressed.

'Dah-la-la la,' Afshan said, throwing her arms out to the side in a theatrical pose. She was wearing a purple *salwar kameez* with a gold *dupatta* (scarf) draped over her shoulder, looking terribly grown up.

'Where are you going?' I asked, suddenly very aware of the blueberry Slush Puppy stain on the side of my white daisy-print dress, one of my mother's recent creations.

'Koran class,' Samira chirped.

'Koran class?'

'Yes, at Aunty Shah's house.'

I was stunned. Being Muslim was something our parents occasionally did when they wanted to celebrate or remember someone who had just died. Or, of course, when it was Eid. That was the one religious event even my father allowed us to celebrate, his reasoning being that Eid could be enjoyed like Christians enjoyed Christmas. Religion did not enter into it. Every evening prior to Eid, he would lead us into the back garden to see if we could spot a crescent moon in the night sky. That was the signal that determined if it was to be Eid the next day or not.

I knew that every other Muslim family in Wembley would be standing in their gardens as well, peering excitedly up at the sky, and I wondered with awe how many other Muslims around the world were also looking up at the sky at that very moment. As this was England and the sky was usually too clouded up for us to see anything, frantic calls to Pakistan would be made to see if the crescent moon had appeared in the East. I would hover shyly as my father tried to talk through the crackles and hisses to anonymous relatives.

Once the relatives told us the crescent moon had appeared, we would rush outside to the street to share the news with everyone. '*Eid mubarak* [happy Eid],' our parents would cry to each other, while we children would skip around dreaming of the presents coming our way the next day. I loved Eid.

But that is as far as being Muslim went. No one of my age actually practised the religion as far as I knew, until that day I saw Samira, Munira and Afshan on their way to Koran class.

'Why are you wearing pyjamas?' I heard Gary McGuinness call out from behind me. I turned and saw that the others had congregated by the front gate, staring curiously at our three friends.

'We're not, stupid,' replied Samira from her doorway. 'It's a *salwar*.'

'Yes,' said Afshan, rolling her eyes, re-adjusting her *dupatta* over her shoulder.

'What's Koran class?' Danny Jobson asked.

'It's where we learn to read the Koran,' Samira replied. 'Like Sunday school.'

'So why don't you go to church?' Michelle asked.

'Because we're Muslim,' Samira said, in an exasperated tone.

'Muslim? What's that?' asked Gary.

Samira's father came out of the house. He frowned when he saw us, his face darkening even more when he noticed Danny swinging on his gate. 'Go away,' he said, shooing us away from the house.

'Go away, out!' said Danny and Gary, mimicking his thick Indian accent.

112

'When are you coming back?' I said, trying not to sound too desperate.

'Come on, *chalo* [let's go],' Samira's father barked, ushering the girls towards the car. 'No play. Big girls now.'

We cleared a pathway for them to pass through. As they walked past, I noticed Afshan was wearing heels. Suddenly I decided to go home and put on a clean dress.

But it didn't make me feel better. Not one of the dresses now strewn across my bedroom floor felt right. Not even my favourite sailor dress from C&A. It looked so dowdy compared to Afshan's outfit. Not that I would ever be found dead wearing a *salwar kameez*. It was just that I wanted to look . . . older? No, that wasn't it. In fact, I wasn't sure what I wanted to look like. As I combed through my wardrobe, trying to find the dress that would make me feel comfortable in myself again, I thought about Afshan. She – or, more accurately, the Khans – was meant to be like us: modern, people who didn't care for all those old-fashioned ways. So why were they sending Afshan to Koran class?

Later that evening, when Mrs Khan came round with Afshan, Samira and Munira in tow, my uncle overheard her enthusing about Koran classes to my mother. He immediately sat up with interest, eager for information.

'This little one,' Mrs Khan said to my uncle, pointing to Samira, 'has already finished her first chapter and . . .'

'Really?' said my uncle, appreciatively, tying his *lungi* tighter around his waist. I heard Afshan giggle. I don't think she had ever seen a grown-up man wearing a bedsheet before. '*Ub kya purrehe* [And where are you up to now]?'

'In three months,' Samira replied, her face lighting up, 'I will have read all of it.'

'All of it!' my uncle exclaimed, very impressed. 'How old are you?'

113

'Eight,' Samira replied, her cheeks flushing red.

And then just to prove that she wasn't telling fibs, Samira recited some words from the Koran.

'Wahh, what pronunciation,' my uncle marvelled.

Samira giggled and skipped shyly from one foot to the other. My uncle had never complimented me. I had always put that down to the fact that maybe it was because I was a girl. But I had obviously been wrong.

'I can read the Koran too,' cried Munira.

'And me too!' said Afshan, excitedly.

'What good girls you are,' my uncle said, nodding his head from side to side with uncharacteristic enthusiasm.

'It's not that I want my daughter to walk around in a *burqua* or hijab like the old times,' Mrs Khan explained in Urdu, thrilled that her decision to send Afshan to Koran class was meeting with so much approval. 'It's just that, I think that they should know in their head right from wrong, especially if they live here.'

My uncle nodded in agreement. 'Sister,' my uncle said, now turning to my mother. 'You must make sure my nephew and nieces go to this Koran class too. We can't have them growing up ignorant. Make them accomplished like these girls.'

No one had ever called me ignorant let alone – in the same sentence – describe Samira, Munira and Afshan as being accomplished.

'Oh, one day they will learn,' my mother replied, quickly dashing off.

Mr Hai had warned her not to get into any exchange about religion with my uncle and she wasn't about to start now. And religion was also the last topic my father wanted to discuss with my uncle. Since my uncle's arrival, he had done his best to stay away from controversial subjects. It wasn't worth upsetting their fragile relationship. But over dinner my uncle kept badgering my father to explain why he wouldn't send us to Koran school. Didn't he realise what a mistake he was making? How would we ever grow up knowing who we were?

What a stupid question, I thought. I knew who I was and even what I was going to be when I grew up: a writer or journalist.

'Think Samsam, what future are you giving your children?' my uncle insisted, raising his voice to drum out the loud noise my mother was making moving saucepans around in the kitchen.

Finally, not being able to bear my uncle's haranguing any longer, my father explained his objections in a firm voice. 'At the school where I teach, do you know who is always at the bottom of the class?' My mother suddenly stopped clanking the pans round.

My uncle grunted to signal that he wasn't interested in discussing my father's job.

'The black children and the Muslim ones,' my father replied. 'Now tell me, wouldn't it be better if our children learnt how to speak English rather than waste time learning the Koran from these illiterate mullahs? And worse, do these children understand what they are learning when they read the Koran?'

'What don't they understand?' I interrupted, surprised.

'You learn the Koran in Arabic. It is written in Arabic,' my father explained, adjusting his tone to sound more educational.

'But they can't speak Arabic,' my brother said.

'Exactly!' cried my father, slapping his hands on the table.

He turned to my uncle. 'Hear that. Even my six-year-old boy understands how foolish it is.'

Now that I knew that the Koran was in Arabic, it seemed sillier than ever that Afshan, Munira and Samira had showed off so much about learning it.

'Is that all it means to you, memorising strange words? Well,

Samsam, all I know is that one day your children will regret it,' my uncle said quietly. 'You can't ignore it, they are Muslims. They were born Muslim.'

Friday afternoons were no longer the same. While the rest of us would all gather outside the Jobsons' house to play, Afshan, Samira, Munira – now joined by Perveen and Shireen, and the children from numbers 8, 10 and 72, in fact all the Muslim kids in the area, apart from us and the wild Quereshi kids – could be seen briskly marching off to mosque school.

'Oh look, there they go in their pyjamas,' Gary McGuinness would joke.

But it didn't sound funny any more. And more so because since they started going to mosque school, suddenly a lot of innocent activities were turning very controversial – becoming big 'umms'.

If I happened to be chewing gum (which was very rare in my case, given that my father had banned gum because it was part of a class of products symbolising American decadence), it was inevitable that one of them would pipe up with: 'Umm, you're eating chewing gum. It's got gelatin in it. That is *haraam* [forbidden].'

If I happened to be wearing my favourite ra-ra skirt, I was guaranteed to be told: 'Umm, you're showing your legs. That's *haraam*.'

Before, I thought the only difference between me and the other Asian kids was that I had read more books and that I had an Aunt Hilda and Uncle Aslam to show me the ways of the English world. But now I was beginning to understand that something more fundamental set us apart. Yet, if circumstances had been different – had my father been different – I knew that would be me right now walking away in pyjamas. Whether I liked it or not, the mere fact that I had been born a Muslim made me a

116

Muslim of some sort, too. I couldn't help feeling a strange empathy with Muslim 'them'.

This became more apparent on Eid that year. I began to notice, and I don't know why I hadn't noticed it before, that while we Hai kids went to school on Eid, most of my Muslim classmates now took the day off.

'Glad you could make it,' Ms Smith would always say, sardonically. In the past I hadn't realised what she actually meant. Being aware now that I was inexorably a Muslim of some sort, I realised that Ms Smith was being rather mean, which hurt me.

In the evening, our Muslim neighbours would always drop by with celebratory dishes. But as Eid often fell on a school night, my father would not allow us to greet them; it was more important to him that we got on with our homework. So I would resign myself to watching the celebrations through the blurry gaps in the net curtains hanging from our living-room windows. I couldn't wait for the day to be over.

The more time my uncle spent with us, the more assertive he was becoming in his views. This was partly because he was spending more time with some of his own friends from back home. Uncle's friends were not like my father's. They might have been educated in prestigious Indian colleges and dressed in smart suits, but they were more traditional in outlook. Whenever they arrived not only did they take their shoes off at the door, but *purdah* immediately came into effect: my mother and the women guests didn't just disappear into the kitchen, they stayed there.

Did I mind our house being overturned like this? Even if I did, the way I felt didn't matter. All I remember was how my brother, my sister and I wandered aimlessly around, unsure of where to sit. The living room was for the men, the kitchen was

117

for the women and all the other rooms were perpetually occupied with one guest or another praying. Before laying their mat down on the floor they would ask us which way Mecca faced. We would point toward Ealing.

Our home now felt very sombre and serious. No one seemed interested in fun, like before. During the course of the evening not one of the husbands would ever stray into the kitchen to joke about how long the food was taking to cook. When it was time to serve, we children were called upon to take the food out to the men, which for me, being female, immediately brought back all those strange feelings of shame and confusion. At age eight was it right for me to make eye contact with the men? Or should I keep my gaze firmly down? As we served the food, I would hear the men speak about Palestine, Afghanistan, Lebanon and Iran, faraway places in turmoil. I wanted to stay and listen to their discussions, but I dared not sit down.

My uncle's friends intrigued me. I had never met people like them before and would have expected them to be rather apologetic about their traditional ways. But they never were. Like the time one of them asked us in Urdu what class we were all in. My uncle quickly interrupted. 'They don't speak Urdu any more, only English,' he said apologetically. His friends looked at us with an air of disappointment. Which of course then made me feel more inadequate than ever.

For my uncle, his friends were proof that you didn't need to leave your culture behind to live in England. This emboldened him.

'You know, Alam's children have all learnt the Koran and they are all in the top class,' my uncle once said.

'That is very good,' my father replied, wearily.

On another occasion, as my brother laboriously recounted how he scored a hat trick during football practice, my uncle interrupted and said: 'Samsam, I wish you would teach your children Urdu. Shah's children speak it so fluently. And they are also top of their class.'

'That is very good,' my father replied.

My uncle always appeared so resolute. Recalling how his friends always seemed so disappointed by English 'us', I couldn't help feeling that maybe I was missing out on something really important. Maybe my mother was feeling the same, because one day she ushered us stealthily into her bedroom. Her mission: to teach us some Islamic prayers. I didn't resist. I was curious to know what all the fuss was about.

'Now, repeat after me. *Bismillah*,' my mother said, sitting us down in front of her.

'*Bismillah*,' I said, giggling at the unfamiliar word. My mother narrowed her eyes and cuffed me round the neck.

'*Hir rahman*,' she continued.

'*Nır rahım*,' I repeated sulkıly.

But even though I was playing up to show my mother that I wasn't about to be taken in by all this religious nonsense, I was secretly fascinated. Maybe it was the foreignness of the words; they were like some secret code, the kind that Nancy Drew and the Famous Five often tried to decipher on their mystery adventures. I felt as if I was being initiated into some exotic club. I liked being part of things, always had done – netball club, country-dancing club, Arsenal fan club. But this club was different.

'So what kind of poetry do you write?' I asked my uncle at dinner that evening. Maybe there was more to him than I had suspected. After all, he couldn't be an important man for nothing.

My uncle was mashing some spinach into the rice with his hands. The white of the rice was speckled with green bits and made my mouth water. He let out a deep sigh and, instead of replying, said: '*Urreh*, Hai, you really should teach your children to read Urdu, too. How else they going to understand our arts and poems?'

'Oh, *bhaijan* [brother],' my father said, dismissively.

I felt tears stinging at the back of my eyes.

My uncle must have realised that he had been harsh with me because, picking up a morsel of food, he leant over towards me and said, '*Lo* [take].'

His dark fingers moved to my open mouth. The *saag gosht* tasted heavenly, deeply nutty from all the melded flavours.

'You never eat spinach,' my mother laughed with surprise.

'But Uncle made it so tasty,' I said, giving my uncle a knowing smile. His face lit up with a broad grin.

'Well there is hope still, I see,' my uncle joked, patting me on the head. My heart swelled with pride. Despite being a girl, I think I had won his approval. Why I had ever sought it, I don't know.

My uncle's six-month-long visit was starting to take its toll on my parents, especially my mother. She was getting fed up with constantly having to cook and clean up after my uncle and his friends. And more so as she had found work as a typist for a small retail firm on Wembley High Street.

I didn't know it at the time, because my father would never have allowed his children to feel insecure, but our financial situation was not good. My mother had offered to help by taking on work as a seamstress, like many of the other Asian women in the area. But my father had firmly opposed the idea. 'If you work on a sewing machine, stuck at home all day, how will you ever learn the ways of this country,' he had said, angrily.

Instead he sent my mother to secretarial college to learn how to type. In a matter of months, my mother became the fastest typist in her class and was soon qualified to take on work. We were so proud of her and never more than when she came downstairs one morning, all dressed up in her work clothes, a formal black trouser suit with a pale blue shirt underneath, correctly buttoned to the neck. She looked a bit like Mrs Hussain.

'Now make sure you behave,' she said to us, ignoring our appreciative stares. My mother was not one to indulge in adulation, especially when she had important business to be getting on with.

This wasn't actually my mother's first day at work. In typical style, my father was timing her to calculate how long it would take her to get dressed — in English clothes as opposed to a sari — and then how long it would take her to get to the new office. Nothing could be overlooked: my mother had to be totally prepared, so that her bosses couldn't find anything to criticise about her.

'That took thirty-five minutes,' my father said, trailing behind her. He clicked a button on his watch, and then jotted down the time in his pocket diary. My mother nodded solemnly, pleased with her result.

Just then my uncle appeared out of the living room. Something about my mother's appearance seemed to disconcert him. He opened his mouth and then pursed his lips tightly together, as if he wanted to say something but wasn't sure if he should. My parents, suddenly aware of his presence, began to busy themselves with preparations for going out.

'Have you got the umbrella?' my father asked my mother.

'Yes, I put it in my bag. Have you got . . .'

'So how long will you be?' my uncle said, rudely interrupting them. He sounded rather tense. He was expecting important guests later that afternoon.

'We will be back as soon as we can,' my father replied, smiling. 'The biriyani is prepared. I can always warm it up if we run late.'

My uncle stared back in horror.

'You warm the food up? Are you the wife or is she?' he snapped loudly. My heart suddenly began to pound. I had never seen adults raise their voices at each other like that.

'Oh, don't you worry, brother,' my father replied amiably, quickly jerking his head towards us three, willing my uncle to stop. 'In England we all have to help out.'

But my uncle was too annoyed to worry about the impact his raised voice was going to have on us. 'Really?' he retorted tartly. 'So how come whenever I go to Mr Sidiqui's house, there is no problem. His wife makes me samosas, kebabs . . .'

My mother was glowering, about to jump in, but my father placed his hands on her arms, urging her to keep quiet.

'Parathas, chicken *salans*, lamb biriyani . . .' my uncle continued. 'Salads, *aloo gogi*, pilau rice . . .'

My mother always made such an effort when his guests came; to mock her was really unfair. My father just stood there, patiently listening. He wasn't going to be drawn in. His indifference must have really wound my uncle up, for in a last-ditch attempt to provoke him, he pointed at my mother, and said something in Urdu, which didn't sound very nice at all.

It was the last straw for my mother.

'Uhh!' my mother laughed, finally welcoming the opportunity to hit back at him. 'You're just jealous. If you had half the chance, you would move here. But you're stuck there!'

'Not now . . .' my father cried, seeing our startled faces.

But my mother wouldn't stop. For every insult my uncle threw her way, she, with great relish, hurtled one right back. Maybe her

122

suit and boots were giving her new-found powers, because she didn't look one bit frightened by him. She stood tall and defiant.

'We are in England now!' my mother cried every time my uncle accused her of being too '*modon*'. 'Not some village back in Pakistan where everyone just bows down . . .'

'Samsam, tell your wife to stop before she regrets it,' my uncle said sternly to my father.

'Mrs Hai, please,' my father said, putting his hands up, signalling my mother to stop. But to no avail.

I should have been proud of my mother for standing up to my uncle. Instead I felt scared. What if the argument led to my parents divorcing? If only my mother would stop. She might have been in the right, but I knew she was crossing the line by arguing with a male elder.

'And look at your daughters,' I suddenly heard my uncle cry out, disgust oozing out of his every syllable. 'While every other girl on this street is being brought up with decency, your girls wildly roam the streets. Shame! Shame!'

'That's enough!' I suddenly heard my father shout, as tears of shame pooled in my eyes. It was the first time my father had ever raised his voice.

A chilling silence descended upon the room. My uncle was breathing heavily, trying to restrain himself.

'I am going to my room,' he said, pushing past my father.

That day the journey to work was called off and so was my uncle's dinner party.

My uncle stayed on for another month, but he and my mother did not reconcile. As for me? Feeling bruised, I took to avoiding my uncle. My father tried to mediate between us all, but it was no use. A strange situation now arose. When my uncle was at home, he remained in his room. My father would cook his dinner and then carry it up to his room. My father would sit with him and when he had finished he would bring the dishes down and wash them up.

It wasn't easy making our way to the Waseems' house, given that my mother and uncle were not talking. My mother ended up walking a hundred yards behind the rest of us, which I am sure pleased my uncle. But it was an important occasion and we had all been asked to attend. The Waseems were throwing a kind of goodbye party for my uncle and they had promised him a surprise.

Except it wasn't quite the surprise they had planned. For as we turned the corner, we saw a crowd of Asians standing outside the Waseems' house. And then beyond them we saw the flashing lights of a police van and ambulance.

We gasped.

'Guess what? Uncle Rehman got beaten up,' cried Irfan excitedly, running up to us. To my surprise, he was dressed in a *kurta kameez*.

'*Qua?*' my mother said, alarmed, grabbing his arms to stop him dancing about.

'By skinheads,' Irfan said, pulling away from her. 'Quick, quick. The police are talking to him right now.'

As we neared the house, the full extent of the commotion hit us. Crowds of Asian men dressed in *kurta kameez* were standing in groups discussing what had happened. By the police van, a group of teenage Asian boys were loitering around, trying to contain their anger at having been invaded so close to their doorstep.

Some of the men were grilling a senior officer for information. He was doing his best to reply to all the questions, but I could tell that he was rather amused by the number of Asians pouring out of the house.

I saw my uncle standing back, watching the scene unfold around him. One of the other uncles was explaining what had happened. My uncle shook his head in despair. That's when I realised that he felt sorry for us. Sorry that we, British Asians, were stuck in this country at the mercy of the English. Suddenly I really wanted him to go back home.

Finally the day came when Uncle Waseem drove us to the airport to see our uncle off. My mother stayed behind at home. So did Mr Rehman, despite his love for Terminal Three. He still wasn't up to travelling after the attack. True to form, we arrived at the airport early. But instead of lingering in the departure lounge, my uncle decided to go through. My father nodded and gave him a hug, which I noticed my uncle did not reciprocate.

'Go on, go,' my father said, pushing us forward to say our farewells. Even though I no longer spoke much to my uncle, I couldn't help tears welling up in my eyes. I knew that I would never see him again and that felt sad. My uncle bent down to hug us. I noticed that his eyes were watery, too. He wrapped his arms around us and I suddenly felt really sorry that my uncle had not enjoyed himself in England.

He went through the departures gate, dressed in his traditional clothes, a stranger leaving a strange land. I thought how different Pakistan must be from England. He was going back to where he belonged, a place still stuck in the past.

Little did I know that he and his friends were the future.

9

Operation Middle Class

'Now!' my father called out.

I grasped the train-door lock and steadied myself against the frame of the door. Behind me five members of the extended Hai family nervously looked on.

'Squeeze it hard, go on, squeeze it,' my father cried.

'You can do it, you can do it,' Uncle Aslam added.

Despite the urgency in their voices, I held back. The train didn't look as if it had dropped enough speed for me to open the door. The faces of the passengers standing on West Hampstead station platform were still fuzzy blurs.

'What are you waiting for?' my father shouted impatiently. 'Come on, come on.'

From the corners of my eyes, I saw the passengers in the next compartment smile sympathetically at me. My cheeks flushed up in embarrassment.

'Come on now. Come on,' my father cried.

This time, I clasped hold of the lock and with gentle pressure attempted to slide it to the right. Despite my clammy hands, it gave way and I was able to push the door open. Relief flooded through me, but it was to be short-lived.

'Don't open it too far,' my father now cried. 'Hold it steady.'

'Yes, steady,' Uncle Aslam repeated, his words reverberating in my head.

And just when I thought things couldn't get any worse, the smell of *aloo buri roti* sandwiches wafted through the carriage. I didn't need to look around to know that my mother was unfolding our packed lunch.

This was the third day in a row that we had made the train journey from Wembley via Willesden Junction to Camden Road. The mission: to familiarise me with the new school journey that I would be making from next Monday, and to accustom me to opening the train doors, which could be problematic at times.

'A little practice is all that is needed,' Aunt Hilda had said.

My father had agreed. So a few days of summer holiday were specifically put aside for the task. But then this was a matter to be taken very seriously – everything about my new school was to be taken seriously.

Camden School for Girls was not like other secondary schools. Its reputation was unique, one of the best in the country. I knew this because, soon after I was accepted, Uncle Aslam had brought over a copy of *The Times* containing a listing of Britain's top one hundred state schools. Camden was near the top. It was circled in red and noted for the attention of Miss Y. Hai. I looked at it with pride. But of course I wasn't half as proud or relieved as my father.

Over the previous months, as my years at Sudbury Junior drew to a close, my father had spent a lot of time scouting local secondary schools in Wembley, trying to decide which one to send me to. He always returned home very disappointed. Being a Socialist, he was loath to send me to a private school. But the alternatives were looking very bleak indeed. Operation Children

127

had reached a critical juncture: the wrong decision on my next school could gravely jeopardise my future success. Heavy discussions about reality vs. political ideals ensued with Uncle Aslam and Aunt Hilda. Nothing so dramatic had consumed our family's attention for years.

It was Aunt Hilda who first suggested Camden. She had heard that Camden School – a state school – sometimes accepted girls who lived in adjacent boroughs. I would have to do an interview, but if I performed well, my future would be guaranteed.

From what I then overheard Aunt Hilda telling my father, I couldn't help feeling excited. Apparently all the girls who went to Camden came from good middle-class backgrounds and spent all their spare time reading Shakespeare or playing the flute. Could such a place really exist? No one played musical instruments at my school, unless you counted the tambourine during country-dance lessons. The more Aunt Hilda spoke about Camden – its historical claim to be the first girls' school in England, the high entrance rate to Oxbridge, the distinguished doctors, lawyers and writers who had sent their daughters there – the more I was seduced by the idea of the place. Camden sounded like something out of an Enid Blyton novel.

For my father, however, the key to Camden's appeal was its middle classness. My father and Uncle Aslam always nodded approvingly whenever the word was mentioned. I thought that to be middle class meant being like Britt and Mrs Sherman: tidy and polite. But listening to the adults talk about Camden, I began to realise that there was another world out there that people like Britt and Mrs Sherman could only dream of being part of. Suddenly Wembley was starting to feel very small and claustrophobic. What would happen if I got stuck here? Perhaps I would spend my whole life without ever knowing any real middle-class people!

Four months later, following an interview, I received a letter offering me a place at Camden. Uncle Aslam and Aunt Hilda were so overjoyed that they bought me an unabridged collection of Shakespeare's plays. I accepted their gift enthusiastically, determined to plough through the collection so that I would be prepared by the time I went to my new school. But my mother wasn't happy. I had only just turned eleven years old and the long train journey to my new school concerned her.

'Oh yes, I was so worried,' she says now, laughing. 'So, I say to your father, "I put her on Pill."'

'The Pill!' I exclaim, wondering, firstly, how my mother even knew that such a thing existed and, secondly, how my father would have responded to what must have been the most explicit conversation on my sexuality that he had ever been part of.

'Well, your father look very shock,' my mother says, as if reading my thoughts. 'But I say, no other choice.'

Apparently my mother had given the matter a lot of thought and convinced herself that it was only a matter of time before some deviant, sex-mad Westerner took advantage of her lonely daughter on the train and left me pregnant.

'And then what?' she'd said to my father. Once I became pregnant, I would become tainted, no one would marry me and then there would be no grandchildren. No, to pre-empt any shame falling upon us, it was best I be put on the Pill.

My father quickly put an end to the idea. 'This is England,' he had said, going on to recount Victorian virtues of modesty and reserve. 'Things like that don't happen here.'

The first thing I noticed as I walked through the Camden School gates was that there were no Samiras or Muniras running around the grounds. All the girls were very English. I would later discover that there was only one other Asian girl and three black girls in my year. Not that the school had a problem with *race*. No, Camden was immensely proud of its colour-blind, 'progressive' ethos. As I quickly learned, that included three guiding principles:

1. 'Everyone is equal!'
2. 'Men are sexist!'
3. 'Nuclear bombs are evil!'

That first day I sat next to a Sophie.

'Hi,' she said perkily, swinging her legs under her desk.

'Hi,' I replied brightly, rather overawed by her sparkling confidence.

Not that Sophie had any reason to look chirpy, dressed in grubby brown corduroy dungarees. I thought middle-class English people were meant to be well dressed. That is why I had come to school wearing my smartest outfit, a brown pleated skirt with white frilly blouse. But as I looked around the room, I saw that many of the girls were dressed just like Sophie. The girl on my left was wearing a crumpled waistcoat, while the one behind me wore a tatty, rainbow-coloured cardigan.

'Hi,' she said, catching me looking at her. Her voice was deep and husky. 'I'm Becky.'

'Umm, hi, I'm Yasmin,' I squeaked back.

It slowly began to dawn on me that maybe it wasn't Sophie or Becky who looked out of place, but me.

When we were asked to introduce ourselves to the class, I mumbled something about coming from Wembley, which no one seemed to have heard of.

'It's near the stadium. Wembley Stadium. You know, where the FA Cup is played, ' I said, trying to inject some enthusiasm into my voice. But I knew it was hopeless. Wembley just did not

130

have the same ring to it as Hampstead, Highgate or Highbury, where most of the girls in my class lived.

I then went on to list my hobbies, which included reading books by Hardy and watching BBC2 programmes. Everyone listened politely, even though I fumbled once or twice. When I finished, the teacher kindly moved on. When Sophie or Becky spoke (listing amongst their hobbies eclectic pursuits such as playing the oboe, pottery and skiing), I couldn't help noticing how the whole class sat up and listened. It wasn't that they spoke poshly, it was just that they sounded very clear and artic-ulate. You just had to listen. I couldn't help being envious at how they had grabbed everyone's attention – was this what being middle class was really about?

During morning break – as my new middle-class friends munched on their apples while I worked my way through my jumbo packet of Bejam salt and vinegar crisps – I decided that, shabby clothes aside, I wanted to be like them. And I knew that there would have to be some radical changes made to Wembley-bred Yasmin Hai.

The need to overhaul everything about me became even more imperative when I found myself put in all the lower classes with the 'casuals', the precursor of the modern-day chav. Casuals was what everyone called the working-class girls who went to the school. (Camden might have had a reputation for being middle class, but I discovered a good percentage of girls also came from working-class backgrounds.) You could tell who the casuals were because they all had names ending in 'ey', like Tracey, Kelley, Vickey; they spoke in Cockney accents; wore a lot of designer labels like Burberry and Lacoste; bleached their hair and danced to Sister Sledge during lunch break. And, like me, when they spoke in class they tended to mumble unless they were playing up. Which was a lot.

It isn't that I minded being dumped in the same class as the casuals, but they did have the rather irritating habit of referring to all Indian people as Pakis. Which, in my presence, they would always qualify by saying: 'We don't mean you. You're different.' And I suspect that was only because, like them, I passionately supported Arsenal. I would smile back as if I didn't care, but of course I did. Still this only made me more determined than ever to become middle class.

The middle-class girls, like Becky and Sophie, were called 'trendies'. They might wear ripped jeans or wear hand-me-downs from Oxfam – but I had learnt that was just an indirect way of saying: 'Hello, I am middle class. I don't care for convention.' The other thing about the trendies was that they were all incredibly 'maaattturre', a quality that I soon learnt I was sorely lacking.

It hadn't taken me long to master the British Rail train doors. In fact, I became so good at them that, like Lara, a Camden girl whom I befriended on the train, I was soon able to perform bold acrobatic manoeuvres, hanging off the train door as it pulled into the station.

I only stopped doing this after overhearing Becky, who was sitting with two rather sophisticated-looking Camden girls from the year above, sneer rather loudly, 'How immmmature!' while pointing at Lara and me as we swung off the window bars, one-handed, at Camden Road. That's when I knew that if I wanted to move into Becky's world, it was imperative that I also abandon the infantile world of my past.

It is amazing what a projected voice, a ripped pair of 501s and eating wholemeal sandwiches can do for one's image. In a matter of a few months, I was moved up to all the top classes – and hung out with Becky and her posse of 'mature' girls on the train.

But to really fit in you needed a north London liberal outlook.

I had an inkling of what this outlook might be from school assembly. When we gathered in the school hall, we didn't pray or sing hymns like we had done at Sudbury Junior; that would have been unthinkable. Rule number one: north London liberals don't believe in God. They are atheists. Instead, during assembly time, teachers and sometimes guest speakers would give talks on lofty subjects ranging from nuclear proliferation to designing one's summer house in France. One time a teacher even gave an assembly painfully defending why she was leaving Camden to teach English at a private school. We all sat there, shaking our heads, as she went redder and redder with what we hoped was shame.

And that was the point. In the north London liberal world, anything and everything was up for discussion. There were no adult–child boundaries. Subjects like sex, drugs and rock and roll – all taboo topics in Wembley, of course – were openly discussed. Middle-class Camden girls didn't shy away from such matters because, ultimately, they were considered mature and sophisticated enough, even at age twelve, to handle such delicate issues.

When Sophie came into school and coolly handed round photos of her mother giving birth, the casuals shrieked with laughter and ran around shouting 'fanny, fanny' to each other.

'How immature!' tutted Becky. And just how like Wembley, I thought, where the mere sight of a pregnant woman on TV had us fumbling with embarrassment and scuttling to switch channels. And in art class at Camden we painted nude models. What would Mrs Khan say about that? Or what would my father say about Celia's creative-writing-course essay, which explored whether it was possible for mothers to fancy their sons?

Every year, the school set a day aside to honour its illustrious founders. So important was Founders' Day that I bought a new dress for the occasion, a cream frock laced at the cuffs with purple silk. Only to find, when I arrived at school, that most of the girls in my class were boycotting the celebration.

'I don't agree with tradition,' Sophie declared to our form tutor, refusing to put on her Founders' Day posy, which we were all required to wear to the ceremony. I saw she was wearing the same brown dungarees that she had worn on her first day at school.

'It's soooo archaic,' sneered Kate, who had come to school, wearing a David Bowie T-shirt, as if to drive her point home.

I couldn't help feeling silly and even more confused when I later found myself secretly enjoying the service. All the hymns that I'd learnt at Sudbury Junior came flooding back.

But I never brought any of these matters up with my father. It was obvious that he didn't have a clue about the modern social mores of middle-class north Londoners.

That is why, on my first parents' evening, I made sure that we turned up early in the evening in order to get our appointments over and done with before anyone else arrived. But there were already a smattering of parents milling about in the main hall when we came in. And, taking one look at my father, I knew I was in for a long evening.

Not only had he come dressed like someone out of the 1950s, in a grey overcoat and trilby hat but, during the evening, much to my horror, I noticed that whenever he passed one of the women teachers or mothers – or worse, my girlfriends – he tilted his hat. Each time he did it, I squirmed, not knowing which way to look, painfully aware of how old-fashioned formalities were frowned upon at Camden. In fact, I wanted to cry in shame. Did my father not realise how he was unravelling all the progress I had made to fit in? But, oddly, my friends looked rather chuffed at the attention.

'Oh, he's so sweet,' they would whisper to me, as my father dipped his hat at them.

About a year after I began at Camden, we received some grave news that Aunt Hilda had been whisked away to hospital. Uncle Aslam phoned my father to tell him that her condition was very serious – she had fallen into a coma.

How did I feel? I can't remember. I don't recall crying, but my mother tells me that we were all very upset. But all I recall is asking my father perfunctory questions like, 'Is Aunt Hilda better today?'

Maybe I was just mirroring my parents' behaviour. At some point, they had decided – in consultation as ever with Uncle Aslam – that our feelings should be protected. Somewhere the message must have filtered down to us. For when we were told that the only time Aunt Hilda showed any sign of consciousness – a gentle squeeze of my uncle's finger – was when he whispered to her that my brother had got into the school of her choice, we had just nodded, partly humbled that Aunt Hilda's last thoughts were with us.

After a week of being in a coma, Aunt Hilda died. But it was decided that we shouldn't attend the funeral. It was feared that the sight of her dead might upset us. And, just as importantly, the funeral was on a school day. It came to be said that Aunt Hilda would have wanted us to go to school that day.

After Aunt Hilda died, Uncle Aslam went into a deep depression; refusing to see anyone for days. My parents were devastated too.

'Not only we lose friend, but we also lose guide to life in England,' my mother says now.

In my third year at Camden, aged thirteen, I found politics. My father took my sister and me on our first political march to

Trafalgar Square in support of the miners. When my Camden friends heard that I had been on a march, I became a celebrity, of sorts, overnight. Even north London supremo Becky took time out to have a chat with me.

'I didn't know you were into politics,' she said.

I nodded, feeling very proud of myself indeed. 'Yes, I am a Socialist.' My political consciousness was still in its early stages, but I had long thought of myself – just like my father, no coincidence – as a Socialist.

'Really?' said Becky. 'So am I.'

I nodded coolly, but inside I felt exhilarated. Finally I seemed to possess a set of ideals that were not at odds with the world I was moving in. Becky was considered to be an ace political activist. Right now, during break-time, which had graduated to smokers' corner behind the school, she was telling us it was rumoured that unemployment would soon reach a record three million! I couldn't help noticing that a new 'Coal Not Dole' badge had appeared on her donkey jacket. It was pinned carefully next to her CND badge, but just above her Sandinista badge, to form a perfect triangle. Hmm, I thought, I might try doing that.

We didn't know how significant three million was. All we knew was that it was very, very bad . . . and it merited a badge.

'Wouldn't it be great if all the unemployed marched to Downing Street?' said Lara. No one responded. Lara was not considered to be very politically astute, so we could afford to ignore her. That is how the power relationship in our group was starting to shape up. The more politically active you were, the higher your standing.

'I tell you, she [Margaret Thatcher] is a disgrace to our sex,' Becky continued.

We nodded, furiously. Becky, as usual, was offering an interesting angle to our discussion. It was a conundrum that we had often deliberated on. Being feminists, should we support Thatcher, a fellow sister, or should we spurn her? We always chose the latter.

I had always kept my distance from Becky in the past, being so in awe of her. But now, our relationship changed. Soon we were spending every weekend together, trudging from one demo to another, marching against nuclear bombs, apartheid in South Africa, the bombing of Libya or unemployment. It all boiled down to trying to oust the Tories from power.

Though it was anger that drove me to attend, I did enjoy going on the marches. There was something exhilarating about seeing the huge crowds with their banners, whistles and horns pouring in from every part of the country . . . Huddersfield, Yorkshire, Liverpool, Glasgow. It was like what FA Cup days felt like in Wembley, except here all these people were gathered to express outrage at what was being done to our country in the name of unrestrained capitalism. You couldn't help feeling uplifted by the camaraderie. It felt good to be surrounded by people whom I felt such a strong affinity with. An affinity based upon who I really was.

But my north London life was in dramatic contrast to Wembley. 'Do you know what's going on in South Africa?' I once asked my old friends down the road. I made a point of looking straight at Jamaican-born Danny Jobson, hoping that the reference to Africa might trigger some response. But he was not interested.

'Anyone want to sign my petition on Palestine?' I asked another time.

'Boring!' replied Ali. 'Let's play Chicken.'

The only person who responded with any interest was Afshan. She loved hearing my stories about Camden; for her, they were not only a window into an exciting, new world, but into a type of English person that she had never come across in her life.

'I can't believe your friends give up their weekends to go on protest marches against Thatcher!' she once said, impressed.

'Yep,' I replied. 'That's what English people in north London are like.'

Of course, my father was chuffed by my growing political consciousness. He finally had someone with whom to share his love of politics and to discuss the abstract; such as which was better, Socialism or Communism?

I must admit I wasn't exactly sure what the difference was between Communism and Socialism. I considered myself a Socialist mainly because I had found the Socialists on the marches to be much nicer and saner than the anarchists or the dippy rainbow face-painted hippies. But I was more than happy to ruminate over such matters, because it always left me feeling terribly adult.

My mother hovered in the background, fuming.

'Mr Hai! No politics,' she would warn. 'You want her to end up in prison?'

'Mum, this is England!' I would cry out, rolling my eyes at my father, and he would wink back.

My father was excited when I invited Graham, the local Socialist Workers Party rep, to our house. Every Saturday afternoon, Graham would pitch up in Wembley Square and vie with the Christian gospel singers for attention. I would watch him as he tried to rally support from Brent's large black and Asian population of shoppers for his organisation's latest cause, usually some crusade against Thatcher. But the revolution in Wembley still had some way to go. Graham would pack up at the end of every Saturday, his voice hoarse, but with no copies of his paper sold and not one signature collected on his new members form. I wanted to tell him that not all black or Asian people were apolitical, but I was so daunted by the idea that a real Socialist could exist in Wembley that I always lost my nerve. However, one day, dressed in a retro red and white baseball jacket, all the rage in Camden, I summoned up my courage and went up to him.

'I'll have one,' I said, in my most earnest militant voice. I pointed to the paper, making sure that I kept my body at a right angle, so Graham could see my CND and anti-apartheid badges.

Graham, so pleased that he had finally been able to engage the interest of a minority, even a fifteen-year-old one, instantly took down my address and promised me that the party would call round for a talk. My father was more than delighted with the news. The next day, I came upon him scrounging around, looking for his old essays and articles in anticipation.

'Let me see,' I said, thrilled that I was about to have a rare glimpse into my father's glamorous political past. My father handed me a bundle of magazines.

'Wow,' I said. The magazines looked like ancient manuscripts and the fact that they were browning on the edges only enhanced their appeal. 'The Myriad Definitions of Democracy: a critique of democratic models' read the headline on the first article. 'Double Tyranny' – a polemic about religion and its stranglehold on the Pakistani masses – read the headline on the next magazine. What's a polemic? I wondered. This was followed by 'Coexistence Vulgarised – A Disputed Road to Communist Paradise', an unflinching opinion on the Russia–China fallout by S. S. Hai. I was thrilled. Graham will be impressed, I thought.

A few days later, Graham turned up at our door with a fellow comrade, Nigel, a rather twitchy man wearing spectacles and a goatee beard. My father let them in. I noticed he wore a tie for the occasion.

My father soon was regaling them with stories of his political past. Nigel was particularly impressed that my father had been in hiding, while Graham was more interested in hearing about my father's invitation to China to meet Chou En-lai, before coyly revealing that he once had a Chinese girlfriend.

At this point I blushed. The conversation had made a detour into a sensitive area. How would my father respond to the mention of a girlfriend in my presence? Would he feel embarrassed? I did. I couldn't quite see Graham kissing a Chinese girl. I quickly collected myself. How silly I was being. After all, this was a sophisticated conversation between liberal adults.

My father nodded back politely at Graham, then tried to redirect the conversation back to the burning question of whether it was Marx or Lenin who had got it right in relation to the class struggle currently being epitomised by the miners' battle against the government.

Graham and Nigel replied they had not yet decided on that question. But my father pressed on, sharing (at length) his current thoughts on the Middle East and the legacy of colonial rule. And then to my horror, I noticed Graham and Nigel's eyes starting to glaze over. I willed my father to stop, but he wouldn't.

No wonder they appeared so relieved when my mother came in with tea and biscuits. They immediately sat up and couldn't stop saying thank you. I think they were hoping that she might stay or offer up her own opinions. But all my mother said was, 'No politics,' before quickly scuttling away, saying that she had to cook dinner. My father, irritated at her quip, waved her off, which I suppose from the comrades' point of view might have seemed as if he was shooing her away. Hence the narrowing of their eyes. Hahh! So Mr Hai wasn't so enlightened after all. He had revealed his true Asian male chauvinistic self.

I can't remember how long the SWP comrades stayed after that. But all I know is that they never called on us again.

Well, I didn't care. I had my Camden friends to fall back upon to talk politics with. And Afshan to talk about my Camden friends with.

'They love Asians and black people,' I once told her, laughing. I loved our cosy chats, for in Afshan I found an eager and lively mind keen to explore and learn about the wider world that lay beyond Wembley.

'The other day I was at a march and this protester asked if I was related to someone called Gurinda. So I said no. And guess what he said?'

'What?' said Afshan, starting to giggle in anticipation of the punchline. Her Farrah Fawcett-Majors flicks were beginning to vibrate, too.

We probably made an unlikely pair: Afshan, in white stiletto heels and eighties shoulder-padded outfits, looking as if she worked in a bank and I in my retro clothes.

'Well,' he said. 'She's from India. She's beautiful, like you.'

Afshan bent over with laughter, and soon I, too, was rolling about on the floor. The idea that brown could be beautiful was totally absurd to Afshan and me, especially as being light skinned was so prized in the *mahalla*. But then, as I often told Afshan, that was liberals for you. You could be dog-ugly, but as long as you were brown or black, you were considered beautiful.

But not on Wembley High Street.

One Saturday, Afshan, Shazia Quereshi and I were standing outside Dorothy Perkins, waiting for the 92 bus to take us home. A group of five or six white girls tottered by and shouted, 'Paki.'

Shazia boldly put her fingers up at them. 'Slags.'

'What do you fuckin' say?' one of them shouted back.

This time, suddenly seething with anger, I replied, 'Slags, didn't you hear us?'

One of the girls, with particularly wavy bleached flicks, ran back, grabbed my hair and yanked me to the floor. I tried to punch back, but she was already on top, kicking her stilettos into my ribs and then in my back. Afshan and Shazia tried to intervene, but the other white girls held them back. Passers-by just stood there, doing nothing.

'You fuckin' Paki,' the girl screamed as she laid into me.

I tried to grab hold of her leg. But it was no use. She had me under her control.

'See how these Pakis speak English?' she said to her friend, yanking me harder by the hair as I screamed at her to fuck off. 'That's cos their own language is crap.'

I suddenly felt paralysed, too ashamed to open my mouth. No way was I going to give this girl the pleasure of hearing me speak in English – *her* stupid language. For she was right, wasn't she? English wasn't my language, was it? My language was Urdu and the reason I didn't speak it was because it was considered crap. In some twisted logic, the 'slag' had a point, and that fact ripped through me.

Finally, a policewoman came and separated us.

For days afterwards I was so upset that I wouldn't go out. I couldn't tell my parents because Afshan begged us not to say anything in case her father stopped her from going out again. I kept to my room, mostly lying on my bed, replaying the incident over and over again in my head, dreaming up revenge scenarios, anything to stop me feeling so bad. When I did finally venture out, I felt terribly nervous and found myself scouring the street looking for angry white faces. If I saw one that looked potentially hostile, I found myself crossing the road, hating the fact that the girls had reduced me to a coward.

But then it changed.

I suppose we were being rather loud as we cut across

Wembley Square that Saturday afternoon, playfully shrieking at each other. But then, for Shireen and Perveen just being out – away from the beady eyes of their parents – was enough to set them off. We were just passing Boots when suddenly, out of the corner of my eye, I saw two English girls, one with a shaggy blonde perm, the other draped in gold rope chains, following us. Their arms were tightly intertwined and though they weren't saying anything, my highly attuned antenna for potential racists sensed menace. I instantly found myself going quiet.

'Let's go that way,' I said, pointing towards the crowded exit route by Wembley train station. But Perveen and Shireen were so busy chuckling at some private joke that they did not hear.

'Shuuuuuuuuuuuut upppppppppppp!' I suddenly heard one of the girls cry. My heart jumped.

Perveen and Shireen turned around to look. The girl with the rope chains collapsed into naughty giggles, burying her face into her hands. But her friend with the shaggy perm remained steady.

'Yeah, you!' she spat out, glaring at Perveen, who was being the louder of the two.

A charge of anger rushed through me. I must have let out a deep sigh or affected a hostile pose, because the girl suddenly turned towards me. Something about my outfit, a trendy blue and white striped top over a tight black pencil skirt seemed to wind her up even more. Maybe I looked too stylish for my own good.

'You wanna slap?' she spat out, when I refused to look away.

'Why? Do you want one?' I retorted, slightly taken aback by the confidence of my voice. But then it was a scenario I had rehearsed countless times in front of the mirror. And now I was getting to play it out for good, word and pitch perfect. I felt Perveen put her hands on my shoulder, pulling me back. But it

143

was too late. The girl was marching towards me, her heels slapping the ground hard.

I put my arms up to ward her off and somehow the abruptness of my movement ended up shoving her away. Much to my horror, the girl went flying back onto a middle-aged man passing by. He quickly collected himself and, muttering a polite apology, walked off.

I froze, frightened by what I had just done. I could feel my body dissolving into a jelly-like state and tears of regret stinging my eyes. But instead of retaliating, the girl looked thrown by my actions.

'Just try that again,' she cried, pulling herself up. But her voice sounded muted.

I had gained the upper hand. I – Yasmin Hai, studious, gentle, Yasmin Hai – had managed to unsettle the girl, maybe even momentarily succeeded in cowering her. I suddenly felt emboldened. It was a watershed moment. Was this all one had to do to fend off trouble?

I soon mastered how to punch, scream and kick back as good as I got. Where I found the strength, especially given my size – five foot nothing – I don't know. All I know is that the sight of a girl with a mousy flick or a Burberry coat scowling aggressively in my direction was enough to set me off. Every limb in my body would tingle with adrenalin – angry energy – and my brain would focus on one thing and one thing only: giving the girl a thrashing that she would never forget.

How dare she and her halfwit peers think they could scare me! And you could see the surprise on the white girls' faces. They had assumed that I was just going to timidly run away. Well, not any more. It wasn't long before I began to find the whole experience of fighting cathartic. Once you hit back, once you see someone tremble, you never forget the charge – the strength – it gives you. I didn't initiate, but I never failed to retaliate.

At Camden we walked around chanting 'violence is wrong'. But in Wembley violence worked. Strutting around in a threatening manner, head held high, chest puffed out as if you wouldn't think twice about thumping someone back if they tried to start on you had the desired effect of warding people off. When I finished defending myself, I walked away feeling proud and strong. No carefully crafted verbal attack could have ever delivered the same satisfaction.

But the euphoria wouldn't last long. Later a deep sadness would sweep over me. Though oddly, never for one minute did I link it to the fights. I suppose I was learning how to organise my world and my feelings.

One summer morning, a very nice woman from the BBC came to our house to interview me. They were doing a programme on young political activists. I recall my father telling my siblings and mother to keep out of the way, so as not to embarrass the BBC woman with their overexcitement. I was grateful because I was nervous. At first the interview went well. I even surprised myself with my reply to her first question about my newest activity: why had I become a volunteer for the anti-apartheid movement?

'As long as apartheid exists and is considered a legitimate form of government, racism will always be seen as acceptable *here*,' I said. By *here* I was referring to Wembley. And I suppose what I was trying to say in my fevered adolescent way was that apartheid's existence anywhere in the world gave all racists (especially the ones in Wembley) tacit encouragement to go and kick the hell out of anyone non-white.

But then the interviewer asked me whether I thought violent resistance was right. I immediately found myself saying no. Of course, I was lying. But the BBC woman looked so much like one of those nice liberal Camden parents that I didn't want to rock her world by telling her the truth about racism; the satisfaction I felt when I made a racist girl cry out in pain. And that sometimes standing up for oneself was all that was needed to put them in their place.

10

Taboos

One evening, Becky invited me to her house for supper. It wasn't the first time I had been invited to one of my Camden friends' homes, but I still felt excited. I knew the invitation signified that our friendship was shifting up a gear.

Becky lived in Highgate, though it might as well have been in Hampstead or Highbury, given the familiar layout of her Victorian house. Every one of my Camden friends had a house like Becky's, all done up in shabby-chic. Cushions covered in natural fabrics were strewn over the sofas, oriental rugs draped the wooden floorboards and proper oil paintings of fruit bowls or Spanish fishing villages adorned the white walls. Not like Wembley, where a Pierrette poster or three flying ducks on the wall was as elegant as it got.

The kitchen, as always, was the heart of the house. Running through the middle of it was the mandatory wooden farmhouse table, cluttered with newspapers, hastily opened morning post and a scattering of breakfast crumbs from the half-eaten, unsliced wholemeal loaf. As I walked into the kitchen, I dreamily imagined

Becky's family gathered around the table, eating wholesome suppers, discussing the latest issues of the day as Radio 4 played in the background. In Wembley, everyone I knew ate in front of the TV and kitted out their kitchens in MFI units.

Becky's mother, who insisted I call her Sylvie, had the straightest back I had ever seen and wore her long, thick, auburn hair in a loose bun held up with chopsticks.

'Yasmin, come over here,' were her first words to me as I came in. She was standing by the kitchen window, her eyes sparkling with mischief. 'Come and see our gorgeous neighbour!'

'Ohh, mum, don't be so cringy,' said Becky, burying her face in her hands, though I could see that she loved her mother's cuckoo behaviour.

As Becky and her mother (soon joined by Lucy, Becky's sister and Doug, her father) busied themselves preparing the evening meal, they swore at each other the whole time, but you could tell that they didn't really mean it.

At some point in the evening, I went upstairs to the bathroom. Just as I was coming out, I noticed a room across the hallway. I didn't mean to pry, but the door was wide open, just inviting you to peer in. It was the messiest and most chaotic room I had ever seen, even by north London middle-class standards. The room was crammed with tables, chairs, shelves, chests of drawers, everything piled high with books, papers, folders, toys and trinkets, resembling a junk shop in a Dickens novel. Everywhere you looked tat spilled out. There was even a wardrobe in the room with suitcases piled on top up to the ceiling.

'My mum doesn't like to throw anything away,' Becky whispered, coming up behind me. I turned around, embarrassed at having been caught snooping. But Becky didn't seem to mind.

148

'It's because we're Jewish,' she explained. 'Mum's family had to flee the Holocaust. They left everything behind, so now she hoards everything. Nuts, huh?'

I smiled politely, but inside I was burning with questions.

Before Becky I had never met a Jewish person in my life. But I often heard my father and his friends speak admiringly of them. They saw the Jews as the immigrant's perfect role model. People who had long been persecuted but who, through hard work and study, had survived and prospered in alien lands. My father and friends were so impressed by Jewish success that they would often recount how similar we, the Muslims, were to them. Now that I had discovered Becky was Jewish, I felt an ever-greater affinity to her than before. No wonder we got on. Like me, Becky was an outsider. But being middle class, she was further down the road of English success.

But Becky wasn't the only one. I soon learnt that a lot of the girls at Camden were Jewish. Lara, my British Rail best friend, turned out to be Jewish too. Why didn't I notice it before? Maybe because she, like all the other Jewish girls at Camden, never went around talking about it, or took days off from school to celebrate Hanukkah or Rosh Hashanah. They were like me; they kept their cultural roots at a distance. But while my Jewish friends might not celebrate their religious holidays, that didn't mean they didn't care for their roots. They did. And this paradox came to fascinate me.

Every other Saturday evening Becky would meet up with friends from the Jewish Youth Movement. On a couple of occasions she asked me to tag along. The Jewish Youth Movement wasn't a religious organisation as such, or at least it didn't feel like one. For a start, whenever they got together all they did was hang out, play the guitar, smoke dope and get off with each other. But what I found most appealing about them was how, in

149

between the snogging sessions, they would talk late into the night about politics and issues pertinent to being Jewish. Was it OK for Jews to have relationships with non-Jews? Was Judaism sexist? Wasn't Shabbat a bit dated? Listening to their discussions made my stomach flutter with excitement, for these were not discussions about religion – they were first and foremost about how you fitted into a country that you didn't totally belong to. I had never known that these issues, which I always kept buried deep inside me, could ever be up for discussion. It was a revelation.

I began telling my father about Becky and the Jewish youth groups. His face darkened. 'Be careful,' he said, his tone turned ominous.

'Why?' I replied, annoyed at his reluctance to engage on what was patently an issue I felt strongly about.

'You start talking about Israel . . .'

'But I am not talking about Israel,' I said, throwing my hands up in the air in exasperation.

'But that is where the conversation will go . . .' my father said, staring at me hard. 'You will find yourself in trouble.'

'Why?' I said.

'Because you are a Muslim.'

I stopped, surprised by what my father had said. It was the first time he had ever called attention to my Muslim roots and then asked me to censor what I could say. Didn't he realise that my Jewish Camden girlfriends would be outraged if they heard how the Palestinians had been treated by Israel? Being Socialists, they would undoubtedly see how wrong it was to take over people's lands and demolish their homes. I was so convinced that my father was wrong, I decided to put it to the test at break time.

'Are you a Zionist?' I asked, looking at Becky.

'Why?' she replied, sitting up with a jerk.

The suddenness of her response startled me. I suddenly sensed I was being warned to back off from the subject. I felt confused. I didn't want to upset anyone.

'I just wanted to know what you thought of Israel, that's all,' I said, warily.

'Yeah, Yas, I understand,' replied Becky impatiently, flicking her hair to one side and furtively looking over at Sophie. 'But it's a sensitive issue for us.'

'And for the Palestinians,' I retorted, put out by her diffident manner.

It was obviously the wrong thing to say, because Becky suddenly sat up and I noticed that her face had gone pale and her lips were quivering. Mine were too. That's when I realised that she, too, was shaken by our exchange. And maybe, if the others hadn't been there, we would have both burst into tears and hugged. But instead, we sank back into silence, feeling rather dazed.

'So who's going to Greenham Common this weekend?' Hannah asked, sensing an opportunity to change the subject.

I nodded. And then Becky nodded too. We smiled politely at each other, but I could sense a new tension between us. Why hadn't I stuck to less loaded subjects that we all agreed on, like Nicaragua and CND? In fact, why hadn't I listened to my father? I had become so used to brushing his comments on my middle-class friends aside that it had never occurred to me that he could have a valid point to make about them. But then, I didn't want my father to be right and draw my attention to our differences – I wanted things to remain as they were. I just wanted to belong.

The catalyst for change was that once-upon-a-time-taboo subject: boys. Our lunch breaks became increasingly preoccupied with discussions about sex.

'What's better, the Pill or condoms?' one of my friends would casually ask to kick things off.

'Is it better to be drunk or stoned the first time?'

'Should you do it on the first date or is it better to wait until you really, really *trust* each other?'

And so on. The prospect of sex was fast becoming a reality for my friends and, given the excitement around the issue, politics no longer held the same interest. New friendships were being forged and others realigned as my girlfriends began to divide into cliques of those who had done it (or sounded as if they had done it) and those who hadn't. The question for me was: on which side should I stand? Should I show an enthusiastic interest in the subject or just keep quiet?

It was a strange situation to be in. For though I did fancy some of the boys that the girls raved on about, I was Asian. And brown skinned. And the boys – all, incidentally, called Ben – were white. Without ever consciously considering why, I never for one minute entertained the idea that they could ever be interested in me. This wasn't something I anguished over; it was just the way things were. And somewhere deep down, I think my friends felt the same way. For while Lara or Jemima might be excluded from being in the 'in' crowd because they weren't cool around boys, I was never subjected to such scrutiny. My friends might coo about how brown and pretty I was, but they would never have considered matching me up with one of their mates. The only time I was drawn into the conversation was if one of their boyfriends turned out to have an Asian friend. 'Yas, his best mate is Asian. He's beautiful.' Or: 'Yas, Ben's best mate, Jay, is half-caste. Half-African. I really think you would get on. Fancy meeting him?'

Though I would shrug noncommittally, the real answer was, of course, no. For the truth about being an Asian girl was that one wasn't meant to think about boys – and never, ever about sex. If I had actually come home one day with the news that I had a boyfriend, there wouldn't have been time for my parents to get angry, because they would have already died from the shock.

I also didn't want to draw my friends' attention to the fact that boys might be a problematic issue for my parents. I couldn't think of anything more mortifying than for them to think of me as one of those sad, oppressed Asian girls, destined for an arranged marriage. Not that my father was in favour of arranged marriages for his girls, despite having had one himself. But then, it wasn't a subject he had ever discussed with me, though I had a hunch this might change – once I got a degree. Imagine explaining this to my Camden friends: my love life was on hold until I graduated.

11

The Bhajis

There were seven of us in the group, cleverly known to ourselves as the Wembley Bhajis. Bhajis, when spoken in a Cockney accent, sounded like the Urdu word for both 'sister' and fried pastry snack. There was Shazia, Aubergine Bhaji, the naughty one. There were Perveen and Shireen, respectively known as Spinach and Potato Bhaji, the immaculately groomed ones who modelled themselves on Princess Diana and Krystle from *Dynasty*. There was Afshan, Cauliflower Bhaji, who was considered the clever one because she was doing 'O' levels. There was Farah, my sister, known as Besan (gram flour) Bhaji. There was me, Onion Bhaji, the odd one, on account of my penchant for wearing ripped jeans. And then there was Nazia, Shazia's younger sister by four years, who didn't have a Bhaji nickname because she didn't really count. She was only there because Shazia's mother insisted she be allowed to tag along.

We were a lively bunch – not that this was necessarily considered a positive thing in the *mahalla*. Modesty and humility were much higher-rated virtues for girls, and they certainly didn't apply to us.

One Saturday afternoon, there we all were, standing outside Dolcis shoe shop on the busiest part of Wembley High Street, attempting to ignore a car-load of Asian boys who had stopped to talk to us. The Bhajis sported tight jeans, high heels and heaps of pastel-coloured make-up. I was in trendy black with a hint of red lipstick, following relentless pressure from Perveen, who had declared she was not walking around with me 'looking like a tramp'.

There must have been about ten boys squeezed into a clapped-out black Capri, jeering for our attention and oblivious to the fact that they were bringing traffic to a virtual standstill. Passers-by tut-tutted at the commotion we were causing, while drivers squeezing past the boys' car beeped angrily.

'Ignore them,' ordered Afshan, as the black Capri beeped again.

But of course Shazia strolled over to them for a chat.

'Trust her!' said Perveen, looking totally peeved at how easily Shazia always fell for male flattery.

Then I suddenly felt Afshan grab hold of my arm.

'Aunt Sidiqui,' she whispered, her large blue-purple eyes (on account of wearing coloured contact lenses) widening with panic.

'Where?' I replied, desperately scouring the crowds of the busy high street. The invincible Aunt Sidiqui was parked in her Mercedes across the road, talking to Aunt Shah. She would only need to turn forty-five degrees to her right to spot us.

My heart began to pound. No one terrified me more than the aunts.

In the distant past I remember them as a bunch of cloth-clad women who spoke broken English and timidly took us back and forth to school. But at some point in the last decade they had morphed. Long gone were the traditional plaits and shapeless tunics that they used to wear; in came glamorous *salwar kameezes* from Pakistan and smart hairstyles, often streaked with red highlights. Mrs Khan had even gone as far as cutting her hair into a bob, which had sent shockwaves around Wembley. But Aunt Sidiqui had trumped all the aunts by learning how to drive.

Still, while the aunts might have been busy becoming modern, God help any of their daughters who had similar ideas in their young heads. No, for us, the rules were clear. We had to remain chaste and pure. Well, at least until we got married. For if anyone caught an inkling of any funny goings-on, family honour could be lost for ever. A one-way ticket to Pakistan or an arranged marriage would definitely result for the offending girl; that is how bad it sometimes got. We all knew the story about Ayesha.

Apparently, while waiting for the number 92 bus on Wembley High Street, she had been approached by a fellow passenger asking for the time. The problem was that the fellow passenger was a young Asian boy. And it just so happened that Aunt Syeda, who had been strolling past, had witnessed their exchange. She immediately ran over to Ayesha's house, reported the incident to her mother, and before Ayesha could reply, 'Four o'clock, the bus is running late,' she and the Asian boy were supposedly down at Wembley Town Hall getting married.

'Don't lie!' I said to Afshan when she told me the story. 'What – fair-skinned Ayesha with braces?'

'Cross my heart, hope to die!' she replied.

Of course, this same anguish was never applied to the boys. In fact, if Mrs Sidiqui was anything to go by, some of the aunts took

156

great pleasure in hearing that their sons were considered risqué characters. Apparently Mrs Sidiqui's boys had once been spotted chatting up some girls on the 182 bus and a few of the *mahalla* aunts had approached Mrs Sidiqui, requesting her to have a word with them. 'Are your girls finding it hard to ignore my boys?' Mrs Sidiqui had replied with a smirk.

So to pre-empt us girls from ever falling into disrepute, the aunts had kindly appointed themselves our moral guardians. They had established a network of spies and an intricate system of intelligence-gathering, which I knew wouldn't take long to rein in the deviants. Meaning: we Bhajis. Or, more specifically, Shazia Quereshi.

Poor Shazia. She wasn't the most popular girl in the *mahalla*. Her clothes were always just a bit too tight and her hair just a bit too bleached for the aunts' liking. But being a Quereshi, I suppose, Shazia was used to their sneers. Not only had her two older sisters run off, but a few years back her father had been sent to prison for money-laundering, leaving behind him a young family shunned by the community. Time had allowed feelings to mellow and Mrs Quereshi (who was a rather simple and God-fearing woman) had gradually been accepted back into the fold, unlike her daughter, Shazia.

'Bloody hypocritical slags,' Shazia would sneer whenever she caught the aunts' eagle eyes on her. Everyone was a slag to Shazia, especially Mrs Khan – not that she would dare say this in front of Afshan. Shazia despised Mrs Khan and Mrs Khan despised her.

'She thinks our friendship will ruin Afshan's marriage chances,' Shazia once spat out to me after being cruelly rebuffed by Mrs Khan at a party.

'What?' I said, surprised. 'Afshan never told me she was getting married.'

'That's 'cos she doesn't know yet, does she?' Shazia replied, glowering at Mrs Khan as she now guided Afshan towards her arch-rival – newly married Ayesha.

Shazia had never liked Ayesha, and all because she had once overheard her tell Afshan that she was planning on applying to British Airways for a job as an air hostess when she left school. Shazia couldn't believe it. She also had plans to be an air hostess, but had set her sights on the more humble choice of Air India or Pakistan International Airlines. (Though she said she might even consider Air Bangladesh if she had no other choice.) British Airways was the big league, not an option for Asian girls like her. Well, now that Ayesha was married, she could kiss goodbye to those dreams.

'Hey,' I cried, waving my hands in front of Shazia's eyes. 'What do you mean about Afshan getting married?'

Suddenly realising what she had just blurted out, Shazia collected herself. 'Forget it. I was just speculating.'

And even though I soon forgot what she said, for a second I do remember thinking that I wouldn't be surprised if Shazia was right and that, unbeknown to Afshan, her marriage was being planned. For that was another thing about Wembley. It was full of little secrets that everyone seemed to know about, except the person concerned.

'Don't run, just walk,' muttered Afshan as we now turned to get away from Aunt Sidiqui.

'I think she's seen us,' said Perveen, completely petrified.

Just then we heard the boys in the car cry out after us, calling us back.

'Keep walking,' Afshan ordered, tugging at Shazia, who was looking over her shoulder.

A bus appeared on the horizon. We started to run, pretending to look as if we were in a hurry to catch it, even though it was going to Brent Cross, the opposite way to where we lived.

'It's all right. It's all right,' Shazia said to us as we scrambled onto the bus. 'They ain't seen us. We're in the clear.'

Thankfully, Aunt Sidiqui was still nattering away with Aunt Shah, oblivious to the drama that had just erupted around her. We sighed with relief, pausing to collect our breath. It had been a lucky escape, for all of us. Including me, for what would my father have said if word had come to him that his prized daughter Yasmin, sparkling mature Camden girl, had been caught behaving like a common *Kanjaree* [loose girl]. I knew he would have been devastated. That morning he'd frowned so disapprovingly when Afshan and Shazia called round that, for a second, I thought he was about to stop me going out with them.

'Want to come to Wembley High Street?' Shazia had screeched excitedly when I opened the door.

'Yeah, OK,' I replied, glancing nervously back at my father standing behind me.

'Just popping to the shops,' I said casually, tactfully avoiding his eyes. My father didn't reply, but I knew he wasn't happy. The way Afshan and Shazia were dressed didn't look as if they were going to the shops – more like the disco.

'*Aslam-al-ekum*, Uncle,' I suddenly heard Afshan and Shazia holler out behind me, making my heart sink. If only they could have said a simple English 'hello'. But thankfully, being a gentleman, my father nodded politely back.

It wasn't that he didn't like Afshan and Shazia. He did. But there was a problem. 'They never care about their studies,' I often heard him moan at my mother.

'Afshan's doing O levels,' I would interject. But to no avail.

'All they do is gossip, put make-up on, watch films and talk about marriage . . .' my father would continue.

'*Shaadi*,' my mother would say dreamily, her face lighting up at the mention of marriage.

In recent months, my father had been giving a lot of thought to *peer pressure*, a concept he had come across while reading up on the phenomenon of *youth*. Like the other Asian parents, he had never experienced teenage life, that Western invention. Nevertheless it was a phenomenon with which he felt he should acquaint himself. Of course, if his Asian neighbours had known that he was paying attention to such things, they would have thought he was insane. They preferred good, old-fashioned Asian parental despotism to manage their children. But my father liked to see himself as a modern man and felt a more sophisticated response was called for in handling us. Which is why, despite his obvious displeasure, my father always let me go out with Afshan and Shazia. He had read that it was important not to impose stringent rules on teenagers, as they would only rebel. And anyway, he must have reasoned, it could only be a matter of time before I grew bored of the Bhajis' company and drifted away from them.

Instead of drifting apart from them, I found that, despite their fondness for white stiletto heels, big hairstyles and bulky Indian film heroes, I began to spend more time with them. But then, the world we inhabited piled contradiction on top of contradiction, paradox on top of paradox – an intoxicating charge for all of us young Wembley girls desperately seeking excitement. Wembley was changing. It was becoming modern but not in a way that my father ever approved of.

While my Camden friends bemoaned the Thatcher years, my neighbours were starting to thrive like never before. Many of the men in the area had long ago abandoned their factory jobs and were now running their own small business ventures, supported by the expanding Asian network. I would often hear how no. 43 had just opened a new shop, how Mr Khan, Afshan's father was diversifying into trade, while no. 75 was joining ranks with Uncle Blah Blah and buying up half of Southall's derelict properties for renovation. Their entrepreneurial spirits had been unleashed and, with more money around, plus a stake in the country, the notion of returning to the subcontinent was starting to fade. Especially as it was just as simple, if not more agreeable, to fly back once a year for visits and be honoured like some rich prodigal son.

It helped that England was becoming a less hostile place to live in. No one banged on about the Empire any more, well, not in public anyway. And those who did, like Alf Garnett, they were just laughed at, weren't they? In fact, we were no longer officially referred to as Asians living in England. Now we were called 'British Asians'. It felt odd using the term at first, as if I was fraudulently laying claim to this country. But I was slowly getting used to it. We all were.

The biggest reminder that Asian fortunes were changing came when Dr Patel knocked at our door. We had just finished eating dinner when the door-bell rang. My brother had gone to answer it. When he returned, he could barely stand still, so excited was he.

'Stop playing games. Who is it?' my father asked, putting his cutlery down.

'An Asian man,' my brother replied, shuffling from one foot to the other.

'And?' my father said impatiently. A huge excited grin broke out onto my brother's face.

'From the Conservative Party!' he cried.

'What?' we all chorused in amazement, even my mother.

Who was this Asian who pledged loyalty and support to Maggie Thatcher? That mad woman who had accused the likes of us of swamping Britain? And who only recently had bombed Libya, a poor, Third World nation! Did this man have no self-respect?

We all rushed to the door. At the threshold stood an elderly Asian man dressed in a green farmer's jacket and flat cap. A large blue rosette was pinned on his left lapel.

'Ahh, Mr Hai,' he said, in the poshest Kiplingesque accent I had ever heard. It was guaranteed to get the back up of any self-respecting Socialist. Though I had hoped that my father would shun his handshake and close the door in his face, he didn't. Instead, for the next twenty minutes or so, my father challenged Dr Patel, on our doorstep, to justify how he could be a member of the Conservative Party. Dr Patel, who rarely got past basic introductions with shell-shocked Asian residents, was more than happy to discuss matters, especially as my father didn't once bring up the question of Kashmir, a rather popular issue with my neighbours.

My father didn't give Dr Patel an easy time. He seemed genuinely amazed that a fellow Asian of obvious merit could so readily abandon the interests of his own people in favour of a party that my father felt espoused jingoistic clap-trap. But Dr Patel was determined to convince my father that Thatcher's infamous 'swamping speech' was just a blip. And that there were many policies in the Conservative Party that would appeal to Asians, especially those entrepreneurially inclined. This got my father's back up even more. And now, hearing Dr Patel's reference to the new prosperity of my neighbours, I suddenly felt ashamed of our situation.

In recent months, no one could have failed to notice the

speed with which my Asian neighbours were getting rid of their lodgers, whose rent had always helped subsidise a mortgage, and starting to do up their homes for their own little family unit. Uncles were beginning to dabble in DIY, while aunties were experimenting with interior design. Unfortunately that only ended up instigating a whole series of new rows, as families began to compete with each other on who could come up with the most tasteful house. For example, Mrs Khan insisted that it was she who had first come up with the idea of having a gold-fish tank installed in the bathroom. But Aunt Sidiqui claimed that she had thought of it first, after having watched a James Bond film.

Weren't the Hais supposed to be the most modern family of all? But while my neighbours might be indulging in new kitchens, patios, loft conversions, MFI furniture and glass showcases to make their lives more comfortable, our only extravagance was more bookshelves. 'It's all about showing off,' my father cried when my mother tried to persuade him that it was time we got rid of our *almarhi* for a more tasteful glass showcase.

Dr Patel's reading of the Asian situation certainly didn't seem to be squaring with the Hai family's experience. But then, when had we ever been a typical Asian family?

Still, while my neighbours' decision to stay in England might be financially advantageous, the problem of how to bring up their children in a sexually permissive society remained. No matter how much you tried to explain to your average Asian parent that wearing jeans didn't mean you were a tart or that sitting in sex-education class didn't mean that you wanted to go out and immediately do it, they would never understand. Faced with their children's budding sexuality, parents of the *mahalla* were

163

floundering and worse, yet they had no one to discuss the matter with. Koran classes had long ago fallen by the wayside and, anyway, most mullahs would have probably choked on their tea if you dared to broach the subject of sex. The parents could have discussed their worries with other parents – but who was going to reveal to the outside world that they were having problems? No, better to keep quiet and administer discipline from within.

However, despite the *mahalla*'s rather tyrannical or, some might say, overprotective approach to parenting, this didn't mean that my friends just caved in to their rules. Using incredible guile and often exploiting their parents' ignorance, they had found their own methods to circumvent the prohibitions. And there was nothing I enjoyed more than listening to the Bhajis speak about boys. They always sounded like they were talking about characters in a Bollywood film, probably because films were their only point of reference for the subject of boy–girl relationships.

In fact, when I first heard them talk about their male friends, Aloo Gobi Ali, Biriyani Belal and Imli Irfan, they cut such romantic figures in my imagination that I couldn't wait to meet them. These were the food codenames we had given them so that no one outside our circle knew whom we were talking about. Maybe, I dreamed, just maybe, I might like one of them and one of them would like me, though I was very aware that whenever the Bhajis spoke about the boys, they never once said, 'Hey Yasmin, you might like this one.'

Maybe they thought I was just shy or maybe the Bhajis thought I preferred white boys, given that I went to a posh school. Well, whatever they thought, I couldn't wait to meet the boys. When I finally got to meet the famous Aloo Gobi Ali, Biriyani Belal and their mates, I discovered that the subject matter of all those intense discussions – and, let's face it, my fantasies – was a mob of gangly Asian boys with bum-fluff on their upper lips and bleached-blond mullet hairstyles.

'Yeah, man, for real,' Biriyani Belal croaked to me, squinting at my 'Coal Not Dole' badge. 'C-c-oaL Not Do-o-o-LE,' he repeated. 'Ha ha, that's funny. It rhymes. What does it mean?'

But the biggest surprise in meeting the boys was being introduced to Imli Irfan. For Imli Irfan turned out to be none other than Uncle Waseem's son, Irfan. I hadn't seen him in years. Despite wearing a red and black, shoulder-padded leather jacket, popularly sported by Michael Jackson, and severely greasing back his hair, Irfan didn't seem to have lost any of his charisma or confidence. He greeted the Bhajis with a kiss on their cheeks. But it was all a front.

'Don't tell my dad, right?' he later said to me, somewhat sheepishly, in reference to his flirty behaviour with my girl-friends.

'Course, I won't,' I replied, happy to collude in Wembley intrigue. To my disappointment, we didn't have time to talk further, because Shazia promptly whisked him away for a quiet tête-à-tête.

'I hope the parents chill out by the time Nazia grows up,' I later said to Shazia after hearing about her near escape with Aunty Sidiqui while talking to Imli Irfan and Aloo Gobi Ali. 'Imagine how nice it would be for Nazia to talk to boys without having to lie or . . .'

'No way,' Shazia slammed back at me. 'Nazia ain't gonna be a slag.' And then, turning to Nazia, who was suddenly very busy combing her Barbie doll's hair, she said: 'Do you get that?' Nazia nodded fast, without looking up.

I was about to point out to Shazia how hypocritical she was being, but I stopped myself. I might harbour romantic ideas of Shazia being some Asian version of Rizzo in *Grease*, a teenage rebel, but deep down I knew she wasn't. She might scoff at the aunts' narrow-mindedness and call her boyfriends 'brothers' in order to ease her conscience, but ultimately she was terribly conservative – still a product of her community. All the Bhajis were.

Maybe that's why talk about boys was always couched in lofty themes such as love, honour, betrayal and disloyalty. It was as if they had to speak in such terms to show that their interest in the opposite sex was not motivated by crude sexual interest but by the most honourable of intentions.

These sensibilities were so ingrained in them that no amount of exposure to the West was ever going to eradicate it totally. I knew this because whenever I spoke to them about my Camden friends – the parties, the freedoms they enjoyed, their relation-ships with their parents – my Wembley friends never sounded envious. If anything, they felt sorry for them and pitied the fact that they were always getting drunk and having to think about sex. The Bhajis equated these Camden freedoms with burdens. I tried to tell them that this wasn't the case, but they never seemed convinced – though frankly, neither was I.

Only Afshan made an effort to understand. But, ultimately, Camden was so outside her realm of experience there was no way she could imagine living with such freedoms for herself. There was one other person in the area who understood the 'other' world I was talking about – bizarrely, it turned out to be Amir Quereshi, Shazia's elder brother.

Everyone kept their distance from Amir. He was infamous. Not only had he been expelled from several schools, but the rumour was he had just been released from a young offenders' institution. Of course, no one knew the truth because if you ever asked the Quereshis about it, they always denied every-thing, claiming that Amir had been away holidaying in Pakistan.

Wherever he had been, he was now back in Wembley and still up to no good.

'Yeah, he's into ganja, big time,' Shazia once told me, in a rare moment of revelation. 'Sometimes you smell it coming out of his room.'

'What does your mum say?' I said, shocked. Smoking pot wasn't something I associated with Wembley.

'Well, how would my mum know what it smells like?' Shazia cried. 'She probably thinks it's some funky brand of Shake 'n' Vac.' Shazia giggled at her own joke. 'To be honest we don't really talk to him. He's weird, my brother.'

And I suppose I could see what Shazia meant, because whenever I saw Amir, usually on his way out or coming back from some all-night party, he radiated darkness. He always wore these long leather coats that floated above his ankles, like he was Huggy Bear in *Starsky and Hutch*. And his face was permanently obscured by his long, wiry black curls. If he did ever happen to look up, in the unusual event of communicating with a member of his family, you couldn't help shuddering at his bloodshot eyes and the scars on his left cheek. He gave you the creeps.

And maybe I would have continued keeping my distance from Amir, if it wasn't for the fact that one day, when I was over at Shazia's, I heard hip-hop blaring out of his room. At the time the hip-hop music scene was still underground. But to discover that, like me, Amir had been seduced by the likes of Grandmaster Flash and Afrika Bambaataa, suddenly altered my view of him, especially as listening to Prince was as risqué as it got in Wembley. I was even more intrigued when I caught sight of the Malcolm X poster hanging on his bedroom wall, alongside a poster of Che Guevara. Who would have believed that arch-delinquent Amir had a political conscience?

'What does your brother do?' I asked Shazia, suddenly very curious.

'Talk about waste of time,' she said, rolling her eyes. 'He goes to some poofy art college.'

Shazia might have sniffed, but discovering that Amir was artistically inclined impressed me even further. It wasn't that I suddenly started fancying him; I just began to feel this strange affinity with him. And I think Amir must have sensed something in me, too, because I began to notice that, whenever he saw me, he would gruffly nod in my direction. One time he even muttered a comment about South Africa, after spotting my anti-apartheid badge.

'What did he just say?' said Shazia, surprised at our interchange. 'God, you're nearly as weird as him.'

'Shut up,' I replied, rolling my eyes at her.

But of course, I knew that in a roundabout way Amir was trying to connect with me, letting me know that he, too, knew there was more to life than being stuck in the suburb of Wembley.

12

Operation Generation Gap

From the moment I entered the club, I knew I belonged there. 'Wow, I didn't imagine this,' I said to Afshan, impressed as the bass from the *dholki*, the Indian hand drum, pounded through the entrance hall. My hips were just itching to dance. Afshan grinned at me knowingly, pushing me further inside through crowds of young Asians – people just like me – who were laughing, talking or just dancing; arms waving madly around in the air and huge grins plastered across their faces.

It was midday and I was at a bhangra day do. Bhangra is a high-energy Punjabi peasant dance. And a 'day do' is a party held during school hours. Perfect, then, for all those young Asians who weren't allowed out during the evening. And there seemed to be hundreds of them here in the club, coming, as I would later learn, from all over London – Ilford, Southall, Tooting, Willesden, Luton and even from as far as Birmingham.

You left home in the morning in your school uniform. But instead of going to school you somehow ended up by 11 a.m. at

169

one of London's premier tacky nightclubs — usually the Hippodrome, Shaftesbury or Limelight — which had responsibly agreed to open their club for us partying under-age Asians. Once in, you made your way to the toilets, where you got dressed into your party clothes, often a little black number, before spending the afternoon dancing away to bhangra or, occasionally, soul. Come 3 p.m., you went back into the toilets, changed back into your uniform and then made your way home before your parents cottoned on what you had been up to.

An ardent party animal like me would normally have given a bhangra day do a wide berth. The idea of dancing to Punjabi folk music, surrounded by a mob of overexcited teenagers during the uncoolest hours of the day was not something I wanted to be associated with. In fact, when Afshan and Perveen had invited me to come along, I was all prepared to spend the day standing on the sidelines, sneering cynically at everyone. But, looking around now, I knew that wouldn't happen.

As Afshan and Shazia went to the toilets to get changed, I waited by the door, revelling in the scene unfolding around me. Here I was, standing in a nightclub. Yes, a nightclub, that most heathen of places, which all Asian parents had warned their children about. But look, there on the dance floor were groups of Asian girls dancing around their handbags, and then there by the bar, Asian boys were shyly milling around, while there in the darkest corners of the club, I was sure Asian couples were smooching as if it was the most normal thing in the world. Even the DJ and MC were Asians — how had that happened?

'What do you think?' said Shazia, suddenly appearing beside me. She was patting her outfit. I didn't reply, so stunned was I. Even though this was an Asian party, I hadn't seen anyone in traditional clothes. But here was Shazia, being her usual provocative self, wearing an elegant pink and turquoise blue *salwar kameez*.

'You think I look all right?' said Shazia, carefully watching my reaction.

'You know you do,' said Afshan, appearing from behind her. There was a note of admiration in her voice.

And from the astonished looks Shazia received from fellow Asian clubbers as we made our way to the dance floor, I could see what a huge statement she was making. 'Love your suit,' people kept calling out. In fact, I was so inspired by Shazia and the attention she was attracting that I decided I would ask my mother to make me a *salwar kameez* too, conveniently forgetting our last foray into dressmaking during my years as an English country-dancer.

But that seemed to be another thing about these bhangra parties. No cool moodiness existed here, just carnival festivity and an uninhibited celebration of who we were. I had never come across anything like it. A new, tentative pride was emerging amongst my Asian friends. It wasn't anything as dramatic as the epiphany of a decade in the future, which had us scuttling to listen to tapes of Nusrat Fateh Ali Khan, adorning *bindis* or celebrating chicken tikka masalas. This pride was different; it was spontaneous and heartfelt; it didn't need race-awareness workshops to facilitate it or PR companies to brand it. It just came naturally. Not that I or, in fact, my Asian peers really understood what being Asian meant at the time. All we knew was that we didn't just want to accept being Asian, we wanted to feel pride in it, too, the kind of pride that the Afro-Caribbeans had in themselves. For it hadn't escaped our attention how Danny Jobson from down our road and some of our other black friends had suddenly developed a *patois* lilt whenever they spoke and began to affect 'black' mannerisms. Being black was becoming cool and we desperately wanted the same. While bhangra parties might not be the coolest event in town, at least for a brief moment they allowed us to be who we were.

And, one time, who should I bump into on the dance floor doing the perfect bhangra? I didn't recognise her at first because she was wearing a designer *salwar kameez*. It was Lulu. Yes, my old nemesis from junior school.

'Yasmin?' she said, after taking a closer look. She was obviously as surprised to see me as I was her.

'Didn't expect to see you here,' I said.

'Yeah, same,' she replied.

That was the thing about bhangra parties: everyone from your past – well, everyone Asian from your past – turned up at some point.

For me the most wonderful thing about the bhangra gigs was that it all felt very British. Unlike our parents' generation, no one cared whether you were Sikh, Muslim or Hindu. When I looked out onto the dance floor, I couldn't help thinking bhangra gigs did something for communal peace that diplomacy in the subcontinent could never have achieved in a million years. We all felt united by our common experience of being British and yet Asian. And that felt good.

But still, bunking off school to go to bhangra parties did mean that we were living on the edge. If, in our youthful optimism, we thought we were going to get away with it, we were sorely wrong. One time as we stumbled out of the Limelight Club at three in the afternoon, our eyes blearily adjusting to the afternoon light, who should we see but Aunt Sidiqui with her husband. What they were doing in Piccadilly Circus, I don't know, but they had obviously stopped to watch all these young Asians pouring out of the club, and now that they had seen us, I could tell from the confused expressions on their faces that they were trying to work out whether their eyes were deceiving

172

them. After all, what could we be possibly doing in the West End during school hours? Maybe we could have got away with it by claiming that we were just shopping, if it hadn't been for the fact that, just then, Shazia strolled out of the club holding hands with a beaming Chapatti Chowan.

'What's up with you lot?' said Shazia, looking at the alarmed expression on our faces. She turned in the direction we were looking and her eyes instantly locked with Aunt Sidiqui's.

'Oh, f—' Shazia cried, shrugging Chapatti Chowan off. With a sudden U-turn, she started to walk in the opposite way. We followed, so petrified that we couldn't even look at each other.

'Don't worry. Don't worry,' Shazia kept saying to us, as we ran towards the Tube. 'We'll just say we were on a school field trip.'

'What? At the Limelight? Are you stupid?' said Afshan.

'Yeah, and what are you going to say about Chapatti Chowan?' Perveen lashed out.

'What are you blaming me for?' said Shazia, looking at her.

Perveen didn't answer. She continued walking.

'Thanks a lot,' Shazia said, quietly.

No one spoke to each other on the way home. Even I felt nervous. What would my father say? I had always managed to avoid trouble, but this time I, too, had been caught doing the inexcusable.

In fact, we were all so preoccupied that we didn't notice the crowd of aunties standing outside Shazia's house. They were talking furiously amongst themselves, but instantly stopped as we approached.

'*Api* [sister], look!' cried Nazia, pointing towards the women. For a second, fear crossed Shazia's face but she quickly collected herself, even attempting to outstare the outstareable Aunt Sidiqui. We didn't need to look at each other, we just knew that they knew what we had been up to. Still, Afshan tried to play the innocent.

'Mum, what's going on?' Afshan implored.

'Home!' ordered Mrs Khan, her eyes boring into her daughter.

And then suddenly, completely catching me off guard, Mrs Khan turned to me and shook her head. 'I never expected this from Mr Hai's girl.'

I saw the women behind her nod in agreement. I felt my cheeks redden with shame and a tightening sensation in my throat. I had never been the subject of the *mahalla*'s disapproval before and it wasn't a good feeling.

'You better go,' Mrs Khan said, jerking her head in the direction of my house. As I looked up towards my house, it took me a few seconds to realise that my mother had been standing by our front gate, witnessing the whole scene. She looked painfully embarrassed. And then suddenly behind her I saw my father come into view, looking so ashamed that he could only hover in the background.

Even though my father was devastated that one of the Hais had been dragged into a lowly *mahalla* scandal, he dealt with the matter very rationally indeed. Instead of berating me as soon as I entered the house, he took me into the kitchen, made himself a cup of tea, and even flicked through the radio listings for that evening. He didn't speak to me the whole time, too busy thinking. All the while I stood, my back pressed against the kitchen wall, rigid with fear. When my father did finally speak, he thankfully didn't mention how I had tarnished the Hais' reputation. Instead he focused on the practical: education.

'Once you have a degree you can do whatever you want,' he began, turning to look at me for the first time. 'You can become a dustbin man, you can waste your time with loafers . . .'

'But I would never do that,' I protested, slightly relieved at the direction the telling-off was taking.

'I haven't finished,' my father said sternly. I flinched, tears welling up in my eyes. 'But until you get your degree you have no standing in life. Do you understand?'

I nodded obediently, thinking again how reasonable and fair my father was being. At least he was giving me the option to do whatever I wanted in the future, subject to getting a degree. It was only when he said, 'But it's best if you kept your distance from Afshan and the others for the moment,' that I panicked.

I stood frozen against the kitchen wall. The prospect of not being able to hang out with the Bhajis ever again was too much to bear. 'But that's not fair,' I said, speaking out for the first time. 'We weren't doing any harm.' I purposely didn't say the word boys or bhangra. 'You know what the *mahalla* aunts are like. They're just exaggerating the problem.'

'Exactly,' my father said. 'That's why I don't want you to have anything to do with them. I don't want them to be gossiping about us. And what is this Asian party you went to?' he demanded, catching me unaware.

My heart started to beat faster. There had never been a conversation with my father that I had ever dreaded more than the one I was now about to have. I knew how much my father hated talk of anything that alluded to multiculturalism or ethnic pride. These ideas were starting to gain currency in England, but my father believed them to be misguided, arguing that they would only perpetuate the ghetto mentality and hold minorities back. And while I understood my father's rationale, right now I couldn't help thinking he was wrong. Hanging out with the Bhajis and going to bhangra parties was the best thing that had ever happened to me. Even better than being at Camden. But I suddenly felt unsure how to explain this to my father.

175

'Asian party one day and next thing, you'll be wanting to watch Bollywood filums and go to the mosque,' I heard my father say scornfully.

'Mosque?' I thought, giggling to myself. Where had that one come from? Who went to the mosque these days?

'Dad, that's not what Afshan and Shazia are like,' I said, attempting a laugh. 'I mean Afshan is doing O levels and . . . and . . . no one cares about religion these days.'

'What do you know?' my father replied authoritatively. 'Underneath they are still steeped in religion. One day you'll see.'

I let out a frustrated sigh, annoyed at how blinkered my father was being.

'I don't expect you to agree with me,' my father said, noting my sulky expression.

'I don't,' I replied.

Instead of getting angry, my father smiled knowingly at my bolshy reply. 'Ahh,' he said, smirking to himself. 'Our disagreement is what is commonly known as the "generation gap". It means . . .'

Even though I pretended to listen to my father, I couldn't resist a private giggle. Had my father just said 'generation gap'? Suddenly, everything felt clear. My father might like to think he had a sophisticated approach to parenting, but the truth was he was like all the other Asian parents in the neighbourhood. He couldn't really listen to anything he didn't want to hear. So, I would behave just like the Bhajis did with their parents. I must have been doing a good impersonation of looking remorseful because my father suddenly added in a kinder tone, 'You will move on soon. This is just a phase.'

And though I remember thinking at the time that he was wrong and that I would find ways to hang out with the Bhajis and

176

still go to day dos with them, what a shame that he turned out to be right.

After the Limelight incident, Shazia was suddenly whisked off to Pakistan by her mother and the Bhajis were banned from going out. I could see my father was relieved, especially as I began to spend more time in Camden. What he didn't know was that I wasn't spending my weekends reading Shakespeare at a friend's house, but instead dancing to hip-hop at warehouse parties.

In many ways the dance-music scene was as exciting as the bhangra parties. It captured the mood of many people of colour in my generation – the black urban experience. And who should I spot at a Soul II Soul gig one night but Jay, that half-caste boy my Camden friends were always trying to set me up with. He wasn't with Ben, Ben and Ben, but a crowd of young black friends. He told me that he no longer described himself as half-caste (he considered the label to be a derogatory term), but as black. I noticed a leather pendulum of Africa hanging from a chain on his neck. He seemed pleased to see me – and I was certainly pleased to see him. Maybe, not that I would dare allow myself to believe it, but maybe Jay did fancy me? For a moment the bhangra gigs happily faded into the background.

A couple of months later, I heard Shazia was back. My mother told me that Mrs Quereshi had invited all the women and girls in the area for a get-together at her house. We were so excited to see Shazia again that none of us stopped to wonder why she hadn't bothered to contact us.

For the first time in a while, we Bhajis gathered to go to the party together. Nazia opened the door to us.

'So where is she?' Perveen squealed with excitement.

'Inside,' Nazia replied, pointing towards the living room.

'You look nice,' Nazia said to me as I entered. But she didn't sound very convincing. I was wearing the *salwar kameez* my mother had made me and feeling rather stupid for it. Not only was it garishly pink, but also my mother had artfully sewn gold sequins around the cuffs, which shimmered every time they caught the light. This was not a suit one would find fashion-conscious Asian girls wearing in upmarket Wembley. But of course the aunts loved it. 'Wow, first-class suit,' they said when I entered the room. 'Proper Pakistani.'

'Yes, first class, first class,' Aunt Sidiqui echoed, while my mother beamed with pride.

I smiled politely back, but I was cringing with embarrassment. The house was so crowded with guests that at first we didn't spot Shazia.

'Where is she?' said Afshan, looking around the room.

Perveen gave her a nudge and pointed towards the main living room. And there, sitting right between Ayesha and Aunt Sidiqui, was Shazia. She was dressed in a sombre, fawn-coloured designer *salwar kameez*. Her bleached hair had been tempered to a sensible chestnut-auburn colour.

'Shazia!' we cried out in chorus.

Seeing us, she smiled and gestured that she would be over soon. Except, much to our growing annoyance, she didn't come over to us once that evening. She always looked as if she was about to, but then something would distract her, like having to hand round delicacies or needing to exchange chit-chat with one of the aunts. In fact, she seemed to spend a lot of time talking to the aunts, which didn't go unnoticed by us.

'I'm really sorry about this,' Shazia said apologetically as she came past. 'I've just got to put some more tea on and then I will be with you. It's just a bit mad.'

'Oh don't worry,' we said. 'Do you want any help?'

'No, no, sit down,' Shazia replied, just a bit too swiftly for my liking. I suddenly sensed something different about her. I couldn't put my finger on it. We all looked at each other. Was Shazia avoiding us?

At some point Shazia's Pakistan holiday photos came round to us. We tried hard not to giggle as we flicked through them. They were mostly pictures of her extended family, but the self-conscious poses they had adopted – set against a fake Niagara Falls backdrop – soon had us in hysterics.

'Look at this one,' laughed Perveen, passing us a picture of Shazia's grandmother sitting in a sparse living room in front of a large, green, metal *almarhi*. Her grandmother was staring sternly at the camera, but the corner of her huge seventies spectacles was ablaze with the flash from the camera.

'Check out *Magnum P.I.*,' said Afshan, passing us another photo. It was a picture of Shazia sitting with her mother and an uncle. The uncle had a large handlebar moustache, which had blurred into a tree branch from the backdrop. We burst out laughing.

'Here, give them to me,' sniped Aunt Syeda, whipping the photos out of our hands. 'Shame on you, *bathamese lurkis* [bad girls].'

We did try to say goodbye to Shazia but she seemed so engrossed talking to Ayesha that we decided not to bother. By then I think we were feeling a bit annoyed.

'Why didn't she tell us?' Perveen cried when we left the house, falling about with laughter. Afshan was leaning against the wall, bent down in hysterics too.

'Tell us what?' I cried.

'She got married, hasn't she?'

'What?' I said, shocked.

'The photos!' Perveen cried.

I was just about to ask whom she had got married to when images of the uncle with the moustache flashed through my mind. My stomach suddenly churned.

'Poor Shazia,' I said.

'Are you mad?' Perveen cried. 'It's what she's always wanted.'

This was news to me.

'But what about Chapatti Chowan?' I asked.

'Dahh, he's Hindu,' replied Shireen. 'How can she marry him?'

'Because we live in England,' I replied, but quietly, to myself.

We didn't see much of Shazia after that. Whenever we visited her, she barely spoke to us, always preferring the company of the aunts or her new best friend, Ayesha. But the funny thing is that she did look much happier and contented, probably relieved that she was no longer the social outcast. And I suppose the aunts were treating her differently now that she was married. They no longer taunted her. In fact, they went out of their way to give Shazia company, as she patiently waited for her husband to join her from Pakistan, and I even heard that Mrs Sidiqui invited her around for dinner one evening. She was finally one of them – and that made the aunts very happy.

As for the rest of the Bhajis, we did continue meeting up on occasion, but we all knew that our time was running out. Perveen and Shireen were going to Pakistan at Christmas and even though we didn't speak about it, we all knew why. As for Afshan, she might be making plans to go to college in September, but I knew what was about to come her way. Once married, the Asian family network would swallow them all up. I was only sixteen, but I suddenly felt very alone and, worse, already on the shelf.

*

To celebrate the end of school term, Afshan, Perveen and I had decided, for nostalgia's sake, to attend a bhangra day do at Leicester Square's Hippodrome nightclub. We knew we were taking a risk, but we promised ourselves it would be the last one. The place was heaving more than usual. A dance competition had been organised and a group of boys were on stage, clambering on top of each other's shoulders trying to do the bhangra.

Even though there wasn't anything particularly innovative about their act, the audience enthusiastically clapped them on, such was the excitement of the occasion. Then suddenly one of the boys, precariously balanced on his friend's shoulders, pulled something from his back pocket and, with a mischievous grin, he threw it high into the air. Our eyes followed the cloth up to the ceiling and as it floated down, it began to unfurl. At first we couldn't work out what it was, but then it opened up to reveal the Pakistan flag – a deep emerald green with a white Islamic crescent and moon imprinted on top. There was a gasp from the crowd and, for a second, silence. And then some of the audience broke out into loud applause, cheering madly while others began to boo. Afshan looked at me, her hands covering her mouth in stunned horror. I felt knots appear in my stomach. In an instant the boys had turned a room full of friends into potential enemies, pitching Pakistani against Indian, Indian against Bengali, Bengali against Pakistani and, God forbid, if the fissures were followed to their logical conclusion, then Muslim against Hindu, Hindu against Sikh, Sikh against Muslim.

'Off, off, off, off,' many in the room began to chant. The mood was changing.

'Trust it to be one of ours,' Perveen said.

By now, one of the boys on the stage had grabbed the flag and, fired up by the crowd's response, was waving it frantically above

181

himself, all the while doing the bhangra. A young guy in the audience tried to jump on the stage, but a security guard blocked him.

'Off, off, off, off!' The chanting was growing louder.

The atmosphere in the room got so heated that the compere had to finally step in to wind the contest down. Reluctantly, the boys left the stage, but they looked exhilarated by the mayhem they had caused. They'd just been fooling around, but their actions frightened me. It felt deeply wrong bringing the tensions of our parents' past into that room.

And while I knew that the British Asian identity was just a construct, a convenient label given by the British authorities to describe people coming from the subcontinent, even I was surprised at how easily it would fall apart in the coming years.

13

Goodbye

The last conversation I ever had with my father was about the Palestinian intifada. It was a cold, rainy February night and my father was getting ready to go to the shops and buy me some chocolates. I had been more than happy to forgo the treat but, tired with hearing me moan at my mother for her failure to stock up on snacks during a critical stage of my exam revisions, he had decided to do something about it.

'I won't be long,' he said, putting his trilby on.

My mother shook her head reproachfully at me. I scowled back at her. Lately, all we ever did was bicker. As my father opened the front door to leave, sleet blew into the hallway. He looked up at the half moon and his silhouette cut a lonely figure. My heart suddenly went out to him. How could I let him go out on his own?

As we walked down the road, the luminous blue glow of television shone out from the windows of our neighbours' warm homes, mocking our excursion outside. The wind blew a hard drizzle across my face, fuelling my self-pity. I hoped my mother felt sorry.

I noticed my father staring pensively at the ground.

'What are you thinking about?' I asked, curiosity getting the better of me.

My father let out a very deep sigh.

'The intifada,' he mumbled.

'The intifada?' I asked, noting the gloom in his voice.

I would have thought my father would be in favour of the Palestinian uprising. David and Goliath was one of his favourite parables. But instead he appeared thoroughly depressed by it.

'They will be crushed, you'll see,' he said, raising his gaze as if looking into the future.

I didn't reply. I don't think I had ever heard him sound so deflated. Usually he was quite optimistic about the fighting spirit of the underdog. 'Foolishly so,' I had often heard Uncle Aslam say. Why was my father sounding so resigned? What had shaken his belief that justice and freedom would one day prevail for all of the world's dispossessed?

I never found out.

Just after midnight my mother rushed into my room screaming. I didn't ask what was wrong. I just knew. As I ran to call the ambulance, I saw my father lying on the bathroom floor. I quickly averted my eyes; I didn't want to see him looking so helpless.

'Is everything going to be OK?' my tearful sister asked as the ambulance pulled away with my mother and brother.

'Of course,' I said, stoically. 'You better go to sleep.'

As I waited for my brother and mother to return, I finished off the economics 'A'-level essay that I had been struggling with earlier. It was about 3 a.m. by the time I finished. As they still weren't back yet, I decided to read a chapter of *Bleak House*, my homework assignment for English 'A' level. I just sensed that it would be a few days before I would find time to do my homework again. I was right.

In the early hours of the morning, my father died.

My family had never been good at expressing emotion. As a grey dawn broke through the winter sky, we sat dispersed around our living room in silence, avoiding each other's eyes, fearful that any contact between us might cause our fragile guard to crumble. With the head of the family now gone, we were scared.

My mother took my father's British passport out from the *almarhi* because the hospital had asked for it. As she flicked it open, we scrambled to her side, desperate to catch a glimpse of our father, as if it were evidence that somewhere he still lived on. Seeing his earnest face staring back at us, we immediately burst into tears. My mother reached out to hug us and we awkwardly allowed ourselves to be consoled. But then, ten minutes later we were back in our places, each of us alone. Thank goodness the doorbell finally rang.

It hadn't taken long for word to get round the *mahalla* that my father was dead of a heart attack. Mrs Khan claimed that she was the first to know.

'I knew. I heard an ambulance last night. Khan said I was dreaming. But I just knew,' she would later prattle to anyone who cared to listen.

'My husband dreamt last night that all saucepans fell out of the cupboard,' Aunt Syeda exclaimed.

'Allah!' Aunt Mahin gasped. 'Well, that is a sign isn't it?'

I looked at my brother, baffled. But we would soon learn, among other things, that saucepans falling out of cupboards was a sign – for some – in the *mahalla* that someone was about to die. Our house was soon teeming with neighbours. And, taking one look at our forlorn state, they instantly took charge.

'Don't worry, sister,' Uncle Waseem said, crouching down to my mother. 'We'll take care of everything.'

'I know a good mullah,' mumbled Mr Rehman, tears streaming down his flabby face.

'And I will go and collect some Koran copies from no. 32,' Mrs Khan added, brimming with purpose.

'I will help you,' said an eager Aunt Mahin.

My mother glanced up and then, seeing everyone gathered in her time of great sorrow, she let go of the tears that she had been holding back all night. Loud howls of grief filled the room. Her cries cut right through me.

'Allah, protect her,' Aunt Syeda said out loud, draping her *dupatta* over her head. The aunts echoed her prayer. But my mother wouldn't be consoled. Her body continued to shake in grief.

No one close to me had ever died. That is, apart from Aunt Hilda. What was one meant to do in such situations?

Watching my mother sob and listening to my neighbours talking about saucepans, mullahs and copies of the Koran, it began to occur to me that death was something I didn't know anything about. My father would have usually handled such situations. But who was going to take charge of us now? Would my mother be able to step up to the challenge? Taking one look at her now, weeping mournfully, I wasn't sure. I felt real panic.

But though I didn't know what to do now that my father had died, our neighbours certainly did. As the morning unfolded, more people arrived to pay their respects. I noticed that, without any prompting, they immediately took their shoes off as they entered our house. I don't know who started it, it just happened. Once their shoes were off, the men disappeared into the living room, while the aunties dutifully filed upstairs or into the kitchen.

'*Bachari* [poor girl],' the aunts would say when they spotted me hovering around the hallway. One by one, they would pull me into their huge chests. 'Have you eaten?' they would ask. I would nod, even though I hadn't. I had been far too preoccupied watching Uncle Waseem and Mr Rehman at work.

The two men had been busy all morning, turning our house upside down. In the living room all the furniture, including the big *almarhi*, had been pushed aside and white sheets had been laid out for the guests to sit on. A huddle of men were sitting on the floor, *topis* on their heads, reading the Koran. Extra copies of the holy book rested on a table in the middle of the room. Upstairs had been transformed, too. The beds were pushed against the wall and scarf-clad women sat in the centre of the room, keening with grief, reading their copies of the Koran. One of them was my mother. Any woman not praying was in the kitchen, churning out snacks and cups of tea for the steadily arriving mourners. Every few seconds the doorbell rang, delivering more guests with Tupperware boxes of *salan* for us to eat. Many I had never seen before in my life.

I was soon starting to feel like a stranger in my home, if not my own body. When Mrs Khan had kindly placed a black scarf on my head, I didn't resist, numbly allowing it to lie there. When Uncle Waseem informed my brother and me that the funeral had been arranged in the Muslim section of a local cemetery, I just shrugged. And even when Afshan, Perveen and Shireen came tottering into the house in their stiletto heels, sobbing their eyes out, I remained calm.

'It's OK. It's OK,' I said, handing them tissues.

'We're here now, don't worry,' Afshan said, blowing her nose. Being well acquainted with the etiquette such occasions demanded, she then instantly placed a scarf over her head.

'Wow, so many people,' said Perveen, glancing around. Many

guests had spilled into the hallway, where they were now noisily exchanging gossip. With so many old friends around, a general bonhomie seemed to have descended upon the house.

'It's been mad,' I said, inappropriately breaking into giggles. I couldn't help it. It all felt so ridiculous.

'Who's that?' Afshan whispered to me, later. She pointed to an old woman, shrouded in white cloth, who hadn't stopped wailing for the best part of the hour. I was sitting with the Bhajis upstairs, in one of the rooms allocated for the women. I shrugged, looking blankly at the old woman. Every time the old woman wailed, my mother collapsed into tears.

'Are you sure?' Afshan said, raising her eyebrows. 'Not some long-lost relative?' I threw my head back laughing, my scarf slipping off. Some of the aunts glanced up smiling, happy to see me cheerful. Others frowned. One aunt frantically tugged at her headscarf, gesturing me to put mine back on. This only made Afshan and me giggle even more.

Our giggles got much worse later when Mrs Jobson and some of her Caribbean friends from church arrived to pay their respects. They quietly squeezed into my mother's bedroom, dressed in their heavy winter coats, but their feet bare. They hushed each other to be quiet, so as not to disturb the aunts, who were busy praying. Except the aunts weren't praying any more, they were now gawping at Mrs Jobson and her friends.

'Praise the Lord!' Mrs Jobson sighed out aloud, settling her ample self onto the bed. She shook her head in gloom at the grief that had befallen us.

'Praise the Lord,' her friends echoed behind her, settling themselves on the bed too. And then, as if in some choreographed dance sequence, they placed their large handbags on their laps, shook their heads in despair and muttered some entreaties to Lord Jesus.

At which point the old wailing woman joined in with an ear-splitting, 'Allllllllllaaaaaaaaahhhhhhhhhh!'

The aunts waited for her to finish and then promptly responded with a loud prayer. My mother burst into tears yet again. Soon the room was filled with fevered cries, wails and prayers as the gathered mourners arduously worked to express their grief and pay their respects to my father. Afshan and I, plus all the other young British-born children in the room, tried to stifle our giggles, but it wasn't easy. We had never seen our mothers behave with such abandon.

I'm not sure what Mrs Sherman and Britt made of it all, either. When they arrived, they just stood awkwardly at the door observing the mayhem.

'Are you OK?' Britt mouthed to me. I wasn't sure whether she was referring to my father's death or the havoc in the room.

At some point Mrs Campbell also wandered in, wearing shabby brown stockings. As she entered the room, the aunts immediately turned to me. Their reflexive response momentarily threw me. I suddenly understood that now my father had left us, it was British-born me – not my mother – who was now expected to be the Hai family's ambassador to the outside world. I dutifully got up, feeling slightly humbled by my new adult role.

'I'm very sorry to hear about your father, Jasmin,' Mrs Campbell said as I approached her. She never got my name right, but seemed genuinely upset. 'He was a good man. Always dedicated to your education. I think he would have been proud of everything he achieved here, for you three.'

It was a strange comment, and the direct reference to my father's British dreams jolted me. Had my father posthumously won Mrs Campbell's respect? I became aware of a lump building up in my throat. She seemed to be the only person in the whole house who had an inkling of who my father really was.

'A lot of people,' she said, peering around. I was listening for disapproval in her voice. Instead I think I heard envy.

'Yes,' I nodded, proudly. 'A lot of people.'

It was a situation I would have to get used to, for over the next forty days this was how things were going to be.

'Forty days?' I whispered to my mother, when we finally settled down to sleep, late that night. We were sleeping in the same room, as some of the aunties had taken over mine and my sister's room.

'That is how we do things,' my mother replied wearily.

'Who does things?' I asked, gingerly.

I knew what the answer what going to be. And though I had been avoiding hearing it all day, I was now ready.

'*Musalman log* [we Muslims],' she whispered, drifting to sleep.

And there it was. For let there be no mistake. My father, Syed Samsamul Hai, might well have dedicated his whole life fighting for a Marxist revolution. He might well have fallen out with his brother over his contempt for religion. And he might well have brought his children up not reading the Koran. But now that he was dead, none of his oddball ideas mattered. As far as anyone in the *mahalla* was concerned, my father had been born a Muslim and he would also die a Muslim.

Did I mind? You would have thought so, given the deep distrust of religion I had inherited from my father. But as the difficult day had gone by, all my hesitations evaporated. In fact, the whole Islamic spirit of the occasion seemed to make total sense, from the women praying for my father's soul to the Muslim cemetery, which was to be my father's final resting place.

There had to be more to him than plain old Mr Hai, the immigrant Marxist, buried in a land faraway from home. There had to be a more profound story that connected his past to the future. The idea that he was all on his own, even in the form of a celestial spirit, was too painful to accept.

I needed antidotes. I needed answers. Transcendental answers, to alleviate the pain boring through me. The *mahalla*, with all its rituals and ceremonies – some that offered to protect my father's soul, others that promised to ease his journey into the 'other' world – was offering those answers. It was reminding us that my father wasn't on his own. He belonged. Belonged to a people, belonged to a history that had not only defined who he was in life, but could also transcend his mortal place on earth. And the best thing was that it didn't seem as if one needed to subscribe to the tenets of the Koran to embrace that idea – it felt broader than that.

After all, why was Uncle Aslam sitting with the men in the living room reading the Koran? He wasn't religious. He was just following a ritual, acknowledging that my father had been born of Muslim people, that my father wasn't going to depart this world alone.

That is when I decided that I wanted to read the Koran.

In the past, whenever I attended Koran readings, I always sat with the girls who couldn't read the Koran – that is, read the Koran in Arabic. Now, only two types of girl sat in this group. The first were girls below the age of seven, too young to have started reading the Koran. The second were girls who were menstruating. Too embarrassed to admit that I had never learnt to read the Koran, whenever I attended Koran gatherings, I always told the *mahalla* that I was menstruating.

But sitting in the non-Koran reading group didn't mean that you were absolved from your religious duties. One still had to recite prayers, which would be done to granules of split lentil peas. We would pick up a pea, say, '*Bis millah, hir rahman nir rahim*' to it and then place it to one side. We would repeat the pattern until all the split peas had been recited to. And then we would start all over again.

But now that this Koran gathering had been organised for my father, it didn't feel right to just sit there, counting humble split peas. I wanted to contribute more – but being my father's daughter, I also wanted to do it with proper understanding.

'Why can't I read the Koran in English?' I asked Afshan, while sifting through another load of split peas. She looked up from her copy of the Koran.

'I don't know why,' she said, shrugging her shoulders. 'Never thought about it.'

'You can if you want,' I heard Samira whisper behind me. I turned around. She was sitting there with Munira, both now reading their fourth chapter. 'I've got a copy in English.'

'Really?' I said, surprised that a translation existed. 'Can I borrow it?'

She nodded enthusiastically. 'Of course, I'll bring it later.'

I don't exactly remember what Samira's copy looked like. All I recall is that the next chapter of the Koran in line to be read turned out to include text about the non-believer.

'Typical, innit?' said Afshan, giggling when I showed her the paragraph.

Samira's copy of the Koran in English – lyrical but also dense in prose – proved to be a tough read, made more gruelling by the fact that I had frequently to consult the reference index to understand what was going on. By the time I returned to my page, I often found that I had lost my place. But still, the mere act of holding the Koran and allowing my eyes to drift across the words felt uplifting, as if there was something sacred in doing just that. Of course, the whole experience would have been more profound if I had been an actual believer. But unfortunately, I wasn't.

'What? You reading the Koran and you don't believe in God?' said Perveen when I told her I was a non-believer.

'Yes,' I replied.

'Well, who do you think made this world?' Perveen said, looking at me perplexed. 'I mean, it didn't just appear, did it?'

I suddenly felt someone's hands on my arm. It was Samira. 'Don't worry. One day you will believe. *Insh'allah* [God willing].'

I felt so safely cocooned amongst my friends and neighbours that I wanted to belong to their lives more than ever before. This obviously came as a shock to some.

'What are you doing?' whispered Amboureen, Mr Ali's eldest daughter. Mr Ali was my father's friend from the Holloway house. Amboureen was crouching down beside me, struggling to maintain decorum. This was difficult, as her pencil skirt kept riding up her legs. Some of the aunts were staring disapprovingly at her.

The Alis had come to pay their respects and were shocked at the state of our house.

'I didn't know you were into all this religious stuff,' said Amboureen, scouring the room in horror. 'And what's with all this scarf business?'

Amboureen tugged at my black scarf. I flinched, for the first time seeing how it all must look through an outsider's eyes. What exactly was I doing? But then I sighed. How would I ever explain to Amboureen what amazing things had been happening to me under the *mahalla*'s influence? The other day, Aunt Syeda had asked me where we stocked our boxes of Kleenex tissues.

'Over there,' I said, pointing to the *almarhi*. 'And watch out for the towels, they keep falling down.'

What was amazing about my reply was that I had said it in Urdu, not English. After all these years, the words just tumbled out of my mouth, and my diction had been spot on. It was as if part of my brain had been liberated. Despite my father's efforts to stop us from speaking Urdu, I could still speak my mother tongue. In fact, being around the *mahalla* was opening up a whole new world for me. I was discovering that many of their practices, which I had previously dismissed as being simply archaic, often had profound meaning underneath.

For example, wouldn't the old Yasmin have been outraged by the forty-day rule, scorning the cultural practice as being impractical. What if you had a job to go to? But now, as I enthused to Afshan, I couldn't help thinking how clever it was. By the time my father's period of mourning came to an end, my grief would surely have subsided, sparing me the worst of the pain. I hadn't cried yet – maybe I could avoid tears all together.

'No, that's not the reason for the forty-day rule,' said Samira, leaning over. 'It's to protect the woman in case she is pregnant so that she doesn't lose the baby through grief.'

'No it isn't,' cut in Afshan. 'It's a tradition borrowed from the Jews.'

Samira shook her head. 'I don't think so . . .'

'I tell you it is,' said Afshan.

But, then, seeing my face fall, she suddenly hugged me and said: 'Don't worry. Forty days or no forty days, we'll still be here for you.'

I hugged her back, tears welling up in my eyes. But I quickly collected myself. It didn't feel like the right moment to cry. 'Thanks,' I mumbled instead.

It was good to have Afshan round. I rarely got to see her these days, now that she was at university somewhere in the Midlands, studying an obscure course in plant biology. But then any course would have done, as long as it got her away from home and her mother's constant rants on 'marriage'.

'You know, you're so lucky,' Afshan said, glancing around the room. 'Having everyone here for you.'

I nodded, aware of a note of envy in her voice. Then it occurred to me that Afshan was comparing our situations. Look how the *mahalla* had gathered to support us in our time of need. What had they done for Afshan when she had bravely stood up against her parents – well, more accurately, her mother – and demanded to go to university? Nothing – the *mahalla* had just labelled her a slag.

The forty-day mourning period came to an end. I came downstairs one morning and saw that the white sheets on the floor had gone and our furniture was back in place. It was as if nothing had happened. I stood in the middle of the room, allowing the silence to envelop me.

'What are you doing?' I suddenly heard my mother say.

I jumped, surprised to see her praying in the corner of the room. That didn't feel right, now that the room was back to normal.

'Have you had breakfast?' my mother asked, rolling up the prayer mat.

I gulped. It was my father who usually prepared breakfast in our house. That's when I knew that I would feel his loss most in the routine of our day-to-day life.

In the event of a death, there are always authorities to notify, forms to fill in, names to be changed on bills, all the details of life that can test the most patient of people. It was all beyond my mother – so fearful of anything to do with English officialdom. Now it was up to me. Only seventeen, I suddenly found myself having to make important – and often emotionally charged – decisions about our future, from family will matters to mortgage choices. It was a role that I privately came to resent. That is why I liked it when the *mahalla* came round. Their jovial spirits offered a brief respite from the mundane tasks of daily life, until one day.

I was in the kitchen washing up, intermittently dipping in and out of the aunts' conversation in the living room, when something Aunt Mahin was saying caught my attention. 'Listen sister, think hard, what have you really got here?'

I quickly turned the tap off to listen more closely.

'Live here with no man! It's madness,' I heard Aunt Syeda say, her voice rising in alarm.

'She's right,' I heard Mrs Khan cry. 'Pakistan is the only answer. You have two daughters to think about.'

'Allah protect them,' they all mumbled in prayer.

Suddenly I heard my mother start sobbing. My heart began to pound. So far I had managed to avoid thinking about the future. Now the aunts' conversation had catapulted me back to reality. It had never once occurred to me that my mother could consider leaving England to go and live in Pakistan. England had always been our home.

But what would happen now? Under my father we had been that liberal family, happily living in Britain. Now that he was gone, and my mother was honorary head of the family, which direction would the Hais be going in?

'I didn't expect your mother to look like that,' Becky whispered to me.

'Like what?' I said, defensively.

Becky looked at me, embarrassed.

'Ummm, all traditional, I suppose,' she said, her voice tapering off.

I glanced over at my mother. Even though she had worn her best trouser suit, with her long hair tied up in a bun, I could

196

see that to strangers she looked like a traditional Asian house-wife.

We were over at Becky's house, picking my sister up. Sylvie had kindly offered to give my sister English grammar tutoring, now that my father was no longer here to provide additional lessons. It was a kind offer, especially as some of my Camden friends had shied away from me since my father's death. I think the concept of death was too terrifying for them. Unlike in Wembley.

My mother was doing her best to follow Sylvie's lecture on educational funding, the latest cause consuming north London's attention, but I could see she was at sea. Still, my mother nodded politely back, occasionally throwing in a 'yes, yes'. She looked so weary, the loose tendrils of hair that had escaped from her bun giving her a slightly untidy appearance. I suppose all this was only making Becky and Sylvie feel more sorry for us than ever. It occurred to me that this was the first time that my mother had come into contact with my Camden world. What did she think of Sylvie's rustic-styled house? Did she think Sylvie was nice? Would she ever consider being her friend? And then a more sombre thought popped into my head: I might have lived with my mother all my life, but I didn't know her at all.

It was a shocking realisation that haunted me all the way home on the bus. I had to bite my lips several times to stop myself from crying.

'Sylvie is nice,' I heard my mother say, leaning towards me.

'Yeah, I know,' I replied curtly, turning away before my mother noticed my tears. The last thing I wanted was for her to know how upset I was feeling about our relationship. When was the last time we'd had a proper conversation? Never was the truth. My father had always been our go-between. My mother was always just the woman in the background who looked after our house, cooked our dinners and was usually talked over. After all, what advice did she have to offer us on life in England?

I looked over at her. She was staring out of the window, lost in silent thought. My heart suddenly went out to her. What would life be like for her now that my father was gone?

'I am leaving my job,' my mother quietly announced one evening over dinner.

I sensed my sister turning towards me. I avoided meeting her eyes.

'Why?' I asked warily, as images of crowded Pakistani streets flashed through my mind.

My mother tried to smile, but it froze halfway up her face.

'Why?' I asked, this time with more urgency, pushing my plate of food aside. It was *saag gosht* [lamb and spinach curry] made by Aunt Mahin.

'I've got new computer job at BBC,' my mother replied, quietly.

'What, *the* BBC – like television BBC?' my sister cried, astonished.

My mother nodded, a shy grin breaking out on her face.

'How did you do that?' I asked sceptically. It wasn't that I didn't believe her; it was just that I hadn't been expecting such news.

My mother looked at me quizzically. 'I apply for job, do interview,' she replied. 'How else does one get job?'

The sarcasm in her voice threw me. When had my mother acquired such a cutting sense of humour? My sister was giggling at our mother's new confidence. And then I found myself giggling too. While I had been running around fretting about my mother and our future, she had been getting on with life. Her husband had died, she had grieved and, with faith behind her, she had regained her strength, ready to take on the world because she knew the rules. And, as I now concluded, it was Islam that had given her the strength. Or so I thought.

'When will you start?' I asked, looking at my mother with newfound admiration.

'In one month,' she said. 'Once you are at university.' I had a place at Manchester University to study politics and modern history.

I allowed myself a weak smile. 'What about Pakistan?' I asked cautiously.

'Pakistan?' my mother replied, looking at me confused. 'What would we do there? We are British!'

My sister giggled at my mother's authoritativeness.

'But you could have gone back, couldn't you?' I pressed.

'No, I am good wife,' she replied. 'I follow your father's wishes. He wanted me to be independent, modern woman, so now I am independent woman.'

I couldn't help being impressed by my mother's clear vision of life, inspired by a curious mix of British, Asian and Muslim values.

Once upon a time, the whole notion of religion would have threatened me. But the past few months had taught me that while I might not believe in a God, as a cultural identity, Islam did have a role to play in my life. It had connected me to a past, connected me to a present and, most of all, connected me to my mother. And the best thing about discovering Islam was that it didn't compromise my Britishness, something my father had always feared would happen. I understood why he had spurned Islam but, as I liked to reason, his views were a product of another time, when religion had meddled in politics. Well, thankfully those times were long gone. If anything, my discovery of Islam felt like the last missing piece in my jigsaw identity. I finally felt whole or some semblance of peace. I became convinced that if my father had been alive, he would have understood.

For the first time ever that year, I decided to observe Islamic ritual and keep Ramadan. Unfortunately, it fell in the summer, which meant long, hot days without food and water. But as Afshan said, 'Typical, innit.'

Still, it was well worth the sacrifice to see the look of pride on my mother's face as I broke my first fast.

When we went to the mosque the next day to celebrate Eid, nothing will ever compare to the exhilaration I felt about being part of the celebrating crowd, even though the gathering looked more like a fashion parade, if not a cattle market. There might have been a strict separation of the sexes, but there were men on the women's side and women drifting into the men's side.

'Check out that guy!' screeched Perveen, as a handsome young man strutted past, coolly throwing his Kashmiri shawl over his left shoulder.

'Look at his Air Jordans!' Shireen cried after her. 'They're the latest.'

The guy suddenly swung his head round and winked at Perveen, revealing a line of gold teeth. Perveen melted on the spot. But she quickly pulled herself together as the *azzan* [call for prayer] rang out over the mosque. As the others slowly filed into the main hall for prayers, I stayed back.

'Come on. Are you just going to stand there?' Perveen said, impatiently.

I was about to nod, but I suddenly thought it would be far simpler to go in than discuss with Perveen my quandaries as a non-believer.

The hall designated for the women was vast, with huge gold chandeliers hanging from the ceiling. Rows of women stood

200

facing towards Mecca, waiting patiently for prayers to start. We found a place near the front of the hall and organised ourselves into a line. It wasn't long before a voice rang out, signalling the start of prayers.

The women quickly settled down and a solemn silence descended upon the room. Then, in perfect unison, everyone cupped their hands together to begin prayers. There was something overpowering about standing in that room, knowing that billions of Muslims all around the world would also be going through the same motions of prayers on this very auspicious day. For that few minutes, surrendering my individuality to be part of a bigger whole was one of the most powerful sensations I had ever experienced. I felt a big weight lift off my shoulders. And then the tears of grief for my father, which had eluded me for so long, finally came.

Part Two

14

Rushdie and Roots

I have been told that, for the next couple of years following my father's death, I walked around with huge dark circles around my eyes. My father's weighty absence permanently resided in my heart. But he was gone. It was time to navigate the world without him manning the tiller. The next years turned out to be some of the most dramatic of my life. And all those ideas of Britishness that my father had so painstakingly instilled into me – they quickly receded into the distance.

I had read plenty of novels about bright young things going off to university and returning home changed people. But that isn't what happened to me. After years of dreaming about going to college, with all the freedom to meet boys and go dancing, when I got there life on campus proved to be rather dreary. Even the presence of Ben and Ben, my old partying Camden friends, who were now also at Manchester, failed to excite me. Not that one would have guessed from the frantic way I threw

myself into student life, signing up to all the clubs and befriend-
ing everyone I met. But I was bored.

I travelled up to Manchester on my own, dressed in trendy
ripped Levi jeans and a long, blue, Parisian-style trench coat (the
fashion in London at the time), lugging a suitcase in one hand
and a saucepan in the other – only to find, when I arrived, that
all my flatmates were dressed in goth clothes and were being
dropped off by their parents, who left them homely gifts like tea
sets and pot plants.

Working my way through Manchester's social scene during
those first few weeks was an eye-opener. At one of my first
departmental drinks parties, after having listened to one of my
peers drone on about his year off in Israel, I provocatively told
him that I was pro-Palestinian. Next day he came to my room to
explain why I might be misguided in my views.

A few days later, another coursemate, ex-public school and
budding Trotskyite, asked me if I was working class. Yes, I said,
because I didn't quite see myself as being middle class, especially given the large numbers of proper middle-England posh
people around. But the comrade wasn't having it. He declared
me to be a self-hating bourgeois and demanded I revise my
position, because going to university made me patently middle
class.

And then there were the feminists from the Women's Society,
slightly piqued at how quickly I had brushed them aside. 'Umm,'
I thought. 'Should I tell them about my lessons in women's solidarity from my fights in Wembley?'

Luckily, I soon came upon Jan and Amelia, who lived in the
next flats along. Both were ex-pupils from Holland Park
Comprehensive in London. It didn't take us long to become
friends and we all soon settled down to college life.

One afternoon, I was sitting with some of my 'goth' flatmates watching TV, when after *Neighbours*, the *Six O'Clock News* came on. A few minutes in, there was a report about the controversy brewing over *The Satanic Verses*. It showed a crowd of middle-aged Asian men standing outside a building up in Bradford, calling for the book to be banned. The editorial line of the report suggested that viewers be outraged by the protesters' demands, describing them as an assault on freedom of speech. But that wasn't what threw me. Rather, it was the sight of protesters, led by mullahs, making demands in the name of Islam. In my experience, one only saw mullahs in mosques, not charging up and down British high streets. At what point had they become so political?

My flatmates, in their sombre, stoned haze, found the whole story hysterical. 'Ha, look at the guy on the left,' one of them guffawed. A protester holding up a placard had a rather large *topi* on his head, which kept slipping down his face. The others giggled, but not me. It was too disconcerting. Even though my flatmates might not associate me with the protesters, I couldn't help feeling responsible for them. I suddenly felt a desire to explain that there was more to this protest than just calling for the ban of a book . . . But if this furore wasn't about some Muslims calling for a book to be banned, then what was it about?

Studying politics at Manchester, I thought I was ideally placed to explore the subject further. But while a lot of time might be spent examining the German proportional representation political model and how it compared to the French presidential system, discussing current issues was not on the course. It was the same in the student union. With no obvious Tory-bashing angle to latch onto, the story just failed to excite the students.

But maybe this state of affairs suited me fine, after all. For when Matthew, a black guy on my course, tried to engage me on the subject, pointing out to me how white liberals, traditional supporters of ethnic minorities, were in the forefront of the attack on Muslims, I quickly walked away. I couldn't bear hearing that nice white liberals, the one group of people in this country who were always on our side, could be against us. That's not how things were meant to be.

I finally did have a conversation about Rushdie. In Wembley, of all places.

I tried to come home from Manchester once a month to assist my mother with managing the house. Not that, I now noticed, she needed help. At some point my mother had reinvented herself. Long gone was the timid housewife. She had been replaced by a rather feisty Mrs Hai, set upon a series of missions to update the Hai household. Her latest project: to give our home a complete *modon* makeover. After all those years of trying to persuade my father that we should knock down the walls to create a larger, Asian-style living space, to get rid of the huge *almarhi* in the living room in favour of a tasteful glass showcase, to replace the poorly glazed door between the garden and conservatory with a swish patio – well, it was all finally happening. Of course, I was overjoyed and promptly offered to help out.

'Help! Why I need help?' my mother said, puzzled. 'You stay there and do university work.'

'But Mum, you don't know what these builders are like,' I cried.

'I am British, I have rights,' my mother replied, trotting out her current favourite saying. My mother was having a bit of a love affair with her British self. Where else would she have been able to own her own home, make her own money, remain independent of the extended family, all without inviting gossip? Certainly not in Pakistan.

'Yeah, but the builders will rip you off. Especially a middle-aged Asian woman like you,' I said.

'Umm,' my mother said. One of those emphatic 'umms' that, translated, said: let them just try.

'Yeah, Mum's gone well scary these days,' Farah later told me.

Despite my mother's protestations, the following Saturday saw me back at home. As I tried skilfully to negotiate a lower price with the builder, a lanky middle-aged Irish man with an empathetic smile, my mother predictably played mute. She stood there meekly in our front garden, a grey shawl draped around her shoulders. Then, at a key point in the negotiation, just as I was about to backtrack on my revised offer, I suddenly heard her whisper to me in Urdu, 'Keep quiet, let man worry about your offer.'

I looked at her, startled. But she was smiling innocently at the builder. I couldn't believe it – was my mother slipping me bargaining tips? It seemed so.

'*Bhole, cum karo* [now tell him to take off another hundred pounds],' she muttered to me as we neared a final price.

'Mum, I can't say that,' I exclaimed, momentarily allowing my guard to drop.

'Just do it,' she muttered in Urdu, again smiling at the builder, who was now confused by the fact that my mother understood my English but not his.

'Sorry, love,' he said, shaking his head at me, but keeping one cautious eye on my mother. 'The work will definitely need four men and at that rate, I will only be able to cover three.'

'Tell him deal is off,' replied my mother to me.

'Umm, I think we'll have to call the deal off,' I said, apologetically. I really was sorry, because the builder did look like someone you could trust.

The builder shrugged. But then he slowly cast his eyes over the house. 'OK,' he finally said, looking back at us. 'You've got a deal.' He extended his hand.

'Good,' my mother said in English, shaking his hand. 'You start Monday.'

Later, some of the aunts popped round to say hello as well as take a quick peek at our plans for a through-lounge, though, as Farah told me, they would have come round anyway. Our home had become the new social gathering point.

While I battled on with sorting through a backlog of bills, the aunts sprawled around our living room, discussed whether Shazia's newly arrived Pakistani husband really was the father of her baby girl. Mrs Khan said she had done the maths and couldn't see how he could be. '*July, mai aya tha* [he only came in July],' she contended.

'But they could have done it . . .' Aunt Syeda cut in.

I heard giggles, followed by a few 'shooshs', and glances in my direction. Voices were hastily lowered and the subject changed.

'Did you hear? Someone has written a book slandering the Prophet,' one of the aunts said.

'What, our Prophet Mohammed?'

'Yes!'

'Shame on these English.'

'No sister, it's one of us. A *Musalman*.'

'A *Musalman*! Is he mad?'

'What do his parents say?' Aunt Syeda said, shaking her head in fury. 'And tell me, what has he gained from insulting the Prophet?'

The aunts paused for a rare moment of reflection. They looked genuinely upset, as if someone had just plundered the core of who they were.

'My husband says some Muslims are telling shops to not sell book,' said Aunt Shah. 'But no one will listen.'

'Why?' said the aunts, looking at each other, baffled.

As I listened to their exchange, I couldn't help noticing that though the aunts spoke a lot about how hurt they felt, at no point did they ever consider notions such as freedom of speech.

But then the term 'freedom of speech' implied having grand opinions – and the aunties had no opinions to speak of. I mean, they had an opinion on what Shazia's husband should do with his wayward wife or what Mrs Sidiqui should say to her mouthy British-born daughter-in-law who wanted to move out of the extended family home. But an opinion on public matters – that was a different thing all together. They knew their place in life.

I suddenly felt this rush of anger towards Rushdie. Up to now, safely cocooned up in Manchester, I had successfully avoided thinking about the issue too much. But seeing the aunts looking so downcast was forcing me to engage. As a British Muslim, didn't Rushdie know how fragile the elders in the community were? The pressures they were under, the fears that made them cling so fiercely to religion? His community didn't consist of Hampstead liberals, politically and culturally sophisticated, able to toy with sacred cows. Couldn't he have been more judicious with his art?

In fact, as I thought about the controversy further, what was the big deal about this much-lauded concept of freedom of speech that the liberals kept banging on about? If anything, it seemed like a rather irresponsible principle to me, if all it did was upset people. I had spent my whole life avoiding telling people uncomfortable truths, especially if they were English. Why alienate people with whom one had to live side by side? But as these angry thoughts ran through my mind, a panicked feeling overcame me. Was I really siding with the protesters against the liberals? Could it be that I wasn't as politically sophisticated as I thought?

And then came the infamous book-burning episode outside Bolton Town Hall. Soon afterwards the Ayatollah of Iran declared the dreaded *fatwa*.

The announcement was shocking. Like most of Britain, I had never heard of a *fatwa* before. Could you really be sentenced to death for insulting the prophet Mohammed? Who in the modern world looked to a seventh-century text for answers? It sounded like pure madness. Now it was Rushdie that I felt sorry for, but at least I could take consolation in the fact that while the elders might support such crude pronouncements because they knew no better, no one of my generation would ever sympathise with such ideas.

Or so I thought.

It was the Christmas holidays and Perveen, Shireen and I were over at Afshan's house, huddled in her bedroom, trying to console her. She had just been unceremoniously dumped by her boyfriend, Jaz. Jaz was a guy she had met at university; apparently they had been in love. That is, until Jaz announced that his parents wanted him to marry some family friend.

Poor Afshan. She was already feeling pretty disappointed by her experience at college. Part of her had been so looking forward to meeting new people, especially the kind of English people that I spoke about knowing in Camden. But now she was struggling to meet anyone she had an affinity with.

'It's not that the *gora* [white] lot aren't nice,' she once told me. 'It's just that they're really different.'

'What do you mean?' After all these years of telling Afshan about white, middle-class people, I was intrigued to hear what she had to say about them.

'Well, I don't think they're like your friends,' she had said. 'They all wrinkle their noses when you mention Indian food.

212

And as for the trendy crowd? Well, they're all into drugs and pub crawls.'

But Afshan had obviously found a crowd of Asian friends to hang out with at college. And it was through them that she had been introduced to Jaz.

'I tell you, I should have known when he kept disappearing off to visit relatives over the weekend,' Afshan now said. 'Can you believe I thought we had a future?'

Afshan had thought that Jaz might offer her an escape from the arranged marriage her mother was setting up for her. But then I suppose she was desperate, having lost her virginity to him – not that she ever said that out loud. I mean, here we all were discussing Jaz and what a creep he was, but not once did Afshan say, 'By the way, I slept with him.' Instead, every now and then she would interrupt the conversation and say, 'What do you lot think about sex before marriage?'

'Why's she making such a big deal about it?' Perveen said when Afshan left the room to get us some tea. 'Why doesn't she just fake it on the night? We'll all have to do that.'

It was in the midst of our consoling Afshan that Shireen brought up the Rushdie issue, as an attempt to change the subject. 'Oi, have you lot heard about what's going on in Bradford?'

'Yes,' we all chorused. Even Afshan, lost in her own pain, sat up. I could feel my heart beginning to race in anticipation of what I was likely to hear. I had never really engaged in a political discussion with the Bhajis before. Usually I spoke politics at them and they politely listened, half bored. But it seemed the Rushdie issue might be different. Maybe by bouncing ideas back and forth with the Bhajis – like Becky and her friends did whenever issues of anti-semitism or questions regarding the Jews' place in Britain came up – I might be able to finally clarify what I thought.

Except it didn't work out like that. The more they talked about the Rushdie affair, especially the media's increasingly damning response to the Muslim protesters – the more wound up they became and then, much to my alarm, opinions began to shift. Britain's response to the Muslim protest was so full of the usual negative stereotypes – of ignorant, backward immigrants – that it had instantly thrust the Bhajis back to the old days. Something about the *fatwa* as a response – its boldness, its indigenousness – spoke to them.

But while I had been quite accepting of the aunts' anti-Rushdie stance, I couldn't stomach the British-born Bhajis defending religious edicts, especially those made in the name of a 'foreign' religion. It was as if they had run out of words to explain how they felt. In that vacuum they were forced to fall back on the *fatwa* to justify what they thought. But I didn't do much better. With little thought-out argument at my disposal, I was churning out liberal clichés, which wound them up more.

The discussion was getting so heated, with everyone laying into me, that I suddenly thought of my father. How many times had I seen him sitting on his own while his friends railed at him about some issue or another? Well, I wasn't going to be like him. So to calm everyone down, I was just about to admit to the Bhajis that part of me agreed with them when Afshan – who had been silent up until then – let out a huge sigh. I realised that her huge, frustrated sigh was aimed directly at me.

'I'll tell you why the book has to be banned,' she said, with a steely contempt in her voice.

'Why?' I said, my voice slightly trembling.

'Because it's a sin to insult our Prophet.'

I felt tears well up inside me. Had Afshan just said 'sin'? How had that word cropped up in a discussion about politics? And why was college-educated Afshan, who should have known better, coming down on the side of the protesters?

'You know they portray the Prophet to be some kind of pimp!' said Perveen, bolstered by Afshan's support.

'But you haven't read it!' I replied, still reeling from what Afshan had just said.

'You don't have to,' Afshan cut in again, slamming her hands on the bedside table. 'It's a sin. Full stop.'

Even though I was still at university, I was spending more time in London. In fact, I might be living in Manchester, home to the Hacienda, and iconic bands like the Stone Roses, where my roommate's brother was managing the Happy Mondays and one of my neighbours was the legendary Peter Hook from New Order, but all this went straight over my head. Instead, most weekends I could be found back in London, standing next to the biggest speakers at the Dub Club in Tufnell Park, bobbing away to roots reggae.

Something truly amazing was happening in London.

You could just sense it as you walked down Portobello Road or round Wembley, areas with a big black or Asian population. The confident gait of the young people and the assured eye contact we would make with each other as we crossed paths was a reminder that we — the children of immigrants —were finally coming of age. And that 'being different' was something we were going to revel in.

After all those years of searching for like-minded people, who understood the complexities of living between worlds, I was finally finding them.

For the first time in ages, I noticed that heavy feeling in my heart starting to lift. My confidence grew and with it my love life. I began seeing Jay, my old friend from the north London party scene. Why I had shied away from men before, I still don't know. The most alluring thing about my new circle of friends was that, after years of struggling to see the world through a white prism, it was liberating to find soulmates who shared my race-tinted view of the world. It wasn't that all we did was bang on about race, it was just that we could talk about these issues without feeling inhibited because we were making someone – i.e. someone white – feel uneasy.

The funny thing about our discussions was that they were also helping us realise just how British we actually were. The experiences of our youth said nothing about Pakistan or Jamaica, but everything about life in Britain. They revealed to us that we were forging our own history in this country. That somehow, we belonged here. Britain was our only home. If I ever doubted that, all I needed to do was think back on the time my mother took us to Pakistan in my second year of university. Bursting with ethnic pride, I couldn't wait to explore my roots and find peace in my spiritual home. Instead, for the first time ever, I heard myself yell that quintessential English sentiment: 'I need space!'

Matters didn't improve when I heard that dozens of marriage proposals had flooded in as soon as our plane touched ground. 'Mum, did you plan this? I'll never forgive you!' I cried in total panic, as visions of forced marriages to men with Basil Fawlty moustaches went through my head. I was already feeling estranged from my mother as it was. Since our arrival in Pakistan, she had suddenly developed a different personality. I had never realised how funny she could be. In fact, she had our relatives eating out of her hands. I should have been proud, but instead I felt threatened by this alternate-universe mother. I suppose the marriage offers only exacerbated my feelings of distance from her. It was only when my very posh Pakistani

216

cousin said, 'Yaar, is that all the proposals you got?' that I finally calmed down. Then I began to wonder what was so wrong with me to attract such little marriage interest.

'So, I hear life is very hard for you Pakis,' one of my uncles said to me one evening. As a guest from England, I was allowed to sit with the men during dinner, unlike my female relatives, who were eating in the next room. 'A friend of mine told me that is the name given to all Asians in England. Even those from India.'

Everyone around the table laughed. Oh, how silly the English were, thinking that all Asians were the same.

'Well it's not true,' I replied, trying to control my irritation. Weren't *they* – citizens of a Third World nation – supposed to envy *us*? Obviously, not. We were the fools, wasting away our lives in a damp and hostile country.

Of course, when I told my friends back home about my trip to Pakistan, they nodded empathetically. Soon they, too, were recounting the unexpected mix of comedy and disappointment that came with visiting your parents' home country. It was another one of those times when we realised how British we really were. But then, despite Maggie Thatcher still being at no. 10, Britain was becoming more receptive to the likes of us. In fact words like 'mixing', 'fusion' and 'crossover' were suddenly very much in vogue. Similarly, with the advent of raves and ubiquity of ecstasy, class barriers were dissolving, too. It was an exciting time to be young, British and black or Asian, or whatever one was, as long as it wasn't straightforward English or posh. So much so that I even changed my look. I no longer worried about dropping my aitches and now swished around with waist-length braids, the ends sealed with pale wooden beads. As I walked, the beads would click together in rhythmic beat, giving my steps a more strident air.

This new pride in my mixed self was doing wonders for my self-esteem, if not my image. When I looked in the mirror, I sometimes caught myself wondering what my father would have thought of this new 'multicultural' me. But then I would quickly brush the uncomfortable thoughts away. I might miss my father, but what was the point of dwelling on such dark matters? It was time to move on.

I had just graduated from Manchester and was finally moving back home. My mother had been eagerly awaiting my return and, having spotted me through the net curtains, dragging my suitcase up the pathway, she had run down to the door to greet me. But now, seeing the new 'me' close up, I could tell that she was regretting my return.

'What have you done?' my mother cried, her eyes widening in horror when she saw my braids.

'But what have *you* done?' I cried back, noting her short, bobbed hair. Her long hair, usually tied in a traditional bun, had all been cut off. I wasn't sure the style suited my mother – it made her look scarier than ever.

'This is *modon* Karachi look,' my mother replied sternly, patting her hair. 'But that . . .' She glanced around to check that none of the aunties were approaching. 'You look like . . .'

My mother couldn't finish her sentence, as her lips were quivering. What she wanted to say was, 'You look black.' But somewhere she knew that if she said something along those lines, I would explode with anger. Instead she cried, 'What would Mr Hai say?'

'Oh no!' I cried, as I followed my mother into the living room. 'What have you done?'

Our new through-lounge had been done up in true Wembley style; hideous shades of lilac and pistachio green. Yes, the

218

almarhi had gone. But the new showcase, made out of cheap brown Formica, in which my mother had placed a tasteful array of plastic flowers and twee chintz figurines, made the room look like a bad soap-opera set. And as for the lighting? Circular UV tubes from BHS. My mother had thought them to be more 'fancy'.

Oh God, I thought, sitting down in alarm. As I sank back into the sofa, a loud crinkly noise made me jump up. It was the plastic protective wrapping on the sofa backs. My mother hadn't removed it – another 'fancy' touch.

'Welcome home,' my sister said.

15

Asian invasion. No case for consternation

'You were complete, one hundred per cent utter rubbish!' cried
Iqbal, his thick Indian-Cockney accent accentuating the word
ruuubish. In the rear view mirror, I saw Iqbal wobble his head in
disappointment, the way only Indians can. The furry dice
attached to the mirror shook rhythmically in time with their
owner.

'You should have put that MP guest in his place, but instead
what did you do?' Iqbal let out a frustrated snort and slapped his
left hand hard on the wheel. 'You let him get away with it.'

Every TV presenter/reporter needs an Iqbal. Someone who
will rudely bring you down to earth. Not that Iqbal ever
watched any of my programmes. No. As he often told me, he
was too busy earning a *'bloodee* living' driving his cab. And
anyway, even if he had time, he still wouldn't have been caught
dead watching the rubbish I made. Iqbal preferred to watch the
BBC, but apparently his wife didn't agree. She was addicted to
TV Asia.

'Take it from me,' continued Iqbal, adjusting his mirror so I was in full view again, 'too many immigrants in this country already. And your MP guest talking all this multi-culti rubbish. Chapatti days for Christmas, Divali lights on Oxford Street, pahh! Well, if that is what he wants, why doesn't he go back to *bloodee* India.'

'Iqbal!' I cried, annoyed at his politically incorrect views. No one spoke like that any more. And Iqbal, being Asian, should have known better.

'Ohh, what do you know with your fancy education?' said Iqbal, speeding over a bump with only one hand on the steering wheel. With the other hand he swept back his long, wispy layered locks, a hairstyle modelled on his heroes Sylvester Stallone and Bollywood actor Sanjay Dutt.

According to Iqbal, the only education that counted was the one acquired at the university of life. NF-trotting skinheads, the Southall riots, Paki-bashing – you name it, Iqbal had seen it all. Not like us second-generation kids, who had nice anti-racist policies to see us through our early life.

'You watch how our *apne log* take advantage of all this multi-cultism,' Iqbal rambled on to me.

I sighed, knowing full well that if I had been an English person sitting in his cab, Iqbal would have been ranting the complete opposite. He was happiest when contrary. Iqbal quickly swerved out of the way of an oncoming BMW, braking to a halt on the kerb. The car lurched forward before coming to rest.

'Bloody women drivers,' Iqbal cried, catching sight of the driver, a rather large middle-aged Asian housewife dressed in a bright pink *salwar kameez*.

'Do you know who I have in this car?' he screamed out of the window.

I sank further into my seat, wincing with embarrassment. I

could already feel Iqbal inflating with pride, ready to deliver his crushing parting shot.

'I am carrying personnel from Tee Vee Asia!'

Riding a wave of multicultural hype and excitement, TV Asia had recently exploded on to the British media scene. 'Home away from home,' was the satellite channel's nostalgia-inducing slogan. Broadcasting mainly Indian films, Pakistani dramas and Bollywood gossip shows, it was rapidly building up a loyal audience in the community. But we, its British-born Asian employees, were far from impressed. Not only did we find the hysterical fascination with Bollywood totally baffling, but also we found the fawning culture of the workplace totally distasteful.

'Fat bitch, she can make her own cup of tea,' said Taz, short for Tazneen, the glamorous but very frustrated receptionist, who spent most of her time hovering round the studio hoping to get discovered. Taz was referring to Pooja, a demanding ex-Bollywood heroine who – in an attempt to revive her fledgling acting career – was presenting TV Asia's keep fit programme. This was the third cup of tea she had asked for in the space of ten minutes.

'Anyone would think that we're in India, from the way she's behaving,' chided Vijay. Vijay, aged nineteen, was TV Asia's resident and very frustrated VT (videotape) editor. Not surprising, given that he spent most of his working day locked up in a windowless room trying to salvage material filmed by camera crews whose previous professional experience had only extended to Indian wedding videos.

'You know what she needs to get into her thick head?' Taz raged, glaring at Pooja. 'She needs to realise that this is bloody England!'

222

That was the funny thing about working at TV Asia. It didn't take long for our British sensibilities to break through. Funny, because we didn't realise that they were so ingrained.

'It would never be like this at the BBC!' I said, stamping my feet.

Atiya, TV Asia's resident press officer, rolled her eyes at Taz. They were used to my tempers. I had anger issues, Atiya liked to say. But then, Pakistan-born Atiya thought all British-born Asians had anger issues, Taz and Iqbal included. Part of me quite liked to hear it: having issues, especially anger issues, felt quite glamorous.

'Well, who wouldn't be angry, working in this dump?' I cried.

For example, to prevent staff from running up huge personal phone bills, the management had blocked all calls outside London. Maybe this was effective at stopping the channel's employees from phoning relatives back home but, being TV Asia's chief news reporter, it also stopped me from doing my job. And if that wasn't enough to drive you mad, then there was the nepotism. It seemed everyone had landed their jobs through one family contact or another – that is, everyone except me. I was the sucker who sent in a letter, accompanied by a showreel from my last job as a presenter on an ITV music programme.

After leaving university, I threw myself into finding work. I desperately needed proper money and the pure mindlessness of the bar and waitressing jobs I was living off drove me mad. So, every morning, as soon as I woke up, I would diligently fire off twenty CVs and make at least twenty cold calls to various TV production companies, whose names I copied down from the Yellow Pages. I persisted, no matter how much the secretaries tried to fob me off. I was desperate to be a journalist, and a television journalist at that. I wanted to change the world and television seemed the best way to speak to the most people.

It was through one of my cold calls that I had heard about the presenter's job for an ITV music programme. Even though I was looking for behind-the-scenes work, the production company had said that the only journalist/researcher they were looking to hire was one who had presenting experience, too.

'Yeah, I've got that,' I had said casually, thinking that as I had got this far and was actually speaking to the managing director himself, I might as well push my luck a bit further.

'Oh good. Can you come up to Manchester for a screen test?'

'No problem,' I said, my heart pounding.

One screen test and an interview later, I got the job. It wasn't difficult. I was so late for the interview – four hours to be exact, following a train derailment in the Midlands – that I had no time to be nervous, let alone to worry about the lie I had told. I obviously performed well enough in the screen test, because the programme director offered me the job on the spot. Over the next year, I presented a music programme called *Bhangra Beat*, which bizarrely developed a late-night cult following. Next I got a job presenting another ITV music magazine programme called *Rhythm & Raag*. I think I was hired to be a foil to the geeky male presenter. But I don't think I did such a good job, because the producers continually berated me for asking the guests – usually middle-aged bhangra pop stars dressed in garish sequinned shirts – earnest political questions.

'Ask them what they had for breakfast, not about Bosnia!' the producers would scream at me. 'And can't you smile more at the camera?'

'And some make-up won't go amiss next time,' added the junior member of the crew, a production secretary.

No wonder I was so pleased when I finally landed a 'real' journalist's job at TV Asia.

But despite the channel's limitations and all my frustrated

bitching, deep down I did have a soft spot for it. There had never been a station like TV Asia, solely dedicated to Britain's Asian community. Hindu, Muslim or Sikh – if you were Asian, the channel catered for you. And, fired with a young reporter's zeal, I was on a mission. I was bursting with ideas, desperate to communicate not only stories about the injustices and oppressions that blighted the world, but also the untold stories of the everyday life of Britain's ethnic minorities, which was, by now, what we were called.

Domestic violence, racism, Asian alcoholism, immigration, interviewing Prime Minister John Major: no story was too big for me. But while Pooja Shrivani got fan mail by the bucketload, I was lucky to receive one. Only my mother seemed interested in what I had to say. Her popularity in the *mahalla* had soared since I started working alongside Bollywood's great and good.

Filing reports for the channel from up and down the country (when I could get my travel expenses paid), I had a great chance to witness first hand the new confidence of Britain's Asian community.

'Oh yes, curry has been voted Birmingham's number-one dish,' said one very beaming Asian food critic to me. 'Next stop, Britain!'

'Oh yes, Britain is searching for next Asian supermodel,' said an Asian cultural pundit before mumbling: 'But she has to be over six feet.'

'Oh yes, drug abuse is rampant amongst our young,' said a self-appointed community spokesperson. 'We are having problems just like English.'

I was never short of stories about how well we Asians were integrating into Britain. Some of us were even finding artistic inspiration in our unique mixed lives.

'What are you doing here?' I said, when I spotted Amir

Quereshi casually reclining in TV Asia's hospitality lounge – that is to say, a three-piece suite outside the men's toilet. I hadn't seen Amir, Shazia's feckless and delinquent brother, for years.

'Yasmin,' he said, jumping up. He kissed me on my left cheek. If we had been in Wembley he wouldn't have dared, but here in 'media land' it was a different matter.

'Come to see someone called Vijay. He wants to use some of my footage for a promo he is making.'

Even though Amir sounded nonchalant, one only had to look at his cream chinos and crisp white shirt, neatly tucked into his trousers, to know how much that meeting meant to him.

'It's a performance film on urban crime,' Amir later explained in Vijay's studio, as images of rundown council estates superimposed on images of NF insignia and harassed-looking Asian housewives shopping in Southall burst onto the screen.

'Asian invasion. No case for consternation,' we heard Amir's voice rap in the background.

'He fink he's black,' sneered Taz.

Usually I would have laughed, but this time I didn't. In a strange way I felt proud of Amir, and I could see Vijay was impressed too. For up to now the only time British Asians made it onto the telly was in BBC 2 documentaries about the British Empire or Enoch Powell's 'rivers of blood' speech. Amir's film spoke about a different British Asian experience: an everyday one, the one we lived, but never saw on television.

'Yep, I'd like to use some of this material,' Vijay said as the film came to an end.

Amir nodded coolly, but I could see he was chuffed.

And yet, all this talk of ethnic pride and multiculturalism did seem to greatly bemuse many of the older Asian journalists on the press circuit. They would always chuckle to themselves while taking notes at the press conferences about some Asian initiative or another being sponsored by the government to redress inequality. After years of handling stories about racism or cultural strife, these feelgood stories probably felt rather hollow. Many of the older journalists had known my father from his days as guest commentator on the BBC Urdu Service.

'Ahh, so you are Mr Hai's daughter,' they would say, coming up to me. 'Hoping to become a great crusading journalist like him, ehh?'

I would nod shyly, humbled by their kind words about my father. For this was how I best liked to remember him – as a distinguished journalist and renowned activist. Suddenly my vocation sounded even more romantic and noble.

'So how is Mr Aslam?' these journalists would always ask me.

'Oh, fine,' I would reply, though nothing could have been further from the truth. Uncle Aslam wasn't doing well. He might answer the door impeccably dressed in a suit jacket and tie but his tired demeanour revealed a weariness with life. With Aunt Hilda and my father gone, nothing seemed to interest him any more. To liven up my monthly visit, I would badger him about the past, especially about my father's political background, hoping to extract insights into my father's life. But Uncle Aslam seemed more interested in gazing idly into thin air or listening to one of his three radios. Identical Grundigs, perched next to each other on the windowsill, overlooking Highgate Cemetery where Karl Marx was buried. The one on the right was tuned to BBC World Service, the one on the left to BBC Radio 4, and the middle radio was tuned to BBC Urdu Service. On the hour, he would switch one of the radios on to get a news update.

'I miss your father more than you ever will,' he would periodically say, his eyes glazed over with rheum. 'He was my best friend, you know. He could have been a great man, but too many foolish principles.'

I nodded sagely, feeling strangely flattered that Uncle Aslam considered me mature enough to have such a frank conversation.

'Oh, how we argued . . .'

The whole time I sat in Uncle Aslam's study, a huge lump would reside in my throat. A lump that would expand even more on the rare occasions my uncle did finally meander into nostalgic stories regarding the early immigrant years my father and he had lived in Britain. How different it was for young Asians like me.

'So, how is your mother?' my uncle would ask at some point.

And I never knew what to say. I no longer lived at home, not that anyone in the area knew. My mother had forbidden me to tell them.

'Only bad girls live away from home,' my mother would say. 'Whenever *mahalla* ask where you are, I say you come home late from TV Asia.'

'But Mum, everyone knows I live in Ladbroke Grove,' I cried, furious that my mother felt the need to turn my life into a lie. 'Afshan's visited me. So has Perveen . . .'

'Umm,' my mother said, disapprovingly, which translated meant, 'You really are a silly girl.'

'Mum, I don't care what anyone thinks,' I would cry. But deep down I knew that wasn't true. By living away from home, living alone, I knew I was breaking one of the cardinal rules of being Asian. And that niggled me no end. What could I do? Hadn't my father brought me up to lead an independent life? He had deliberately made sure that all those Asian rules of family duty and obligation would never impinge on my life. I would often hear him say to my mother, usually after an episode of *In Sickness and in Health*, starring Alf Garnett: 'Don't expect your children to look after you when you get old. This is England.'

The thought of living out old age on her own – something totally unheard of in Asian culture – must have terrified my mother, but she would always nod sanguinely. Unlike me, who would hastily leave the room, vowing that I would never leave my mother to such a sorry fate.

But by moving out of home, hadn't I effectively abandoned my mother, a nagging voice inside my head would often ask me. No, I would quickly reason, I wasn't abandoning my mother. My brother and sister were still living with her. 'And what happens when they move out, too?' the voice would ask. 'Well, that won't be for ages,' I would argue back. 'And anyway, by the time they move out, I will have established myself in a career, earned loads of money, bought a house and my mother could come and live with me.' In fact, thinking about it, that is why I needed to live away from home at the moment. I needed to focus on my work. But no matter what I said to myself, the guilt remained.

While for most of my English friends their twenties might be about expanding one's horizons, seeing the world, having experiences, for we Asians it was different. When we reached our twenties, family responsibility suddenly became this pressing burden. It was expected that now we had come of age, it was time we took charge, which is why I found being at home so uncomfortable. I didn't want to be reminded of my responsibilities or, more accurately, how I was avoiding them.

16

A Proper Muslim

One afternoon when I was visiting my mother, a group of Asian men came knocking on her door.

'Is your father there?' mumbled the man closest to me. I say mumbled because, like the rest of his colleagues, he instantly lowered his head as soon as I answered the door. Right there and then, I wanted to slam the door in their faces. This wasn't just any group of Asian men. This was a group of Muslim men. It wasn't the first time that Muslim groups had come knocking on our door, but never before had they made such a fuss of being in the presence of a female.

'Hello, this is England,' I wanted to yell out. I wouldn't have been so angry if I genuinely believed that they were just clumsily trying to be respectful. But their actions had been too self-conscious, too deliberate, designed to show off their pious credentials – and I, for one, wasn't impressed. This wasn't the Islam I knew – and I was annoyed at them for suggesting that is what it was supposed to be.

'No, he's dead,' I replied to their question regarding my

father, employing my stroppiest Wembley voice. But the man in front of me, still staring at the ground, just muttered a prayer, which then made me feel somewhat churlish.

'Is there any man we can speak to?' a faceless voice from the back asked. 'We were told Muslims lived here.'

'What's this about?' I said, a dozen separate thoughts racing through my mind. Part of me was feeling nervous that I had revealed too much about our family affairs; that there was no elder male living in the house. Part of me was annoyed, that we – the Hai family – had been defined as being Muslims. And then part of me felt flattered that we had been described as just that. Why could my response never be simple?

'Umm, no worry. Local campaign,' the man in front of me said, turning away. And with that the men moved on. They might have been a ragtag group, but I could tell – even then – that local men, campaigning under the banner of Islam, was the beginning of something new.

If I thought the Rushdie affair was a blip, I was wrong. It hadn't escaped my attention how, in recent years, many of the elders in the *mahalla* had started to become more absorbed by religious matters; another reason why I found returning home so trying. No longer did the aunts happily parade around Wembley dressed in colourful *salwar kameezes*, with their hair fashionably coloured. Now many were starting to favour more sombre attire in shades of white or beige, with a scarf draped around their heads. To be fair, they were not the only Asians becoming more religious. Back at TV Asia I covered events like the opening of Britain's first Sikh state school or the opening of an alcohol-recovery home only for Hindus.

'See, I told you,' Iqbal would say scornfully as he drove me back from similar stories. 'This is what multi-culti achieves. Everyone taking the piss . . .'

But even though I agreed with Iqbal, Afshan and I couldn't help being intrigued by the phenomenon. How was it that despite the more tolerant and meritocratic nineties' Britain we were living in, so many Asians were starting to retreat into their religious cultures? We would spend hours discussing the matter, though careful not to upset each other with our views, given our last exchange on Rushdie.

A jadedness had set into Afshan, which always made me feel tense in her company. I tried not to take it personally, as I knew she was going through a difficult time. University had come to an end and her mother, so desperate to preserve the family good name, was again furiously trying to arrange her marriage. Afshan was feeling trapped, unable to see a way out. I also think she had reached that point in her 'independent' life where she wondered: 'Is that it?' Young Asians like her were meant to hanker after Western freedoms, but now that she had taken advantage of them and had lived life to the full, it all felt like a bit of an anticlimax. I knew this because every time I spoke about my life, she might have laughed in all the right places and nodded her head when expected to, but I could see my stories no longer interested her. So desperate was I to hold on to our friendship, I preferred to ignore what I sensed, redoubling my efforts to listen to her, especially when she ruminated over the *mahalla*'s increasing religiosity.

'It's 'cos they're getting old,' Afshan once said to Perveen and me.

'Yeah, you're right,' said Perveen, as she carefully fed her baby son, trying not to get any stains on her designer clothes. Perveen might have become a mother of three, but she wasn't about to compromise on her dress style. 'It's 'cos they're just panicking about the day of judgement, aren't they?'

Afshan nodded.

232

But how did that explain Uncle Waseem? He was still young and had always been our trendy uncle who never cared for religious ways. But only the other day, much to my alarm, I had seen him talking to the orthodox–religious Shahs who, worryingly, had become more prominent in the community since the opening of a new Muslim centre in the area. When Uncle Waseem had spotted me, he had quickly averted his eyes, leaving me feeling, of all things, wanton. And what about Aunt Bilquis? She had only become more religious when her husband died. And what about Afshan's own mother, Mrs Khan? After Afshan broke off a near engagement, Mrs Khan had been so mortified that she hadn't shown her face in the area for days. When she finally came out of the house, she was no longer wearing one of her fancy *salwar kameezes*. Instead she emerged dressed in a long brown woollen coat and a scarf on her head.

'She looks like a right refugee,' Shazia had said. Over the months, Shazia had slowly drifted back into our crowd. It seemed her relationship with the aunts had soured.

'Shoosh,' her mother, Aunt Quereshi, had cut in. 'Is that any way to talk about *shareef* [pious] lady?'

Still, this brilliant diversionary tactic on the part of Mrs Khan meant that no one bothered after that to ask her what had happened to Afshan, too awed were they by the fact that *modon* Mrs Khan had discovered Allah and gone humble.

I'm not saying that personal calamities were responsible in every case, but one couldn't help noticing a pattern emerging. It was as if instead of confronting the problems or the moral fallout, of living in the West, some in the *mahalla* preferred to save face and lose themselves into religion. As if that might redeem them. And then something strange began to happen to Afshan, too.

233

To please my mother I had agreed to go to Aunt Sidiqui's house for a Koran blessing. This is how the *mahalla* aunts now preferred to spend their spare time.

'You know, you could wear that suit I bought you,' my mother said as we got ready. 'It will make you look so pretty.'

'No!' I said firmly, shuddering as I recalled the gold *salwar kameez* with puffball sleeves my mother had brought me from her last trip to Pakistan.

'Do you know how many people walk around with no clothes on in Pakistan?' my mother sighed.

'But I didn't ask you to buy it!' I snapped. I didn't mean to be rude, but my mother's comments had a way of winding me up – reminding me of all the do's and don'ts which still dictated *mahalla* life.

On this occasion Aunt Sidiqui hadn't organised the Koran gathering to pray for Allah but, rather, for the aunties to come and admire her new knocked-through living room, in preparation for her son's arranged marriage. The special feature was a Mogul-styled arch, in the shape of the Taj Mahal, made of pine-coloured plywood, which now linked the two old rooms.

'Wah,' said the aunts, as they came in, marvelling at the arch. How had Aunt Sidiqui pulled off such a design coup?

Perveen, Shazia, Afshan and I were sitting in the corner of the old back room beside the fish-tank, which, as Shazia astutely pointed out, contained no fish. Our heads were buried deep in our copies of the Koran (an English copy for me) when I suddenly heard Shazia say: 'I know that bitch is talking about me.'

'Who?' asked Afshan peering up from under her scarf.

'Aunt bloody Sidiqui. I swear I heard her mention Aloo Gobi Ali's name,' Shazia whispered angrily.

The aunts had long memories of past scandals.

'And I heard them mention the word *budhi* [old spinster] and *shaadi* [marriage],' said Perveen, talking over me to Afshan. 'They must be talking about you.'

Afshan put her copy of the Koran down and one could see from the way her body tensed up that she was furious.

'Well, they could have been talking about me,' I said helpfully, knowing full well they weren't. I just wasn't interesting enough to incite gossip in the *mahalla*.

'No, they're talking about me, all right,' spat out Afshan, staring at the aunts, daring one of them to look up. But not one of them would. Never in their years had a young woman – and an unmarried one at that – ever deigned to speak back to them. 'Yeah, well, they might think they're being proper Muslims, but they're not,' said Afshan, raising her voice so that they could hear. 'But Allah will have the last word.'

The Bhajis giggled at her audacity. I would have too, if I wasn't reeling from shock. Had Afshan just mentioned Allah? Suddenly memories of the Rushdie argument came flooding back.

'And you know what?' Afshan said, looking over at Mrs Sidiqui's son's dowry collection on display at the back of the room: packs of shirts and underwear from M&S, Old Spice aftershave bottles, fake diamanté jewellery sets and so on. 'Someone needs to tell them that dowries, as well as arranged marriages, are a Hindu tradition.'

Mrs Khan narrowed her eyes at Afshan, warning her to stop.

'Really?' whispered Shazia, turning to Afshan. 'What? You're not allowed to marry someone you don't want to be with?'

'No, not in Islam,' Afshan said defiantly, still staring at the aunts.

'I didn't know that,' said Shazia, impressed.

'Yeah, well, how would you?' snapped Afshan, turning to

her. 'Look how we were taught the Koran. By Mrs Shah in her living room. Did we ever understand what we were reading? I mean, did *she* understand what she was reading? No, she was ignorant just like *them*.'

At the words ignorant and them, Afshan once again raised her voice. Perveen and Shazia tried not to giggle but couldn't help it.

'Where did you learn all this?' said Shazia.

'Been reading up, haven't I,' Afshan said, matter-of-factly. 'You can get these leaflets from my old uni that explain what proper Islam is.'

Proper Islam! The words boomeranged around in my head.

'It will tell you that Islam demands women be treated with respect.'

'What, like feminism?' said Perveen.

'Yes, but the Koran was talking about it years ago,' Afshan replied, sitting up proudly. 'Centuries before the West cottoned on.'

It was the first time in ages that I had seen her look so alive. After that, I began to notice that every time Afshan and I got together, it was guaranteed that at some point our conversation would veer towards what Islam had to say on the matter under discussion. For example, if we were talking about how miserly Mr Sidiqui had become since his kebab shop took off, Afshan would interject: 'Well it says in the Koran that profit . . .' And say we were talking about the growing number of homeless people in Britain. On cue, Afshan would say something like: 'Well in the Koran, it is a duty of all Muslims to give a fifth of their income to charity . . .'

And though I would patiently nod as Afshan imparted her knowledge on Islam, inside I was bubbling with rage. Citing the Koran just felt downright mad. That was for our parents, not

British-born us. But the refrain of Afshan's that came to annoy me most was: 'That's not Islamic. That's culture.' Afshan would often shout this one out whenever she heard of some irrational act that an aunt in the *mahalla* had carried out in the name of Islam, such as when Aunt Bilquis had tied a string round her granddaughter's wrist to ward off the evil eye.

For some reason, separating out practices – those that were truly Islamic and those inspired by her parents' culture – had suddenly become very important to Afshan. It was obviously made more pleasurable by the fact that the practices and values that Afshan identified as being Islamic were always so noble and rational and those located in Asian cultural mores were always so superstitious and irrational. I didn't believe in what she believed and yet part of me was seduced by what she was saying. I had never realised the Koran was so egalitarian and just in spirit. After years of having to go along with the myths of what England was about – tolerance, fair play and so on – it was refreshing to be presented with a vision of Islam that not only spoke of our heritage, but was also grounded in notions of equality, liberty and justice. But then I pinched myself, remembering that in this day and age, no one sane spoke about religion.

Why couldn't Afshan be more like my friends, Atiya, Irfan or even Amir from down our road? They were proud Muslims, too. But, like me, they saw it as a cultural identity and an important one at that. That's why when Amir started super-imposing images of burqua-clad women and other Islamic icons as backdrops on his films, we just saw him cleverly trying to draw attention to the plight of oppressed people around the world. Amir was using the Koran metaphorically, as an inspiration. The problem with Afshan was that she was reading it too literally.

'Well, how else is it meant to be read?' she said to me tartly when I tentatively put that point to her. She folded her legs under her, sitting taller.

Perveen narrowed her eyes at me, urging me to stop.

'Well . . . umm,' I stuttered, 'The Koran was written in the seventh century, so one should—'

I didn't finish because Afshan suddenly threw her hands down in frustration and cried, 'Don't you know that the Koran is timeless? I hope you're not saying that they have better values?' she said, pointing out of the window. By 'they', Afshan was referring to the English. 'Divorce, drunkenness, leaving the old to die. You think that's better?' Afshan shook her head as if she was astounded by my stupidity.

'Not all the English are like that,' I said, trying to keep calm. Her remarks had a way of making me feel exposed, as if an English person was actually in the room listening and thinking: 'See how nice we've been to them. Letting them in, being all tolerant, while they banged on about their roots. And look at the thanks we get.'

'All I'm saying is that as a Muslim—'

'What about being British and Asian?' I interrupted, aware of how desperate I sounded. But then it was slowly occurring to me why I found Afshan's religious talk so frightening. It was all very well asserting our Asian roots as we had done in the past, but asserting a religious identity felt like opting out of everything that my father's generation of immigrants had worked so hard to achieve in England. The way I saw it, there was a set of values that underpinned the multicultural ideal, and secularism was the most important of them. To now assert Islam as an alternative authority just felt like breaking the deal.

'British Asian!' Afshan jeered in a mocking tone. 'That's the label the English gave us. You just don't get it,' she continued, chuckling unkindly, 'but then, how could you!'

'What does that mean?' I said, thrown by her venomous tone.

'Face it, Yasmin. You're not a proper Muslim.'

17

Mad Mullah!

A friend of mine from the BBC rang with the news that the *Newsnight* programme was looking for a temporary researcher.

'Temporary? Who cares!' I cried.

Not only did I finally see a way out from TV Asia, but the opportunity to work on such a prestigious programme in the 'white world' (as I now called media outside TV Asia), even if it was for just a couple of weeks, felt like a dream come true. In so much reverence did I hold the programme that I had never before considered sending my CV to them. *Newsnight* was the big league. One nervous phone call to the *Newsnight* office, plus two interviews with the programme editors, and I got the job.

Apart from the huge database of contacts or the instant access to top stories and the generous budgets to creatively realise news items, just saying, 'Hello I am from *Newsnight*,' opened doors. But the best thing about working on the programme was that after a year of making films for such a small viewership, I finally had the opportunity to communicate to a wider and more influential audience.

I felt a small flicker of pride on my father's behalf. Having worked for the BBC Urdu Service himself, would he ever have imagined that, in one generation, his daughter would be working for a BBC news programme that was so central to shaping the national debate? It felt like an achievement and of course, I was pleased with myself, unlike my mother and the aunties in the *mahalla*, who saw my move to work on *Newsnight* as a demotion. For a start, they had never heard of the programme, let alone seen it.

'But where were you?' my mother cried in dismay. 'I watched the programme, and you weren't on it. Only a man called Jemmy.'

'Jeremy!'

'Are you sure Tee Vee Asia won't take you back?'

'Mum!'

'Well, at least now everyone believes why you come home late.'

My new colleagues took some getting used to. What a culture shock it was to commute across multi-ethnic London to arrive in the offices of *Newsnight* in White City. Aside from the cleaners and a couple of receptionists, there was only one other ethnic-minority staff member on the programme. During my first week, I overheard two of my new colleagues moaning about the equal-opportunities initiatives that the BBC had introduced in its recruitment policies. 'It's not as if we can't recognise talent when we see it,' she said resentfully. 'We're only going to end up being force-fed minorities—'

The woman quickly broke off when she saw me listening. She smiled sheepishly, as if to reassure me that she wasn't talking about me. I smiled back, to let her know I didn't take offence. Actually, my emotions were more complicated. I got the job on my own merits, not because of any scheme. Or at least, that's what I believed – until then. But for a moment I began to wonder: was I just another minority being force-fed to my colleagues? I suddenly felt very uncomfortable.

Still, working on the programme, learning about Britain – how power was organised, who its movers and shakers were – I was starting to receive the practical political education I had always craved at university. Nothing inspired me more than watching good journalism in practice, day in, day out. Whether it was tracking down elusive contributors, the rigorous scrutinising of facts, formulating questions that would deliver the most concise and informative answer back, or reporting a story so it remained fresh and alive by the time of broadcast – not easy by 10.30 p.m. – the standards were incredibly high. But now that I was working alongside some of Britain's finest journalists, I was keen to buckle down and prove myself.

'Get a mad mullah, get a mad mullah,' the day programme producer screamed at the desk staff. She was so excited that she could hardly contain herself. We had started the morning thinking that it was going to be a dull news day but, just around midday, news had come in that there been a bomb attack on one of the government offices in Oklahoma City. And it was big.

'Get a mad mullah!' she screamed again.

I looked over my shoulder at the programme producer, unsure of whether to smile indulgently at her mischievous spirit, like the rest of my colleagues were doing. Part of me couldn't help wondering why we needed a mullah in the first place, let alone a mad mullah. No one had yet taken responsibility for the bomb. But everyone else seemed to agree with the day producer, because right now they were poring over the database looking for mad mullahs and experts on Islamic terrorism. Great, I thought. Muslims finally make the news – and look what it's for.

And yet, distasteful as the programme producer was being, the journalist in me knew she had a point. In light of the 1993 World Trade Center bombings, the horrible truth was that the story was leaning that way. And whether I liked it or not, I had to engage with the possibility of a Muslim terror connection. Of course, my task could be made easier if the day producer would just shut up for a minute. But she wouldn't. 'Anyone found a mad mullah yet?' she cried again.

I think I must have let out a frustrated sigh, because I suddenly saw the producer sitting opposite me turn to his senior producer, who then turned to the day producer and fired her a sharp look before jerking his head towards me. I didn't turn round to see her response, but she suddenly stopped. There was a strange silence around the news desk which, of course, made me feel more uncomfortable than ever. When it was later announced that some 'mad' Christians had been responsible for the bomb attack, I felt a great sense of relief.

That is not to say the programme editors didn't want to hear what I had to say on issues regarding Islam or ethnic politics. I soon found that whenever such stories emerged, they often assigned me to work on them, keen to get insight into a world they knew little about. And while I relished the opportunity to show off my expertise in these areas, the truth was, when it came to airing them into the newsroom, I found myself floundering. I had never anticipated a situation where I would have to articulate what my religious/cultural identity meant as a political phenomenon. Up to now, it had always been a private matter.

But these issues were not about to go away. And I soon realised I would have to learn how to cut through my emotions and clarify what I thought. With Britain fragmenting into smaller regions, stories on race and identity were erupting all over. But no discussion about English identity ever turned touchy as quickly as the one about British Muslims, especially Muslim women – an issue that, from my perspective, seemed to hold some strange fascination for my colleagues. My colleagues just could not understand why Muslim women were embracing Islam. And I must admit that I found it baffling, too. Who were these women who considered themselves secondary to men, shrouded themselves in black cloth to hide their female shame, allowed their husbands to have other wives, walked several steps behind them and happily gave up their careers to be the primary carer at home? Truly baffling – until I remembered that my colleagues were talking about the kind of women I had grown up with. And I didn't know one who usefully fitted their description.

'Look it says so in the Koran,' said one producer, picking up a copy of the Koran from her desk and turning to a page marked by a yellow stickie. Consulting the Koran was becoming a regular activity amongst my colleagues. They probably knew more about the Koran than 99 per cent of the people back in the *mahalla*.

'Ahh, here it is. Good women are obedient . . .' the producer started.

'Sorry, is that a valid translation recognised by Muslim authorities?' interrupted one of the programme editors.

'Oh, yes,' replied the producer, 'I rang Regent's Park mosque.'

'That might not be enough.'

'I've also checked with the Islamic society up in Oxford and Professor . . . and . . .'

The programme editor nodded, satisfied. The producer continued.

'Now where was I? Ahh, here. As for those from whom you fear disobedience, admonish them and send them to beds apart and beat them.'

The production team sighed knowingly at the citation.

Meanwhile I sat there wondering if it was possibly true. Did the Koran really give a man permission to beat his wife? Was that really written in the Koran? And if so, how come Afshan had never mentioned that bit of the Koran to me? I later found out it did say that, but I couldn't think of anyone in the *mahalla* who took their cue from it. In fact, hadn't Afshan said to me that Islam was the first religion to take women's rights seriously? The other religions hadn't even bothered mentioning the issue.

Seeing an opportunity to counter my colleagues' view of Islam, I decided to tell them about my most recent trip to Pakistan, where overnight all my female relatives seemed to have undergone a radical social transformation. Now that they had discovered Islam they no longer sat in the back room, but in the front room with their menfolk, holding their own in political discussions. 'But are your cousins proper Muslims?' asked another producer. 'I mean, they're not like you, are they?'

Like what, I wondered, recalling Afshan's comment on my Muslim identity? But now that my colleague had also brought the issue up, I was starting to wonder in what sense I could really call myself a Muslim. It wasn't exactly the most appropriate of places or times to be deliberating upon my identity, but I couldn't help it. I thought I was a Muslim. But according to my colleagues' definition – not to mention those Islamic fundamentalists out in Iran – I probably wasn't.

Still, my comment about the Koran as a source of female liberation must have made an impact on one of the editors because, for my next assignment, I was asked to develop a long film that

245

explored the phenomenon. I couldn't have been more pleased. Over the next few weeks I threw myself into the project, speaking to Muslim women from across the world. Some were engaged in re-interpreting the Koran from a women's perspective, others saw the whole exercise as totally futile. 'The Koran is a product of its time,' said one Muslim female scholar. 'Only human rights can give Muslim women genuine freedom.'

Speaking to Muslim women made me realise that a very fierce and sophisticated debate was raging around the relationship between women and Islam, often shaped by very local political concerns, and rarely did the issue of headscarves or 'wife-beating', get a look in. Yet these were the issues that my bosses wanted to be at the heart of the film we were making. 'We've got to find a Muslim woman who defends the line in the Koran about wife-beating,' the senior producer repeatedly urged.

I groaned. No matter what research or explanation I might offer on Muslims, they would always be out of kilter with what the Koran had to say on the matter. And the Koran was my colleagues' ultimate book of reference on Muslims. Why look at sociocultural factors when the question at hand was obviously one of religion?

'Well, what did you expect?' said Iqbal, the next time I bumped into him and told him about my frustrations. 'You think you can change things with your big job.'

'No,' I replied, 'I am just trying to contribute to the national debate.'

Iqbal laughed out loud, making me feel more naïve than ever.

After *Newsnight*, I became a freelance producer, mostly working on documentaries broadcast on Channel 4 or BBC 2. But, unfortunately, whenever stories regarding Islam cropped up, my old anxieties returned. My colleagues never intended to wilfully misrepresent or be malicious about Muslims. It was just that I noticed lazy editorial jumps could be made on Muslim stories that would never be allowed on other subjects. Mention Muslim – get mad mullah. Talk about Muslim women – consult pages in Koran about wife-beating and hijabs. At the end of the day, the Muslims were far too alien – too cultish – for the rational Middle England world of my colleagues.

I soon found ways to manage my unease. Firstly, try to avoid working on such stories. And secondly, if found working on such stories, then stick to the general editorial line but just temper it by throwing in a bit of 'community' insight. Like I did the time I interviewed the dreaded members of the EC1 Massive for a documentary. I wasn't exactly thrilled to be making a film about Asian gangs. In Wembley I had never been able to buy into their affected 'street' attitude. But my executive producer was beside himself with excitement. 'This is exactly what we need, hard-hitting, earthy stories and, Yasmin, you're the perfect person to do it.'

After mulling over the issue for a while, I decided that if I could get the boys to articulate their need for belonging, then maybe the film could acquire some depth. But that was obviously wishful thinking.

'It's all about empowerment, right?' croaked little Abdul, the tiniest member of the Bengali EC1 Massive.

'Yeah, empowerment,' his friends chorused behind him in enthusiastic agreement, flicking their fingers.

'But what does that mean?' I said, struggling to suppress my impatience. Where had the energy that had spawned our initial race consciousness gone?

'Yeah, well, our yoof worker Mrs Byron told me we're alienated,' replied Abdul, his baseball hat sliding down his small head. He swept it back up. 'And that deprivation is brutalising . . .'

'Yeah, yeah,' his friends replied, 'bruutalising.'

I could see they were really impressed by little Abdul's command of intellectual-sounding multicultural clichés. Abdul shuffled in pride.

And as for my bosses, they were very pleased with my footage, too. 'Ahh, great stuff,' they cried when they saw the interview. 'Brilliant insight. That's why we took you on.'

My career started to flourish and some big people in TV began to take notice. 'I would like you to come in to talk about your future,' said one channel director of programmes. 'Have you ever thought of commissioning in the future?' two Channel 4 commissioning editors, at different points, asked me, when looking for young people to fast track. I had learned how to play the game. This was the world my father had encouraged me to aspire to. But now that I had arrived, all I could feel was disappointment.

I dreaded going to Uncle Aslam's at the best of times. But as I made my way to his house that particular day, I felt more deflated than ever. Something was bothering me and I couldn't put my finger on it. As we settled down in his study, I decided to tell him about my neighbours and how in recent years they had grown more Islamic. I suppose that I was desperately craving a discussion with my father, someone who would have laughed off the *mahalla*'s expression of Islam and provided me with much-needed arguments and perspective to counter the media's fixation with radical Islam. Maybe even tell me where his secular, liberal daughter could fit into this increasingly confusing world. With my father not around, I was falling back upon Uncle Aslam.

It was obviously a winning topic for discussion, because Uncle Aslam immediately sat up when I started speaking. But the more

I spoke, the more agitated he became. In fact, when the grandfather clock in the hall rang four, Uncle Aslam didn't even bother turning one of his radios on. However, one quick glance at the window sills revealed that the radios were no longer there. Uncle Aslam must have moved them.

'I tell you, these fundamentalists will be the undoing of us Muslims,' he said, wagging his finger in the air. I smiled, bracing myself for an anti-Muslim rant. But that wasn't what happened.

'Do you know what it is meant by the saying that the Prophet is the last messenger?' my uncle said, leaning forward. There was an intensity in his stare I had never seen before. 'The meaning behind it is more profound than you will ever believe.'

'Allah has delivered his last words of guidance to humanity through Mohammed. From then on, it is up to mankind to use the words with the instrument of reasoning to live our lives. Never again does one need to look to Allah for guidance.

'But who out there is using reason?' my uncle cried, jerking forward, his finger dancing angrily in the air. I sat up, surprised at the surviving passion in that old, tired man. But then, why was I surprised? Weren't my uncle and my father the products of the spirit of Islam, which revered the mind? After all, their whole education and lives had been steeped in Islam. And just because I was only being exposed to Muslims like Afshan and Uncle Waseem these days didn't mean that there was not another way.

But who was right any more, I thought. Had there ever been a time when so many of the world's Muslims were literate, all keen to understand the Koran as a guide to life? Not just to rote-learn it – but to engage with it as a tool of empowerment. No longer did Western-influenced elites like my uncle and father have the monopoly on interpreting the Koran and disseminating its truths.

'What do you think about Islam?' I said, concentrating hard on my uncle's face so that I wouldn't miss his response. I had never asked my uncle the question, always assuming that he took the same position as my father. But I was wrong. My uncle laughed. 'Ninety-nine per cent of Muslims are scoundrels,' he replied. 'But for the one per cent it is worth being one.'

I suddenly felt tears welling up in my eyes. Why had his comment moved me so much? Was it because I suddenly felt permission to call myself a Muslim – that maybe that one per cent would understand me?

'I've got a book that I should lend you,' I heard my uncle say. 'But I can't.'

'Maybe next time,' I said, bringing myself back to the present.

'There won't be a next time,' my uncle replied quietly.

'Why?' I replied calmly, my throat tightening.

'I am flying to India next Tuesday to see my last few days out.'

'For good?' I replied calmly. If Uncle Aslam wasn't showing any emotion, it didn't feel right that I should.

'Yes,' he replied.

'Oh, what a shame,' I replied politely, as a thousand emotions exploded inside me. Was this it? Would I never see my uncle again, my last connection to my father's world? And why was he, the epitome of the English gentleman, choosing to leave England and be buried back in India? These are the questions I would have liked to ask. But instead I said, 'So what about your house?'

'Aunt Hilda's relatives are taking care of its sale,' he replied.

'So I will never see you again,' I said, gripping hard onto the chair's armrests.

'No,' Uncle Aslam replied.

'But what if I need you – need to reach you?'

Uncle Aslam pulled out a Mont Blanc fountain pen from his

250

breast pocket and then scribbled an address down in my diary. 'Yasmin, I am tired now. I think it is time for my nap.'

I got up. Uncle Aslam came to see me off at the door. 'Bye bye,' he said, as I passed through.

I lingered by the doorway, hoping for a more dramatic parting. But it didn't happen. And that was it. I never saw Uncle Aslam again.

It was only when I turned the corner onto Swains Lane that I allowed the tears to run down my face. I cried for my uncle, I cried for my father and I cried for a lost world that they had once inhabited, which now appeared so innocent and simple. But it hadn't been innocent, had it? The Empire and then the post-war years, still under the shadow of colonialism, had sown the seeds of today's turmoil.

How predictable that the former subjects were now choosing to break free from the West's clutches. Yes, it upset me that they were choosing Islam as their mode of revolt, but at least Uncle Aslam had left me with the knowledge that there was a tradition in Islam that was bigger and more accommodating than the versions Afshan and her ilk were presenting to me. Yes, it wasn't being heard at the moment, but it helped to know that it existed. And surely, once the current popular resurgence had settled down, it would re-assert itself.

But it was all about to get much worse. The Muslim populist revolt had only just begun.

18

Mothers!

We might forget to send her flowers on Mother's Day, we might forget to send a card on her birthday and we might even forget to ring her on Eid. But woe betide any one of us who failed to turn up at Heathrow Airport Terminal Three when Mrs Hai returned from her annual trip to Pakistan. After we all forgot to turn up, back in 1992, my mother wouldn't accept any explanations – refusing to speak a word to us for a week.

One could say that the reason for her insistence on the matter was because she had missed us terribly. And, given how protective she was of us, it probably was quite tough for her to be away from her children for over a month. My sister and I had offered on numerous occasions to accompany her. But, recollecting the disastrous last time she had taken us to Pakistan, our mother would shudder and cry, 'Never again. Your husband take you, not me.' Which obviously meant that we wouldn't be boarding the plane for a long time.

This Hai family airport event was not so unique after all.

Walking into the arrivals hall you would see legions of young British Asians waiting to pick up their parents. As we would wait, we would exchange furtive glances – as if looking into a mirror to see who we were. Some of us came dressed in *salwar kameezes*, others in fashionable English clothes. But from the slightly diffident way we held ourselves, you could tell we were British. That meant, unlike our parents, we didn't get overexcited about being at the airport. We were indifferent to the whole business.

Having been kept waiting several hours, the sighting of an Indian woman coming through the arrivals gate raised our expectations. We now craned our necks towards the doors, in the hope that our relatives might be the next to arrive.

'Arranged marriage,' I heard my sister whisper. I looked at the pretty young Indian woman, weighed down in gold jewellery and obviously wearing one of her best saris, a pink chiffon print. This was a game my sister and I often played. I think my sister was right. The young woman was now shyly greeting an Asian family, while a young Asian man, dressed in a tracksuit, hovered bashfully in the background, mumbling, 'Shame man, shame,' as his mates playfully tried to shove him forwards towards her.

'Darth Vader,' laughed a young boy next to me as another woman, draped head to foot in a black *niqab*, appeared at the gate. I shuddered. In fact, I think the whole arrivals hall shuddered. These days, one occasionally saw a Muslim woman wearing a headscarf, but rarely full Islamic dress. And then, just behind the woman with the *niqab*, through the crowds and trolleys piled high with luggage, I spotted my mother wearing a new tailor-made green *salwar kameez*.

'She's here,' we cried in unison, running towards her.

From the look of excited anticipation on my mother's face

as she searched us out, I could see that there was something almost magical for her about returning to Britain. Somehow the whole ceremony of getting off the plane, having her passport checked at immigration in the British passport holders queue (as opposed to non-British passport holders queue), walking through the customs gates and finally seeing us all there waiting behind the barriers, affirmed something in her that no birthday or Mother's Day celebration ever could.

It was good to have her back. We were hugging away, our eyes full of tears, when we heard a voice call out to my mother, '*Bhaji* [sister]!' It was Aunt Quereshi, Shazia's mother. Of course, she and my mother then had to spend ten minutes chuckling about the fact that they had both been on the same flight and neither had known. 'Next time, you tell me, OK?' said Aunt Quereshi, wagging her finger at my mother in jest.

'Oh yes,' my mother laughed. 'And you tell me.' Though I knew neither would. Once you told anyone in the *mahalla* that you were off to Pakistan, the next thing you knew, your neighbours were arriving on your doorstep with gifts to forward to their relatives back home. The same thing happened when you were getting ready to leave Pakistan to come back. One time my mother had to buy another suitcase just to accommodate all the presents given to her for delivery.

'*Abas are he?* [you are expecting Abas]?' my mother asked as she spotted Aunt Quereshi anxiously looking around. Abas was Shazia's Pakistani husband, Aunt Quereshi's son-in law.

'Umm . . .' said Aunt Quereshi, her cheeks reddening. 'Don't worry, someone coming.'

My sister rolled her eyes at me. It was obvious that Aunt Quereshi was expecting Amir, her eldest son, and that he hadn't turned up. I would have offered to call Amir on one of his three mobile phones, but I knew it would be a miracle if I ever got through on any of them.

'Maybe he's stuck in traffic,' I said hopefully.

'What, for four hours?' my sister mumbled under her breath. My sister didn't have time for Amir and no matter how often I told her that behind the happy, druggy image there was a rather clever young man, she never believed me. But then, while many of our peers were starting to get their lives together, Amir was struggling to hold down a job. Apparently he had an authority problem.

'Oh, he'll come,' Aunt Quereshi said, waving her hands dismissively. But it didn't take a genius to see how much her son's irresponsible behaviour pained her.

'Sorry to hear about . . .' my mother stopped, seeing Aunt Quereshi's face fall. A couple of months before, Aunt Quereshi's distant nephew (related to her through her ex-husband, who had walked out on her after leaving prison) had been shot dead in a gang fight in Pakistan. The news had been shocking, even though one often heard of some Pakistani relative or friend who had gone missing or died in a violent attack. Such news was always a reminder of what dispensable lives our relatives led back in Pakistan.

'*Hota he hunna* [what can you do]?' said Aunt Quereshi with resignation. 'It is in Allah's hands.'

We nodded despondently.

Aware that her news had brought our mood down, Aunt Quereshi said chirpily, 'So, any news?' She looked at my mother and then nodded mischievously in my direction. Annoyingly, I saw my mother's grip on the trolley tighten. She shook her head. '*Bachari* [poor girl],' Aunt Quereshi said and I could see that she felt genuinely sorry for me. 'Don't worry. Someone turn up.'

My sister giggled. That was hardly the problem. These days, I spent most of my time hanging out with my rather ebullient group of alpha-female girlfriends. Young, pretty and living in Ladbroke Grove, west London, with healthy incomes, we were determined to have fun. And, despite what Aunt Quereshi might think, on the man front things couldn't have been going better.

'Oh, you know, Mr Hai always said she find her own husband,' my mother waded in, not one to ever let the *mahalla* have the last word. I bristled, aware of an underlying tension in her voice. 'And she is career woman,' my mother continued, brimming with false cheer.

Aunt Quereshi nodded understandingly, though I could see she wasn't sure why she was nodding. I cringed even more. I wasn't against the idea of marriage, but the way the *mahalla* went on about it, elevating it to this highest of ideals – especially now that, aged twenty-seven years, I was apparently passing marriageable age – just left me feeling cold. Who you chose to marry so defined who you were and the life you hoped to lead. At the moment, I wasn't sure of either. Was I my father's daughter, who would choose to lead a more independent life? Or was I my mother's daughter, who would choose a life and a partner that kept me close to my roots?

But what roots? The *mahalla* was hardly the same place that I had grown up in. No longer was my old road only inhabited by Asian, Afro-Caribbean and white families – now there were also Somalians and East Europeans in the mix. As for my old friends, specifically Afshan, well, she was no longer interested in revisiting the past. In fact, the other day I had gone over to her house to congratulate her on getting married. I joked that it wasn't like the old times when we all used to go out. 'Well, we didn't go out that much,' Afshan had replied, very quickly, before muttering an Islamic prayer.

'You know what I mean,' I'd said quickly, trying to placate her while wondering why I was doing that. The truth was that we had gone out quite a bit. Much more than most of the *mahalla* girls.

'Well, we were all young and naïve then, weren't we?' she said, sounding extremely adult. 'I mean, your father had just died, Shazia was having all that family stress, Perveen and I were on the verge of getting married – we just wanted to let go.'

It seemed Afshan had it all worked out. I would have loved to argue back, but with Mrs Khan sitting there, all smiles and charm now that her daughter was finally getting married, and to a pious Muslim of all things, I could hardly say, 'Don't be such a hypocrite, we went out all the time.'

'Aunty, do you want a lift?' my brother asked, as conversation between my mother and Aunt Quereshi drew to a conclusion. I could see that Aunt Quereshi wanted to say yes. But, taking a look at all my mother's luggage, she shook her head.

'I wait; he come,' she said, waving us off. She promptly sat down on a chair to illustrate how comfortable her wait would be. She looked so alone sitting there amongst her suitcases, as other families and their loved ones darted around her that I vowed then and there to have a word with Amir. But Aunt Quereshi's desire for Amir to give up his wild ways and return to the family fold would soon come true – in a way she couldn't have imagined.

I promptly forgot to have a word with Amir. The truth was that our paths rarely crossed any more. Amir was lost in his world of drugs and dance parties and I was busy with work, mostly abroad. And, anyway, getting hold of him wouldn't have been easy. He had done one of his famous disappearing acts, something he often did when he was avoiding trouble, but I would periodically hear that he had been spotted at some rave, dancing more frantically than usual. 'He looks awful. He's taking his cousin's death really badly,' acquaintances would tell me. I would nod sympathetically, before recalling Aunt Quereshi sitting alone at the airport. But by the time I did bump into Amir, a month later in Portobello Market, it was too late for recriminations.

Besides, in the meantime something worse had happened. Perveen told me about it. Just a few days after Aunt Quereshi got back from Pakistan there had been a big family bust-up at the house. It ended with Amir being hurled out onto the streets by Abas, Shazia's husband. 'Don't come back here until you've learnt some manners,' Abas had yelled. 'Son like father.'

'And you won't believe what happened next!' said Perveen breathlessly. 'Well, poor Aunt Quereshi, she sees Amir lying on the ground, so she rushes to help him, but Shazia stops her and says, "Mum! He's got to learn the hard way." And then they close the door on his face. Imagine being kicked out of your own home. It's like they're English.'

'What was the argument about?' I interrupted.

'I don't know,' said Perveen, impatiently. 'But Amir was swearing and shouting, mimicking Abas's Pakistani accent, and then he threatened to come back with his posse and beat him up . . . I tell you, this is serious.'

But now, standing in the middle of the Portobello Market, waiting for Amir to tear himself away from a sexy blonde stallholder who was selling hemp-made bikinis, nothing in his demeanour suggested that he was contemplating some vengeful plan to get back at Abas. In fact, he looked his usual jovial, if somewhat eccentric, self. Amir was wearing pink PVC combat trousers and a black puffa coat. But then, maybe he had dressed up for the cameras. They were filming *Notting Hill* on Portobello Road, a feel-good British film designed to celebrate the new Britain of Prime Minister Tony Blair. All the locals were out in their full splendour, hoping to be captured on film. Little did they know that, despite their enthusiasm, most of their black faces would end up never really being seen. I guess they just didn't fit into the idealised version of what Notting Hill was supposed to be like. But that was New Britain for you full of false hopes that looked good on the surface.

'Yasmin,' Amir cried, with his usual exuberance, when he saw me. He pecked me on both cheeks, while simultaneously knocking fists with two black guys who were walking past. 'Respect,' he said to them over my shoulder.

'So, how have you been?' I asked. It was an innocent question, but from the way Amir's eyes narrowed – I now noticed they were bloodshot from heavy spliff-smoking – I could tell that he knew that I knew about the shameful bust-up with his family. 'I'm sorry about your cousin,' I said, quickly steering the conversation away from the argument.

'Why? What did my stupid mother say?' Amir snapped, glaring at me.

'Don't talk like that about your mum,' I replied sternly, though I did feel slightly nervous. Ninety-nine per cent of the time, if you stumbled upon Amir you would find a very charming, cheeky chappie. But, just below the surface, was a more unpredictable and volatile Amir; a side of him that he kept carefully in check.

Amir let out a tired sigh in the way of an apology. But I

could see he was still angry. 'Well, at least he's in peace now,' he said, punching his chest with his clenched fists, in noble salutation to his cousin's memory. Amir started to walk, inviting me to follow. I fell in behind him. 'He was like my older brother,' he continued, nodding at some rastas standing by the falafel shop. One hailed him by holding his hand up in a solidarity sign. 'He was a right laugh. Like a Punjabi Robin Hood.'

'Really?' I said, unsure of what he meant by that description.

We had now reached the end of the road. Amir stopped to watch a crowd of young men pouring out of the mosque. They were congregating into small groups around a stall distributing Islamic leaflets. In the past we would have probably walked by, totally indifferent to them. But in recent months that had changed. No longer was the crowd of men made up of elderly Asian men who went to the mosque for solace. No, these men were young. In fact, with their natty dress sense and trim goatee beards, they could have easily been part of our circle of friends. And yet with their devotion to Allah, that couldn't have been further from the case.

But it was the way they huddled together, like they were in some special brotherhood earnestly thrashing out the meaning of life, that intrigued me. Or, perhaps, humbled me. It was such a contrast to the anything-goes spirit at the heart of Amir's lifestyle and my own. I couldn't help feeling this grudging respect for the fact that they were engaging with the bigger issues troubling our world. They felt like our conscience. I didn't want them to be my conscience. I might share their anger at the state the world was in. Yet it rankled me that they were the only ones taking a political stand in this country.

It was the same in Wembley, where everyone had suddenly become very Islamic.

'Did you see the news? A Muslim Kashmiri man's head was cut off and stuck on a pole on top of a church. Woe us, how we suffer,' said Mrs Khan.

'Mum, that was Bosnia,' Afshan replied impatiently. 'They don't have churches in Kashmir.'

'So how come we don't see anything about Palestine on the news?' Ali had said, directing the question to me. Yes, the same Ali – who once strutted around in hip-hop gear and who ten years ago had shouted 'boring' when I had asked him to sign a petition on Palestine – was now a born-again Muslim.

'It's hard,' I answered, glancing at Afshan, who instantly lowered her head. That hurt. I could tell she thought I was colluding in the conspiracy against Muslims. It seemed that my job no longer excited my neighbours. 'The thing is, we do cover these stories,' I quickly added, wondering how one explained editorial concerns without it sounding like a feeble excuse. 'Too worthy. Think counter-intuitive. Think *Daily Mail*,' commissioning editors would usually say if you suggested foreign ideas. And I suppose they did have a point, because any film they broadcast on Africa or Asia always saw viewing figures plummet. But the problem was that while British television might not be covering these stories, the Asian satellite stations certainly were. And now you could find them on the internet as well.

'Do you know how many Muslims died this week?' interjected Irfan. Yes, Irfan, Uncle Waseem's trendy son, who now sported a fashionable Islamic goatee beard.

'Well, it's not only Muslims,' I replied. 'I've just been in Rwanda and . . .'

'Rwanda?' Irfan said, his face falling. 'I heard about what happened there. It was really bad, man.' And then that was it. He promptly turned the conversation back to Muslim Kashmir.

'I tell you why we don't hear about our Muslim brothers,' interjected Ali. 'It's 'cos the media is controlled by Jews, bruv.'

'No,' I replied, annoyed.

'Yes, it is,' Ali replied, looking at me slightly confused. 'I went to this meeting at uni the other day, through the Islamic group.' Yes, Ali and Irfan might not have a GCSE between them, but they had found a university willing to take them on. 'And this guy who was giving the speech was saying how the Jews don't like criticism of Israel . . .' Ali continued.

'There are lots of Jews who don't agree with what the Israelis are doing to the Palestinians,' I replied. Irfan and Ali looked at me in surprise and, out of the corner of my eyes, I saw Afshan tilt her head up too. I could see Irfan mulling over my reply. Not that it would change his opinion. That wasn't what his Islamic group was telling him. And yet, despite how uncomfortable Irfan and Ali's questions made me, I had to applaud the fact that at least they were taking an interest in the world. More than any of my so-called politically conscious English friends.

Amir and I were still absorbed in watching the young men outside the mosque. Just then, one of them looked up and gave Amir a brotherly salute. Amir nodded back.

'Do you know him?' I said, surprised.

'Yeah, he used to be a dealer,' he giggled, amused at the irony. Still, from the extra bounce that Amir put into his step as we began to walk away, I knew he felt chuffed. Despite his decadent lifestyle, he had been recognised as being held worthy of respect by a fellow brother.

'So what are you going to do about your mum?' I gingerly asked. Our brief stop outside the mosque had helped defuse Amir's anger. I felt it safe to broach the painful subject.

'What do you expect me to do?' he said, trying to sound defiant, but failing. The fight had gone out of him. He looked tired. 'She'll never get who I am.'

'Yeah, but whose parents do?'

Amir looked at me and I could see his mind racing through all the adult figures in the neighbourhood. 'Yours,' he said.

'It is a bit more complicated than that,' I replied.

Amir paused to think again. 'Yeah, you're right,' he finally said. 'They're all crap. Mine, especially.'

And even though we both giggled as we continued to walk on, part of me felt frightened for Amir. It was as if all the tensions that had dogged his life through the years, which he had worked so hard to keep at bay, were finally starting to catch up with him.

I had wanted to go along with Amir when he said that the Hais were a successful Asian family model – but I couldn't. Despite all my freedoms there was an emptiness in my life that I knew was connected to my relationship with my mother. I would always feel it most strongly when she rang me up.

'Moany, what you doing?' she asked. 'Moany' was the nickname she had assigned me, following my stroppy outbursts at her.

Given that my mother always rang me just before *EastEnders*, the answer was always the same. 'Cooking.'

'For yourself,' she said.

'Yes, Mum. For myself.'

'Oh, *bachari* [poor girl],' she said.

Though I huffed impatiently back at her, I knew what she meant. It was unheard of amongst Asians to cook for yourself. Only saddos like me did that. But then what did that make my mother? I could hear the latest drama on TV Asia playing out in the background. Now that my sister had also moved out and my brother was working late, the Pakistani epics were my mother's sole company these days.

'Mum, what do you want?' I asked, trying to keep the tension out my voice.

'Nothing,' my mother said. Except it wasn't nothing. It didn't take long for our conversation to drift onto the sore subject of marriage, as it always did these days.

'I am my own woman with a career,' I huffed indignantly.

'*Careeer?*' my mother said. 'You have had career.'

'What do you mean I *have had* career?' I blasted back. 'It's not a hobby you do for a few years and then stop!'

'No shouting. I am Asian mother,' my mother cried. 'Always angry.'

'But Mum, have you ever wondered why I am so angry?' I said, suddenly thinking an injection of psychology might help ease the problems between us. There had never been a precedent for this in my family, except the time when my father tried to discuss my teenage angst via the concept of the generation gap. But it wasn't too late to start. 'I mean, I don't like being angry,' I said, my voice softening.

'If you smiled more and didn't moan, you wouldn't be angry,' my mother replied. 'Look at number three's girl. Always smiley – always happy.'

'Uhh,' I screamed in despair, which only set my mother off again. I tried to be patient, but for some reason I couldn't allow her to have the last word.

264

'You know what your problem is?' my mother finally said.
'What?'

'Your father gave you too much freedom. Now you've seen too much.'

'What does that mean?' I said, my voice starting to shake at the mention of my father. In one quick swipe my mother had taken our argument to a darker level. She had reminded me that the freedoms my father had given me were taking me further away from my roots and, more importantly, her. In the past, I had avoided thinking about these issues, choosing to believe that I had successfully found a balance between my two lives. But now — with questions over my future reaching some sort of climax point and with some difficult decisions needing to be made — I no longer could.

'Hello, are you there?' I heard my mother whisper.

'Got to go,' I cried, quickly putting the phone down before my emotions got the better of me. It was only when I put the receiver down that I realised my mother had been choked up with tears, too.

That evening, for the first time ever, I found myself questioning my father's ideas and how he had chosen to bring us up. All my life I had blindly followed him. When he had ordered us — as children — to be English, we had become English. When he had demanded we drop our mother tongue, we had dropped our mother tongue. When he had encouraged us to go out into the open world and be independent individuals — well, that is exactly what we had done. But what peace had his ideas ever brought me? None at all.

Hard as it had always been to admit, I knew I was never going to lead a life that my mother could be totally part of. We were too different. I would always be an outsider in my mother's world and she an outsider in mine. My mother was right, I had seen too much. There was no going back for me. And, whether I liked it or not, she would end up living on her own: being distant from me.

I wanted to be angry at my father for the situation he had put us in, but I knew it was pointless. He was dead.

19

Jahiliyya

It was around about now that travelling took on new significance in my life. London was starting to feel claustrophobic and intense. 'You've got to cut half your brain out to live in this country,' I said to my friend Tam. Tam wasn't very happy living here, either.

Despite our good jobs in television, our lively social lives, something about living in Britain troubled us, and we both knew that race had a large role to play in our angst. (Tam was mixed race – half Indian, half English – and adopted.) We were always flying off the handle about issues of race and identity, unable to take comfort in the racially tolerant environment that we were constantly being told we lived in. Our anger was also the dynamic that helped feed our creative passions, but sometimes it just felt all-consuming.

If I thought that by travelling I could successfully manage to put my tensions aside, I was wrong. For I soon discovered a pattern to the countries I was drawn to visiting. They were all struggling with problems of ethnic conflict and integration. The first big trip I made was to Israel. This was a controversial choice, because I had grown up hearing my father and his friends say how they would never step on Israeli soil as long as Palestinian land remained occupied. Still, after years of being told by Jewish friends that I didn't know what I was talking about, that Palestinians didn't really have it that bad, I just felt I had to go and see for myself. Maybe my father had got it wrong. It wouldn't be the first time.

While at university, I had spent time studying Zionism. Initially I had just been interested in learning how the concept for a Jewish homeland had arisen in the mid-nineteenth century. But the more I read about the early Zionists, the more I became fascinated by the experience of Diaspora. Zionist Jews argued that as long as they lived in Diaspora, they would always be defined through their Jewishness. Only by having their own home would they be able to cast off the burden of being Jewish and live as 'normal' citizens. For me these ideas were riveting. All I remember thinking was, how far was I a 'normal' citizen? I began to wonder what an alternative Yasmin brought up in Pakistan or India would have been like. Would I have been less neurotic and angry? Would I have more easily fitted into my profession? Given all this, one can see why I might be curious to visit Israel. What would a nation made up entirely of immigrants be like and how 'normal' would they be?

One of the first things I noticed as I sat in Ben Gurion airport, waiting for dawn to break and for the buses to start, were the Israeli teenagers. In their Levi's and hooded tops they looked so familiar – just like the Jewish kids one often saw in north London or New York. But as I watched them, it occurred to me that I hadn't heard one speak English. Given the way they were dressed, I just expected they would, but instead they were all chattering away to each other in Hebrew. Once I had asked a group of young girls for the way to the bus station they struggled to understand me. It wasn't much of an incident, but it totally threw me. I had never seen Israelis as being indigenous to the land they were in, but look, here they were, young born and bred Israelis, living in the only home they knew, and creating very hard facts on the ground. In fact I soon learnt that hard facts were being created everywhere – and Arabs were not part of the equation. Like the time I was in the Old City and joined in on an historical walk.

'So what happened between AD 100 and 1917?' I asked the tour guide. We were looking at an ancient wall by the East Jerusalem gate, dating back to the Roman period. The tour guide had hinted that until the excavators came along in the early twentieth century, the wall had been in a ruinous state.

'Nothing,' said the tour guide, abruptly. 'All desert.' He swept his hands out as far as they would go to illustrate the huge size of the area he was talking about.

Slightly irritated, I was about to ask what had happened to the Arabs who used to live here, but decided not to. It wasn't the right place or time. The tour guide was already feeling tested by a rather irritating middle-aged American man in the group who, keen to show off his born-again Jewish credentials to his twelve-year-old son, was making a point of refusing to enter any non-Jewish sites. The American only mellowed when we finally clambered up to the top of the walls. From our high vantage point we had a clear view all over the Old City.

'Look son, look,' he said, pointing excitedly to the Jewish quarter. Neat rows of houses with bursts of colour from window boxes dotted the horizon. What a contrast to the Christian quarter, where only crosses and domes dominated the view. And then what a contrast to the Arab quarter, where a heart-sinking sprawl of satellite dishes and TV and radio aerials brutally assaulted the skyline.

In the Old City every ethnic and religious group jostled with each other to co-exist. Who were you? Where were you from? These questions weren't far from anyone's lips, identity being such a key issue for them. Once the facts of your identity had been established, a short exchange would follow as you discussed your respective immigrant experiences. What a contrast to England, where such issues were only spoken about between friends in private.

In the West Bank it was the same. 'We are the new Jews. We are the ones in Diaspora,' one of my Palestinian friends said, deliberately hijacking Zionist jargon.

I would return to Israel and the West Bank on several occasions, and the obsession with identity was always the same. How did one meld a society together when people come from such diverse backgrounds? Later, while making a film for Channel 4, Nathan Sharansky, one of my interviewees, would say it was ultimately a choice between 'melting pot' or 'mosaic society'. Different notions of integration, each with its own implications for citizenship. But what did such notions mean for the Arab population, who didn't neatly fit into the Jewish society? And where were we heading in new 'multicultural' Britain? Not far, I concluded, after living in South Africa for a few months.

These were the immediate post-apartheid years and South Africa was basking in euphoria, celebrating its rainbow nation. One of the things that struck me about my non-white South African friends was how developed their race-consciousness was, despite having lived under apartheid. Granted, many of them were filmmakers, artists and writers who had spent a lot

270

of time thinking about these issues. But if we were sitting in a group, you could probably spot the black and Asian Brits in the crowd a mile away. We were usually the overexcited ones, prone to angry outbursts whenever discussions of race and culture cropped up. Our South African peers would watch us, bemused, as our rants disintegrated into tears. I suppose their ease with being black stemmed from being in the majority in their country, while we British-born ethnics had always been in a minority, politely suppressing our ethnic identity. Yet it wasn't always that simple.

'Hey, the new South Africa!' an excited passer-by cried out to us in Cape Town. I was walking with Lara, my school friend from Camden, who was white, and Tam, who was mixed race. We giggled, none of us having the heart to open our mouths and reveal that we were British. The truth was, what we might lack in terms of a secure identity, we made up for by our relative ease in mixing with other races. This was the proud result of being brought up in multicultural Britain and being educated in the state system. As clichéd images of England, commonly found in a Hovis advert, ran through my head, I had to concede reluctantly that while it was trying at times living in Britain, at least an effort was being made by a decent many to forge a way ahead. That's when I remember feeling my first pang of homesickness. Suddenly I couldn't wait to get home.

I had heard Amir had changed while I was away. But I didn't understand how much until he finally came by to see me. He suggested we go on a drive.

'Should I turn it louder?' Amir shouted, reaching over to the volume button as more loud jungle music bombarded my eardrums.

'Actually, do you mind turning it down,' I said, keeping my gaze focused outside. It was a late summer afternoon and London was bathed in balmy sunshine. Seeing normal life unfold out of the window was helping to keep my nerves steady, as well as my tears in check. Amir really had changed and I wasn't sure I liked the new him. 'So, tell me about your father,' I asked warily, as he finally lowered the volume.

While I had been away Amir had made contact with his father. 'Let's just say he didn't want to know me,' he grunted bitterly, 'now that he's got a new family and all that.'

'What, you've got brothers and sisters that you didn't know about?' I said, turning to face him.

Amir made an attempt at a laugh, but nothing came out. I could tell he was hurt. I was about to offer a sympathetic remark when we pulled up at some traffic lights. A group of young girls dressed in short skirts were giggling hysterically at an Ann Summers window display on the other side of the road.

'*Jahiliyya* [hell],' Amir muttered under his breath.

He could not have used a more extreme word for what he was seeing. *Jahiliyya* was from the Koran, a reference to a state of ignorance and barbarism. But this was Oxford Street on a summer's afternoon in late twentieth-century Britain. My heart started to pound. This is what everyone meant about Amir changing. I don't know how exactly it had happened, but at some point while I was away, Amir had found Islam or, rather, his own brand of it. When I was first told, I had just laughed, dismissing Amir as trying to be controversial. After all, these days, all Muslims were flirting with Islam. But now hearing him utter that dreaded word '*jahiliyya*' – a sure sign of someone turning their back on the West – I realised how wrong I was.

'So, when did you become . . .?' I couldn't even say it.

But Amir didn't seem remotely put out by my question. My

272

world might have just turned upside down with the realisation that another close friend – the unlikeliest of my friends – had turned to Islam but, for him, it was the most normal thing on earth.

'A couple of months back,' he said. There was a lazy, slightly self-congratulatory smile on his lips. 'I saw the Koran on the shelf, picked it up. Reeaaaaaaadd it. And it just made sense.'

'And that's it?' I said, disappointed. I had been hoping to hear a much more dramatic story, with some kind of epiphany thrown in. Especially given the run-up of events before he found faith.

'You know Faisal, that guy we saw outside the mosque that time? Well, one day he got talking to me and he told me about Islam. And he said I should check the Koran out for myself. And so I did. You know, he's right. This world's fucked. We're living in *jahiliyya*. I mean, look at all these poor women,' he said, jerking his head towards another group of women walking down the road. 'Living alone, having to sell themselves in those clothes.'

'How do you know they live alone?'

But Amir wasn't listening. 'And all our drug-taking – it's a conspiracy to stop the common man from thinking, asking questions.'

'But I didn't know you believed in God,' I said provocatively

'Yeah, course,' he fired back. I paused, expecting Amir to now waffle on about Allah's mercifulness. But he didn't. Instead he launched into a lecture about the virtues of the Koran and how right it was. Obviously, it wasn't the spiritual aspects of Islam that appealed to Amir, but the rules. Those same rules that had been missing from his life.

The strange thing about Amir was, given that he had now decided we were living in *jahiliyya*, you would have thought he might be in a rush to get away from it. But instead, whenever I went out over the next few weeks, he came along too. 'Why's he tagging along?' my friends would ask me, slightly bemused. It was all rather bizarre. And more so because if we ever went to a club, halfway through the night we would see Amir leaning against the big speakers, stoned out of his brains, mumbling something about the decadence in the room.

'What an idiot,' my friends would giggle. And while I would giggle too, I felt relieved that he kept coming out. Maybe he wasn't giving up on the British way of life, whatever that might be.

As the months went by Amir did drift away, more than happy to be seduced by the brotherhood. Part of me wanted to shake him. I wanted his outlook on life, his anger, to remain couched in reality, not hijacked by religion, but part of me also felt envious, for every time I saw him, he seemed ever more motivated. He even gave up smoking dope.

'That's impressive,' I told him, chirpily. I had called round to his studio to pick up some videotapes that Amir had said he would dub for me a year back. I had given up hope – but here they were. As part of his change, Amir was determined to keep his promises.

'Well, I'm keeping myself clean, aren't I?' he replied, matter-of-factly. 'Not that it's a sin to smoke. In Islam there is a difference between sins that can be forgiven and those that can't.'

'Really? Who told you that?' I asked, noting Amir's selective understanding of Islam.

'That's what we – the group I go to – talk about. Drugs, drink, sex, women, you know, all the stuff that concerns us young lot. Not like those stupid mosques we grew up around.'

Amir got up and started pacing around the room, abandoning all pious protocol. 'You know, the problem with us Muslims is that we've turned away from the truth. We've become weak. That's why Bosnia, Palestine and Kashmir is all happening.'

I nodded, but obviously not enthusiastically enough because Amir suddenly said in an ominous voice, 'You don't believe me, do you?'

'Yeah, course I do,' I said, feeling slightly nervous at his tone. He might have changed, but I guess he still had his temper.

'You want to see this?' he said, marching over to his bookshelf. He rummaged around and pulled out a tape. 'Secret filming,' he said, a bashful grin lighting up his face, as he held up the tape.

'Oh,' I said. The cynical journalist in me prayed that I wasn't about to be subjected to hours of homemade videos of an imam delivering a ponderous lecture in some badly lit community hall.

'Muslims being slaughtered,' Amir said, lowering his voice conspiratorially.

'What?' I said, alarmed, noticing how his eyes had taken on this mischievous glimmer.

'Do you want to see it or not?' Amir asked insistently. 'You'll see what I'm talking about.'

'I don't know,' I said. Yet the journalist in me knew I had to see the tape. 'OK,' I said reluctantly. 'Is it scary?'

Amir didn't reply. He slid the tape into the machine and I sank back in anticipation of the horrors that were about to unfold: unwelcome images of cracked skulls, mobs of feral youths wielding machetes, and dead bodies splayed along dusty roadsides rushed through my mind.

'You won't regret it,' Amir said, as the screen fuzzed up

before a hazy image began to take shape. The footage was grainy from being duplicated so often. In the film a crowd of twenty to thirty Far Eastern-looking men were standing in a line, smiling inanely at the camera. They were chewing enthusiastically on chunks of food. The camera panned slowly over them in close-up. Hardly secret filming, I thought.

'Where did you get it from?' I said, feeling bolder. The images weren't harrowing at all. Just a bunch of men eating dinner.

'A brother gave it me,' I heard Amir reply. 'He got it off someone else in the group.'

'Yeah, but who filmed it?' I asked.

'Don't know. But whoever it is, was well brave, don't you think?'

'Yes, if you say so,' I said wearily, wondering what the big deal was.

'I mean, you know what they're eating, don't you?'

'No,' I replied, my stomach suddenly tensing up.

'Muslim flesh!' he cried, his voice rising. 'Look, I'll show you.' Amir pressed hard on the rewind button of the remote control. 'And you can see how they kill this Muslim and then cook him . . .'

'Turn it off,' I shouted as Amir's words began to register. I didn't want to see any more.

Amir did as he was told. We sat there for a while, in his tiny studio flat, not saying anything to each other. Outside I could hear cars whooshing by on the Westway. The sound of everyday British life was soothing. I looked at Amir – this vulnerable young man. In his current state, he would believe anything. He needed to believe whatever the people around him believed.

So many questions were running through my head. Where

had this alleged massacre taken place? Who were these cannibals supposed to be? Who filmed the scene? How did it get into the hands of Amir's Muslim friends? And what was looking at tapes like this – the pornography of violence – doing to young men like Amir?

These were the kind of questions I had been trained to ask. I was a journalist. The truth was supposed to matter.

But Amir was living in a different world. He wasn't about to ask any questions that would only undermine his ties with the one group of people who had finally given him a sense of belonging and renewed purpose in life.

Amir was watching my face, waiting for a reaction.

I didn't know what to say. Finally, I resorted to the truth.

'How can you watch stuff like this? It's propaganda.'

He got angry.

'No, it's not. Do you want me to turn my back on what the West and infidels everywhere are doing to our people?'

As far as Amir was concerned, you were either with him and his friends or against them. I could have argued back that there were other ways of showing solidarity with the dispossessed, but I knew my protestations would only fall on deaf ears.

I couldn't wait to get out the door. Amir's blinkered view of the world, his readiness to go along with anything he was being told by his new friends had done my head in.

The last thing I wanted to do was attend Nazia's wedding as I knew I was likely to bump into her brother, Amir. I hadn't seen him since the video incident and I wasn't sure I wanted to.

It was Afshan who spotted him first. 'There's your mad mate,' she said.

I looked up and, darting around the men, acting the perfect Islamic host, was Amir. Gone was his street look. Instead he was wearing a red and cream *sherwani* suit. He looked very much like the model dutiful son, and I think the men agreed, because every now and then one of them would heartily slap him on his back. Amir would reciprocate with a hearty slap on their backs. At some point, Abas came over to him, placing his hand affectionately on his shoulders as he whispered something. Amir nodded politely back.

And then, in that uncanny way Amir always had of knowing when he was being watched, he suddenly turned around and caught me staring at him. For a second, I saw his face cloud over, but then a big grin appeared. He waved. Picking up some plates, on the pretext of being busy, he made his way towards our table. 'Yasmin,' he said, greeting me.

'You all right?' I said, as he laid the plates down.

'Yeah, cool.'

'Uhh, they're not driving you mad?' I asked, looking towards the men.

'They're all right. But I tell you what,' he whispered, bending down towards me. 'They're not proper Muslims. They're circumcised Hindus.'

'He's so weird,' said Afshan, as Amir walked off. 'Did he just say what I think he said? I tell you, I don't know why you hang out with him.'

I was about to tell her I no longer did when I saw Aunt Quereshi, dressed in a pretty green Banarasi sari, approach. 'Such a good boy,' she beamed, watching Amir walk off. '*Marsh'allah* [a blessing]. Five times *namaz* [prayers].'

I wanted to be annoyed at Aunt Quereshi for being so blind to Amir's crude and disturbing embracement of Islam. But how could I begrudge her, of all people, the chance of happiness? Over the years, she had gone through so much upset – her husband deserting her, her children's wild behaviour, and the *mahalla*'s gossip – but never once had she complained. And now here she was, surrounded by all her children, with her youngest daughter finally getting married. Yes, her son Amir might appear strange with his born-again Islamic talk, but could anyone have ever imagined that harmony would, one day, prevail in the Quereshi family? What a contrast to relationships in the Hai family. I had to be happy for Aunt Quereshi.

'Yes, Aunty, he is a good boy,' I said, hugging her.

Aunt Quereshi pulled me to her chest and kissed me firmly on both cheeks. Having felt so distanced from the *mahalla* in recent months, it felt good to be reminded that the warmth and kindness was still there. 'Now, make Mum happy!' she said, pulling away. 'Find husband.'

20

9 / 11

We were watching a top-rated Pakistani soap opera on one of the Asian cable channels, *Go Round the Sacred Wedding Fire Seven Times*.

'I don't get it. What's his problem?' I asked my mother as the poor, beautiful heroine dutifully swept the kitchen floor, which her wicked sister-in-law had littered with wet chapatti flour. This, while her gormless husband looked on. I wasn't really interested in the answer. I was just trying to make conversation.

'Can't you see?' my mother said, tears streaming down her face. 'Poor girl, dark skinned.'

'What?' I said.

'Because she is dark skinned. Very bad.'

I pursed my lips hard to stop myself from speaking. But still a heavy sigh escaped.

'You sigh. But this is life in villages back home,' my mother explained, her eyes remaining fixed to the screen. Now wicked sister-in-law was busy stealing the valuable family jewels.

'How can you take such rubbish seriously?' I exclaimed. 'You sound like one of the aunts from the *mahalla*.'

My mother looked up, annoyed. Nothing wound her up more than being dumped in the same category as the *mahalla* women. She turned back to her soap opera, but I could tell by the way her body tensed up that she was hurt.

I had spent the train journey vowing that I would be attentive and warm when I saw her. But as soon as I entered the house and saw the alabaster lilac walls, as soon as the familiar house smells hit me, a combination of cooked spices and Lily of the Valley air freshener, I instantly seized up, mustering only enough energy to mumble: 'What's for dinner?'

My mother hastily placed a plate of food in front of me. She was convinced that the regularity of my visits was due to the fact that I missed her cooking. As I ate, comforted by the soothing tastes, I tried to make polite chat. As always, I soon gave up. It felt like such a grinding effort, explaining to my mother what was going on in my life. So I did what I always did when I visited her. I turned the TV on. Hence, the Pakistani drama we were now watching at midday.

'Tut tut tut, he's already married,' my mother cried, as the plot now revealed that dense husband already had a wife locked up in some mental asylum. 'Tricky men, everywhere,' my mother muttered to herself.

'Sorry? What do you mean by that?' I said. It was an innocent comment. But I took it personally.

'*Kya?*' my mother said, turning to me with irritation. But it was too late. From the look on her face, I could tell that she knew what I was referring to.

'Face facts, Mum,' I cried at her in frustration. 'I am with Jay.' Yes, Jay, my ex-boyfriend from ten years ago.

'Umm, him! The married one,' my mother replied, contemptuously.

'He's separated!' I snapped back, but it didn't help matters that I was already feeling rather tense following a discussion I had with Jay that morning. It wasn't my plan to give him a hard time about our relationship, but it sort of came out. Didn't he realise that I had just turned thirty-one – thirty-one! – and was starting to panic about the future?

And now my mother had dredged up the whole sore issue. Well, I didn't care if Jay was separated, or that he was black. Mixed race, actually. That's how he described himself now. We had an affinity – we had a future.

The soundtrack suddenly jumped to a crescendo and the credits began to roll. 'Finally,' I said, grabbing the remote control before my mother got any ideas about watching what was coming up next, *I Am Leaving My In-Laws' House to Go Back to My Mum's House*, or rekindling the painful subject of Jay.

I was flicking through the channels when I suddenly saw a 'news flash' graphic over a picture of New York's Twin Towers on a very sunny morning. Black smoke was coming out of one of the buildings. I turned up the volume, transfixed.

My mobile phone rang. It was Perveen. 'Have you seen what's going on?' she screamed frantically down the line. The spectacle was unfolding in front of me. It was the strangest thing I had ever seen and the fact that it was happening live, on TV, made it even more bizarre. As I sat in my mother's stuffy living room in Wembley watching clouds of smoke billow out of one of the Twin Towers, people were inside the building, dying. Dying, right now, in front of me.

'I've been there. I've been there,' Perveen cried, as the camera zoomed closer into the building. 'It's so high, you can see all of New York.'

'I know,' I replied.

'God, it's so mad!' she said. 'Imagine a plane going into a building. What's the pilot on?'

'Well, they say it might be a terrorist attack,' I replied, my calm disguising just how apprehensive I felt. Perhaps the whole shocking affair would soon be revealed to be pilot error.

'That's why I'm calling you. I knew you'd know what's going on,' Perveen said.

'It might not have anything to do with terrorism,' I swiftly added, hoping to dash any such notions, 'but if another plane hits the other tower, that'll confirm it.' I was only repeating what one of the pundits had just said but Perveen seemed very impressed by my insight.

At the corner of the screen, I suddenly saw a moving black dot. I heard the commentator's voice tense up in horror. As the dot transmuted into a plane, it careered towards the second tower. As the plane smashed into the back of the tower I suddenly felt this uncontrollable rage. My mind exploded with a multitude of incoherent thoughts, trying to make sense of what I was seeing. These were quickly followed by an almost suffocating sense of panic. 'Please don't let it be Islamic terrorists,' I said to myself. I got up, suddenly unable to deal with the thought that had just passed through my mind. I felt scared.

Over the next few hours I remained glued to the screen, like everyone else. I devoured every piece of information on the terror attack, growing more suspicious every time some supposed expert brought up the Muslim connection. How stupid was that? If you looked carefully at the facts, it was clear that the disaster couldn't have anything to do with Islamic terrorists. The attacks were far too sophisticated and clever to be the work of men living in caves and coming from poor, developing countries. Didn't anyone know how disorganised and chaotic Arabs and Pakistanis were? And as for an Afghani connection – how ridiculous. They were all peasants and farmers. No, the experts didn't know what they were talking about.

Then I wasn't so sure. As more information came to light, I could feel my whole understanding of the world being turned upside down. 'Al Qaeda'. Never heard of it. 'Osama Bin Laden'. Who was he? And yet the name was familiar. Where had I come across it?

In the past, I had always downplayed the threat that Islamic extremists posed, seeing them as severely misguided and often brutalised men, sorry victims of a world that abused and rejected them. But never had I imagined that their despair could drive them to terror on this scale. Looking at the TV, there was no longer any need to imagine anything. It was all there. And I had to accept that I had been terribly wrong.

'It could be as many as eight thousand deaths!' speculated one announcer.

'Possibly twenty thousand,' said another, ratcheting up the terror in my heart.

I nervously glanced up at the clock yet again, willing the hands to spin back a few hours to a more innocent and happier time. Even back to the argument I was having with my mother about Jay.

'So, do you condemn it?' the newscaster sternly asked a mullah from some obscure Islamic organisation. He was the latest expert to be wheeled out to comment on the attacks and their implications for wider racial harmony. I put my head in my hands, unable to watch, incensed that the newscaster even presumed that the mullah might support the attacks. That 'we' Muslims would fail to condemn them.

'We Muslims?' I thought, suddenly aware of how I was looking at the attacks through Muslim eyes. But that is how I felt at that moment – a Muslim, and a defiant one at that. I wasn't going to allow these Islamic extremists or these Western pundits to dictate what being Muslim meant. By identifying with the Muslim part of myself, I was just about to enter the most conflicted period of my life.

'Sorry, I didn't hear you,' I heard the newscaster rebuke the mullah. He was an old man, now looking rather anxious. 'Does Islam condemn . . .'

Looking out of the window, through the white-laced net curtain, life was no longer the same. Everything, from the neat terraced houses across the road, the commuter cars parked along the kerb, the passers-by busily darting to and fro, seemed to have taken on the tone of menace, a shade of grey. I realised that I was scared of going outside. It wasn't physical assault I feared. It was the hostile questions and the ignorant comments that I knew would follow, angry people damning British Muslims for being the traitorous enemy.

After 9/11 it wasn't as if all of us Muslims began ringing around asking each other what we thought. Our response was rather muted, restrained. Maybe we were just trying to digest the enormity of the event. Or maybe we were confused as to why we were being asked to account for terrorists. Or maybe we were doing what British Muslims had always done, keeping our heads down. Or maybe we were just busy re-reading the Koran, checking up on whether Islam did, in fact, endorse violence and suicide. Or maybe we were just perplexed about how to respond to questions that were predicated on the idea that history recommenced on 9/11?

'Do you see condemnations when villages are destroyed in Palestine? Do you see "news flash" when Kashmiri children are murdered?' Uncle Waseem cried at Tanveer and me.

I had bumped into Tanveer, Shazia and Amir's younger brother, on my way home from my mother's. He was dressed in his traditional *kurta kameez* with a beard sprouting from his chin. His head bent down low and he was walking with a slouch. I wondered whether, in some strange way, he felt culpable.

'Bad, huhh,' he had said resignedly, as if he had been programmed to deliver that response.

But before I had a chance to reply, Uncle Waseem, who had been lingering outside the Khans' house, butted in. 'They deserved it,' he said. A triumphant smile played on his lips. He had come a long way from the man who built Wembley's first home cocktail bar.

'*Salaam*,' we both said politely, before quickly looking around to check that no else else had heard him.

As Uncle Waseem turned away, I looked at Tanveer, but an awkward silence had descended upon us. We both wanted to say more – talk, discuss, analyse, explore, examine – anything that could help us understand how something so terrible had been done in Islam's name. But instead we said nothing. It was all too enormous to contemplate.

But our silence, our inability even to ask these questions of each other, was proof that in some way they didn't matter. The politicians and media had set the parameters for the debate and anything less than words of condemnation, especially from a Muslim, would be seen as tacitly supporting terrorism. We knew what was required of us.

Over the next few weeks, I found myself wandering around in quiet despair, bracing myself for another momentous disaster. Something big and terrible had happened; surely something big and terrible would follow. Maybe everyone felt the same, because the saying 'nothing will ever be the same again' became a kind of mantra, then a cliché. What did it mean, I often found myself wondering. I wished the future could speed up so I could see what it would bring, putting me out of my misery.

I suppose I was dreading the change that I knew was coming, even if I couldn't be sure of its form. Whatever it was, I knew it wasn't going to be good news for Muslims. You could tell just from the tone of stories starting to dominate the front pages. Or from the bellicose pronouncements being made by the American president: 'You're either with us or against us.'

I didn't talk to white friends or work colleagues about how I felt because I didn't want to validate the notion that 9/11 could have anything to do with ordinary Muslims like me. But the news kept on getting worse. A month after 9/11 the US invaded Taliban-controlled Afghanistan. I could barely watch the news, so stunned was I by the injustice of it all. Didn't anyone know about Afghanistan – the recent proxy wars, the fierce tribal codes that had rendered the place lawless, the beleaguered condition of its population – all factors that had allowed the Taliban to seize power in the first place? How was such a rash military offensive going to solve the real problems which could pre-empt terrorism in the future? But no one cared, too consumed by revenge and the desperate need to secure results on the ground.

'I can't believe it!' I said to Jay, surprised by the extent of support for the invasion. It was first time in my memory that I felt so frighteningly out of line with the public mood. It's not where I wanted to be. We rarely saw each other these days. I suspected it had something to do with my questions about the future, but Jay said that he just had a lot of work on. A low-level tension had developed between us that only vanished when talking about politics.

And while on the outside I remained defiant, something inside me was changing. I might have looked like Yasmin enjoying a cappuccino at work while scanning the paper for stories, but every time I turned the page, a wave of dread swept through me, in case another damning story about Muslims cropped up. Britain liked to see itself as tolerant, but I believed that not much would be needed to shake it. We were living in strange times.

I would have given up reading newspapers altogether if it wasn't for the fact that, professionally, I had never been so sought after. Every day I would get a call from a different TV company looking for a Muslim producer/director. And, given the gravity of the terror attacks and its aftermath, I had abandoned all my usual reservations about working on 'Muslim' stories in an English environment. 'Yes, I am Muslim but not a religious one,' I would reply. When talking to English people one always had to make that distinction.

'Religious? Oh that's not important,' the caller would say, relief in their voice. In the aftermath of 9/11, they never knew when they were going to get a 'mad Muslim' on the phone. 'We've been commissioned to do a documentary on why the Middle East hates America so much and . . .'

'Yes,' I said eagerly, excited by the prospect of working on a film that would put the attacks in a global context. But if I had thought that 9/11 could end up being seen as some isolated event, organised by Muslim extremists in faraway places, I was wrong. The story was soon going to have some very real implications for British Muslims too. People like me.

'Who's that?' shouted Shazia, jerking her head towards the TV screen as she shoved a samosa into her mouth.

'I don't know,' I said, reluctantly tearing myself away from the *chaat masala* I was devouring. As the TV sound was on mute, I manoeuvred myself to get a better look at the Muslim cleric being interviewed. It was hard to see with the dozen children running wildly around the room, even more excitable than usual because the Ramadan fast had just broken.

288

'Quick, quick, I don't want to miss this!' cried Afshan, theatrically. Because, unlike the rest of us, she's a proper Muslim, isn't she? I found myself thinking bitterly. The sight of her headscarf only served to wind me up even more. It wasn't just draped over her head the way we often wore it during Koran gatherings, but it was securely tied around her face with no hair in sight. Only *hijabi*s wore their scarves like this. Afshan had become a scarf *wali*.

The children instantly went into search mode, throwing cushions and pillows into the air, trying to locate the remote control. But of course, with the usual chaos in the Quereshi household, no one could find it. It was the first time since 9/11 that all the Bhajis had come together and it was the first time since 9/11 that I had found myself alone with Muslims. And I was deeply aware of it. If I had been sitting with my non-Muslim friends, I would have been carefully listening for any possible Islamophobic remark. And though I'd like to say I felt relaxed sitting with Afshan, Perveen and Shazia, I didn't. Instead, I found myself dreading that one of them might open their mouths and a pro-Bin Laden or an anti-British comment would come out.

'Oh, here it is,' said Shazia, laughing as she spotted the remote control on her lap, hidden in the folds of her *salwar kameez*. As the volume went up and up and up, because now that we were watching TV only a volume level fit for the truly deaf would do, we caught the tail end of a regional news programme, with an item on *jihad*.

The children sat down, hazily aware that the programme had something to do with them. These days you couldn't turn on the TV or tune into the radio or pick up a paper without questions over British Muslim loyalty or diversity hurling themselves at you. Being a TV journalist, I knew that these were valid issues for discussion. But the novelty of seeing them cavalierly thrashed out in public by people who didn't have a stake in the consequences was taking some getting used to.

'What rubbish are they going to come out with today?' I heard Afshan say, leaning towards the screen. I knew how Afshan felt but again it didn't stop me from feeling an irrational wave of anger towards her. As if I blamed her for the charges of disloyalty being thrown at us. How many times over the years had I heard her – and in fact many of my other Muslim neighbours – slag off the British way of life? It is true that many of her remarks were no less offensive than what many white Britons said about their country. But we weren't considered properly British, yet, were we? Afshan should have known that. But no, she had the audacity to think that she could be special – that she was free to be a Muslim in Britain.

'Samosas!' we suddenly heard Aunt Quereshi shout from behind us. And then, as her eyes caught sight of the TV screen, she let out a loud screech. To our horror, who should be on screen being interviewed? Uncle Waseem, dressed in his best *sherwani*. He was nodding at the camera.

'Oh my God!' said Perveen.

'That's Uncle Waseem,' shouted one of the kids, jumping up excitedly. And so shocked were we at seeing him that we all instantly burst out laughing.

'Shh, shh, I want to hear,' Afshan cried, urging everyone to calm down.

'. . . it is Jewish imperial conspiracy . . .'

'Umm, OK,' said the Asian presenter, quickly moving on.

'This is wrong!' said Perveen, as the camera panned to the next guest. 'What's he doing there? Did you see it? His title – "community leader". I want to complain.'

'What, go on *Points of View*?' said Shazia, giggling at her joke.

'No point,' said Afshan, very knowingly. 'They won't listen to Muslims.'

'You should write a letter of complaint,' I said, feeling really annoyed at Afshan's continuing put-downs.

Perveen suddenly went coy. 'Don't be silly,' Perveen said, shuffling with embarrassment. It was one thing being privately angry, but to write an official letter of complaint? That isn't what people like her did.

'Why not?' I said, looking at her hard. 'How else are you going to get heard?'

'Won't make a difference,' I heard Afshan crow again.

Perveen looked at me, and then shrugged. But though she returned her attention to the TV, whenever I glanced at her, I could see that she was starting to write a letter in her head.

A few days later, she called me to say that she had sent it.

I began to realise that I had been getting it wrong. I had always been reluctant to explore stories which would put the community in a negative light. I thought I was protecting it from a world that didn't understand. But those feelings which, in the past, had even left me indignant at Rushdie for writing *The Satanic Verses* – well, they were gone.

Everything was different now. We British Muslims could no longer afford to remain aloof. We had to stop behaving like immigrants, hiding in our mental ghettos and start asking ourselves some uncomfortable questions about our place here. It was time we faced the fact that we were British citizens.

'So you think it's obligatory for all Muslims to support the *jihadis*?' I asked Amir down the phone line. I was sizing up potential contributors for a programme on British Muslims and loyalty that I had been asked to develop.

'Yes,' he replied, resolutely.

'How can you say that?' I cried out in frustration.

Tom, the researcher on *Celebrity Pets' Ten Worst Moments*, who sat across from me, motioned for me to chill out. He seemed to think the high emotions my project was generating were hilarious.

''Cos it's true,' Amir replied.

I was just about to argue back when I remembered that I was meant to be talking to Amir in a professional capacity. So I reluctantly kept quiet and jotted down his comments.

From the corner of my eye I saw Zakia, a fellow Muslim researcher on my project, shuffle in her seat, a thin smile creeping up her face. I could tell she was enjoying hearing me squirm. She had yet to make her mind up on whether I could be trusted or not, unlike the executive producer, who thought I was fantastic: I looked like the other journalists and yet, being Muslim, I had access to the sexiest story of the day.

Right now the exec was veering towards my desk. Today, he was wearing a metrosexual purple polo shirt tucked into a pair of Carhartt jeans. Very street indeed – if they hadn't been belted unfashionably high at the waist. I saw that he was holding the sheet of paper I had written up on my potential contributors to the programme.

'OK, what next?' I heard Amir mutter.

'Well, some people say that it says in the Koran that all Muslims must respect a contract. And that if you've got a British passport then that constitutes a contract with this country. And so you can't go off fighting against your country . . .'

I heard Amir grunt. I could tell he was feeling compromised by talking to me. There he was, the Muslim loyalist – and there I was, a stooge of the British press.

'I've heard that one and let me tell you, those Muslims who say that are blatant sell-outs,' he replied.

'Right,' I said, scribbling down his answer. I saw the exec gesturing to me.

'Look, I'll call you later.'

'OK, sister, you take care. *Allah hafiz* [may Allah protect you],' he said with clipped precision.

'Yeah, you too,' I replied.

'Umm, Yasmin, just been looking through your notes,' the exec said, casually leaning against the photocopier. 'Not sure.'

'If we're looking at loyalty, I think it is worth interviewing some moderate Muslims on how they are trying to understand their Britishness through the Koran.' Even as I said it, I could already feel the television producer in me starting to yawn, but I had to remain focused. This was too important a line to drop. Zakia obviously thought so, because from behind her computer I could see her looking at me with grudging respect. But the exec wasn't. His eyes had glazed over with boredom.

'What about that Hiz-group?'

'Hizb ut-Tahir,' I said.

'Yes. Have you called them?' he said.

'Extremists more like,' said Zakia in mock horror, standing up.

'Yes, exactly. Call them,' said the exec. 'What we need is radicals! Some mad mullah types!'

'But that's like asking the BNP to represent how the British people feel,' I replied, trying to keep the desperation out of my voice as past experiences of covering Muslim issues came flooding back into memory.

'Umm, not quite,' said the exec, raising one eyebrow as if he had given some deep thought to the matter and had come to a sophisticated conclusion. In that second, everything changed between us. I didn't reply, but from my icy stare he could tell I wasn't happy.

293

'Prat,' mumbled Zakia under her breath, as the exec strode off.

I was furious that I had allowed him to have the last word. Why hadn't I put my foot down? But what was I going to do, refuse to make the calls? Walk out? God, how Afshan and Amir would laugh at me if they were here now. I picked up a list of radical Muslims I had been given by the production team, but the brusqueness of my action caused all the sheets to fall to the floor. Sighing, I bent down to pick the sheets up – and that's when I saw the memo. It was addressed to the exec from the commissioning editor of the TV channel that had commissioned the programme and had obviously been mistakenly included with the contact sheets. 'Hello . . . you need a good Muslim journo (who isn't really Muslim – you know what I mean, a Muslim name would do). Do you have anyone in mind?' As I read it, I felt myself going cold, particularly as the writer had a Muslim name. Was the Muslim journo – who isn't really a Muslim – me? I quickly glanced around to see whether anyone had seen me. I caught Zakia's eyes.

'You OK?' she said. I could see she was keen to have a bitch about the exec. For a second I was tempted to show Zakia the memo, but I held back. It was dawning on me that I had stumbled onto something potentially embarrassing and, even worse, something that in a strange way compromised me.

'Yes, I'm OK,' I said. 'Look, I'll be back soon.'

With that I grabbed my coat and left the building.

'I don't know if I can work on this project,' I said to Jay as soon as I got outside. I was shaking with so much anger that I could hardly hold my mobile phone straight.

'Yeah, but you've got to,' he replied. 'And this proves it.'

'But I am that fake Muslim they wanted,' I said, stopping in mid-stride.

'You're not,' replied Jay.

'If I make the programme I want, then they'll accuse me of having an agenda.'

'Funny how they always accuse us of having an agenda! What about theirs?'

I suddenly felt fired with new resolve. This really was no time for angst. I had to get out there and do my job. There was too much at stake to back down now. The need to show who British Muslims were was more urgent than ever.

But who were British Muslims?

21

Oi Paki!

'OK. Come up then,' Tariq said on the phone.

'Really?' I replied, wondering whether I dare repeat the request in case Tariq heard correctly this time round. He didn't exactly sound as though he was on the ball. Tariq was the brother of one of the British *jihadis* rumoured to have been found in Afghanistan. I was trying to persuade him (as he drove between his cash-and-carry and his dry-cleaning businesses) to meet with me.

'Yeah, sure, come up. We'll talk. I mean you are Muslim, right?'

'Yes,' I said, wondering if I should tell him that I wasn't religious. But then most Muslims had never heard of such a thing as a non-believing Muslim. Oh, that is, apart from Salman Rushdie.

'You know, we had Sue Lawley up the other day.'

'Sue Lawley!' I cried, wondering how on earth Sue Lawley could have possibly beaten me to the story.

'Oh sorry, not Sue. Her name was Kate. Or, hold on, was it

Fiona? God, it's gone right out of me head. Her cameraman is called Nigel, though. Top lad. Do you know him?'

'Uhh, no,' I said, as my grip round the phone tightened. 'Umm, what did they want with you, Tariq?'

'Oh, nothing to do with me, love. Pictures of the mosque for the news, they said.'

'Oh,' I replied, relief flooding through me. 'Look Tariq, I am just coming up for a chat. No cameras.'

'OK,' he said, the signal growing faint. 'Let me know when you get in. I will be free from seven.'

'What, seven tonight?' I said, my heart sinking at the prospect of cancelling a dinner date with Jay. But I knew I had no choice. Tariq was too strong a lead for me to lose.

Of course, my mother was beside herself when I rang her to tell her from the train that I was on my way to interview potential contributors for a programme on British Muslims.

'Are you mad? An Indian girl on her own! They (the community) won't treat you like you are English journalist, you know. They will think you are prostitute and all the *goondas* [gangs, bad boys] will come after you.'

'Mum, we're not in Bollywood,' I sighed, trying to keep my voice down. But I knew she had a point. Some of the Muslim communities I was visiting were notoriously traditional and segregated.

But it would be a great way of exploring the arguments of the multicultural-bashers. Their logic went like this: if it hadn't been for multiculturalism then Muslims wouldn't have segregated; if they hadn't segregated, then many wouldn't have become radicalised; and if they hadn't radicalised, then some of the Muslim menfolk wouldn't have gone to Afghanistan and so betray this country. It was such a seductive idea, I could see why many people were falling for it. But something about it jarred.

That's why contacting Tariq was such a breakthrough. Not only had his brother gone to Afghanistan, but he also came from one of those segregated communities that the multicultural-bashers argued were responsible for producing radicals. Maybe by spending time with Tariq, I might be able to explore these issues further.

'Why you talking to people like these?' my mother asked, interrupting my thoughts. 'Is he a professor?'

I giggled. I suppose it was rather baffling to her. Only experts and politicians went on TV, not normal people – and certainly not poor, uneducated Muslims, like Tariq or Uncle Waseem. What was the world coming to?

Except now, standing on my own in the winter dark, waiting for Tariq outside the station, the last thing I felt was bold. What a pitiful sight I would appear to any Muslim passing by right now. Not that anyone would – the place was frighteningly deserted. I reached into my bag and rummaged around for the headscarf I had brought with me, to put on when Tariq arrived. No point offending him with an uncovered head. I toyed with the idea of putting it on now, but then decided that I didn't have the nerve to do that. What if some yobs saw me?

From where I stood, I looked down into the dark and mist-filled valley that the station overlooked. The cosy orange glows sparkling from the houses below only made me feel worse. I could imagine how the Asian families, who I assumed inhabited the houses, would now be gathering around to eat their evening meal – hot *salan* with chapattis. The *salan* would be especially hot with loads of chillies and intense flavouring – proper *desi* style – because I knew that is how the community up here spiced their food. I suddenly wished I was a normal Asian girl tucked up in the comfort of my home surrounded by family. I missed my mother.

In the near distance, I heard the rumble of a car. And then a big BMW came swinging round the corner, blaring out Celine Dion. Startled, I stepped back into the shadows. The car stopped outside the station. I tried to peer into the windows, but they were blacked out.

'Is that Yasmin?' I heard a voice shout out as the electric windows rolled down.

'Tariq?' I asked surprised, cautiously stepping forward. I had to ask, because Tariq didn't look how I imagined he would. For a start, there was no beard. Instead he had an eighties' mullet hairstyle and was wearing a cheap, brown imitation-leather jacket.

'Ai, you must be freezing, jump in,' Tariq said, opening the passenger door. As he leant back into his seat, I noticed that the top of his head just missed hitting the car roof. He slid on his seatbelt, wheezing as he adjusted it.

'Right, shall we go?' he said.

Tariq took me to a pub near the station. It was a shabby workmen's pub and the smell of toilet-cleaning products and urinals hit you as soon as you entered. A surprising choice, I thought, for a brother of a *jihadi*. Maybe he wanted to go somewhere where he wouldn't be recognised, though from the response of the few customers, lounging around, he seemed to be a regular.

'Hey, Terry. Who's the girl?' one asked cheekily.

'She's from a TV company,' Tariq replied, as he ordered a drink from the bar. Though he spoke with nonchalance, I could see he was rather chuffed from the way he stood up taller.

'What, you famous now?' someone else piped up.

'No,' said Tariq, chuckling, trying hard to repress a bashful grin. 'Just a chat. Just a chat.'

'So do you know where Imran is?' I asked when we sat down. Tariq had found us a seat right next to the front door. He seemed impervious to the cold draughts that came through it. But then, I suspected he was impervious to most things in life.

'Oh no,' he said chuckling, pulling himself up on his seat. A rather large beer belly protruded from under his shirt. 'He went to Pakistan a long time back . . .'

'Really?' I said, making a mental note. 'How long has he been there?'

Tariq breathed a deep sigh, while his eyes lazily flitted over the tired, bosomy barmaid. 'Well, put it this way. Our Imran was always a bit on the lively side.' He stopped and I noticed that he was looking me up and down. 'You know what?' he said. 'You don't look Muslim. Don't you wear a scarf?'

'Umm, no,' I replied.

'What, you one of those modern Muslims?' he said, tilting his head up in interest.

'Uhh, yes, I suppose so,' I said, suddenly feeling uneasy. Thankfully the barmaid came by.

'She's from a TV company,' he said blankly, nodding his head in my direction.

'What's it about?' said the barmaid, eyeing me up suspiciously. She put a protective hand on Tariq's shoulder.

'It's about the little one,' explained Tariq.

'Oh, him,' said the barmaid, rolling her eyes.

'Trouble he was, from day one. In here all the time and . . .'

'Really?' I said, as a worrying thought occurred to me that maybe I had got all my contacts confused and was talking about the wrong Imran.

'So how come he was in Afghanistan?' I asked Tariq as soon as the barmaid walked off. I had decided to abandon all tact and make sure I was on the right track.

'Wanted to be a martyr,' said Tariq, a shy grin creeping up his face.

'And you supported his decision?' I asked, relieved that we were talking about the right Imran.

'Oh, me? No,' said Tariq, chuckling. He took another sip of his pint.

It was hard trying to get information out of Tariq. He wasn't very forthcoming, or articulate, for that matter. But I persevered. As we spoke, interrupted on numerous occasions by acquaintances coming over to say hello, it dawned upon me that the pub was like some sort of second home to Tariq. It was a place where he took refuge from his family and all the responsibilities that came with it. In fact, it didn't take me long to work out that Tariq was a rather lost and lonely man, always on the lookout for a drinking partner and that night that poor sod was me. Still, with the help of another pint, he did eventually loosen up. That's when I learnt that Imran's story was more complicated than I'd originally imagined.

'So, why did he leave Britain and go to Pakistan?' I asked again, looking over my notes and seeing the details still remained sketchy.

'Got hooked didn't he?' said Tariq, sighing. 'So we sent him over to get away from it.'

'Hooked on what?' I said, stunned.

'Heroin.'

'I'm so sorry,' I said, amazed at the turn in conversation, yet wondering how it was going to fit into my story of loyalty. 'Was he cured?'

'Yeah, of course,' replied Tariq. But I noticed that he didn't quite look me in the eye. That's when it occurred to me that maybe Imran had never really got over his addiction. And maybe, like so many British-born Pakistani boys sent back home to get disciplined, Imran had fled to Afghanistan to deal in heroin. Maybe Imran had got caught up in the fighting. I don't know. What I did know was that Tariq was never going to admit the truth to me. He might happily sit in the pub, drinking the night away, but somewhere all those conservative Asian values still resided deep in him. Maybe that is why it was preferable to him that his brother was seen by the community as a heroic freedom fighter rather than a junkie.

I didn't know what to make of this turn of events. I had come to find out more about *jihadis* but, speaking with Tariq, I seemed further away from the story than ever. The TV producer in me could have exploited Tariq, urging him to go on camera and hail his brother as some hero, but I decided not to. It didn't feel right.

'Tariq, it's getting late. I better go,' I said, looking at my watch.

'Oh, where you going?' said Tariq, his eyes widening in disappointment. I think he was starting to enjoy our conversation. 'I'll give you a lift.'

'No, it's all right,' I said. 'I'll get a cab from across the road.'

'OK,' said Tariq, looking slightly relieved that he wouldn't have to leave his cosy cocoon after all. I quickly said my goodbyes and left.

I might not have got much from Tariq, but still it should have been a sign, because over the next few days, as I travelled to Muslim communities the length and breadth of the country, nothing I found easily or conveniently explained the state British Muslims were in. Of course, that was to be expected. Only fools treated the Muslim community as one monolithic mass. As for the Muslim radicals I met, many reminded me of Amir. Few seemed to have respect for the communities they had been brought up in. 'They practise culture, not Islam,' the young radicals would spit out at me when talking about their parents or Muslim peers. 'They're all ignorant.' Then, eyeing up my combat trousers and trainers, which suggested to them the kind of lifestyle I might be leading, they would add: 'I used to be like you, clubbing all the time. Until I found Islam.' I would nod politely, wondering what to make of their comment. Did they see me as a potential recruit?

But during my travels there was something shocking that I did discover about Britain. I had never realised how deeply segregated parts of it were. At times I'd drive down rows and rows of streets teeming with those drab, old-fashioned back-to-backs, without seeing a brown face in a supposedly modern, multicultural British town. Everyone was white. From the youths skulking miserably on the deserted street corners, dressed in tracksuits with gold chains dangling at their chests, to the mothers ambling to the shops with their prams. Even the newsagents were run by white people! But then, turn a corner into another narrow street lined with old-fashioned back-to-backs and this time one didn't see any white faces, just brown. Asian brown. Or, as someone corrected me, Muslim. Yes, everyone was Muslim. From the youths skulking on the street corners dressed in tracksuits with, maybe, a white embroidered skull-cap, to the mothers swathed in black, pushing prams to the shops. Even the fish and chip shop was run by a Muslim! Just like their white neighbours, who apparently had fled the area as soon as the first brown face appeared, the Muslims, too, were living out everyday British life.

And yet, as I knew only too well, living a British life was one thing, but feeling British was another. Walking through these 'Muslim' areas, I assumed (like most of white Britons) that their loyalties must lie elsewhere.

In fact observing the way the youths with the wiry beards menacingly eyed up my uncovered head, I felt rather threatened. I couldn't help wondering how long before words like 'infidel' and 'kaffir' would start to be hurled at me. This was exactly the sort of community that my father used to get so upset about. It was strange that I should remember him now. I hadn't thought about him for years. I mean *really* thought about him. How often had he criticised these traditional communities for their God fearing ways and their suspicion of modernity?

But then these youths with the wiry beards didn't care what people like my father thought about them. They were defiant, prepared to embrace anything that set them apart from their white neighbours and their morally bankrupt, sexually licentious, spiritually defunct, culturally devoid, modern ways. They didn't care in the slightest if their white neighbours saw them as barbaric, uncivilised and backwards.

And what was to blame for all this division? I thought angrily. Multiculturalism? My idea of multiculturalism was London, where all the cultures happily mixed and were tolerant of each other. But for many, up and down the country, what I was witnessing was multiculturalism. Permission to live in segregation and practise Islam. But this was the most conservative interpretation of Islam I had ever seen – it went even beyond what I had seen in Pakistan. It was the same interpretation which, as Saquib, a young Muslim community leader told me, caused a local mullah to tell parents not to let their children participate in the school nativity play as that would be *haraam*. *Haraam!* I hadn't heard that word for years. In the end, the English children had to be bussed to a different school to watch a nativity play at Christmas.

'That's so wrong,' I said to the community leader.

'But what can we do?' he said, shrugging his shoulders. 'Most of these mullahs are uneducated. We tell the authorities not to let them in but they don't want to upset anyone. But, ultimately, you know what the real problem is?' Saquib shook his head. 'These mullahs practise culture, not Islam.'

I groaned inwardly. Wasn't that refrain past its sell-by date? In fact, wasn't it high time that Muslims took responsibility for their situation?

'All right, can I help?' I heard someone ask me in a playful northern accent as I walked in. I had wandered into a fruit and vegetable shop on my way back from a meeting at a local community centre in Huddersfield. From the traditional way the woman was dressed – with a black scarf around her head – I hadn't expected her to speak English.

'Umm, I'm a TV producer,' I said, desperate for some female interaction.

'Why don't you hang around? I could introduce you to some local women,' said Naima, after hearing me out.

'OK,' I replied.

A broad grin erupted on her face, as it did on Sanya's, her assistant. I think the idea of aiding a journalist in her duties must have seemed like a pleasant diversion from their everyday tasks. And more so because of the exotic creature I must have appeared to them. I was a young Asian woman like them, and yet I didn't behave like one.

'So, what, you just staying at a B and B on your own?' Naima asked warily, as if it was the strangest thing she had ever heard.

'Uhh, yes,' I said somewhat sheepishly.

'And you don't have any relatives up here?' asked Sanya.

'Well, I'm here for work, aren't I?' I said, trying to sound enthusiastic. I caught Sanya throw a look of alarm at Naima.

'Wow, my mother doesn't even allow me to go into town on me own,' said Sanya in utter amazement. 'But you are Muslim, aren't you? With a name like Yasmin.'

'Yes, I am Muslim.'

'But your mother's white, right?'

'Uhh, no. Both my parents are Muslims.'

'Oh, you don't behave like a Muslim. I mean, no offence, but . . .'

'Don't worry.' I smiled, desperate to change the subject. 'So, do you live with your family?'

'Oh, yes,' said Naima. 'Three teenage boys.'

'Teenagers!' I exclaimed. Naima looked as if she was the same age as me, if not younger.

'Oh yes, *marsh'allah*,' said Naima, proudly.

Just then an old man dressed in *kurta kameez* and a religious hat entered the shop. Naima instantly readjusted her scarf over her head and lowered her gaze. 'Me husband,' she whispered to me.

On cue, I lowered my head, though, in the duty of reporting, I allowed myself to have a peek. I was thrown by how old he was. His face was gaunt and withered and though he had the build of a Pathan, strong and burly, he carried himself with an air of timid resignation. In a different place – i.e. Pakistan – maybe he would have walked with greater confidence. But here in Huddersfield he appeared diminished, fearful of life, unlike his British-born wife, who seemed scared of nothing.

A few minutes after her husband left the shop, a young pasty-faced Englishman with a shorn head marched in. 'Oi, Paki,' he said, throwing some apples and potatoes onto the counter.

'What, honky?' said Naima, reaching for a brown-paper bag.

I relaxed, suddenly realising that this must be some private joke between them. But it wasn't. Apparently, stocky pasty man was a local racist of sorts, but over the years had developed a

306

grudging respect for Naima because she could give back as good as she got.

'What, another of your relatives?' stocky skinhead sneered, spotting me glaring at him.

'No, she's a TV producer,' said Naima proudly.

'Oh,' said skinhead, looking at me with new interest.

'Oh look, there's yer friend, Osama,' he said with a cruel chuckle, glancing at a car that had pulled up outside the shop. It didn't park directly outside, but a few yards up.

'That ain't me friend,' said Naima firmly, but I noticed her cheeks colouring.

'Whatever you say, Paki,' said the skinhead, menacingly tapping his fingers on the counter. As he left the shop, he burst out laughing.

'Ugh. Who is he?' I said.

'Oh, he's all right,' Naima cried, grabbing her coat and a black scarf. 'Look, I'm popping out, but Sanya will look after you while I am away, OK?'

And before I could reply, Naima was out of the door. I looked at Sanya, in confusion. 'Where's she going?'

'Driving lessons. Don't tell anyone. Her man would go spare,' Sanya said conspiratorially.

'Oh,' I said, slightly amused by the fact that, apart from Sanya and me, only the skinhead was in on the secret.

Later on, when Naima returned, she invited me for tea. As we walked up the stairs from the shop floor, she whispered, 'If me husband asks, just say you're having a *salwar kameez* made up. Don't tell him that you are a journalist.'

'Oh,' I said, uneasy at my controversial status. But I didn't have to worry because, their being a traditional family meant that, as soon as I entered their living area, *purdah* came into effect.

'Wait here,' said Naima ushering me into what must have been the boys' bedroom. Outside the room I could hear some commotion, which I assumed was the husband and sons being moved to the living room.

'OK, coast clear,' said Naima popping her head back in. She beckoned me to follow her. The hallway was poorly lit and smelt of damp, which only accentuated the unease I was feeling. But when I entered the kitchen, it was a different matter.

'Wow,' I said, marvelling at the décor. It wasn't exactly my style – kitchen surfaces of green Formica, patterned, tiled walls so cooking splashes could easily be wiped away and a huge industrial-sized freezer situated in the corner – but I knew my mother would have been impressed.

'Me husband and boys did it up for me as a surprise,' Naima said, lowering her gaze shyly.

I nodded again with appreciation.

'So, you married?' asked Naima as she rolled out some flour to make chapattis. My mouth began to water.

'No,' I said, unfazed by the abruptness of her question. It was obvious I wasn't married, but I knew Naima wanted to know more.

'How come?'

'Haven't found the right person,' I replied, deciding that it would be unwise to tell her that I had a boyfriend, let alone one who was married.

'What, you finding your own husband?' said Naima, giggling at the idea.

I nodded, smiling.

'And your mum, she all right about you not being married and travelling around on your own?' said Naima.

I was about to say, yes, but something about Naima's sisterly

308

manner, made me say, 'Umm, no.' I caught Naima looking side-
ways at me. I could tell she thought that, despite my exciting
career, my life was in a mess. Sitting here in Naima's kitchen, in
the heartland of 'Asian Muslim Britain', I couldn't help thinking
that maybe she had a point. I felt my cheeks flush as I recalled
my last visit to my mother with Jay.

I don't know why I wanted her to meet him, but I did, and
finally my mother had given in and invited us over to dinner. But
she hadn't taken to him at all, not one bit. In fact, the instant
Jay walked through the door, dressed in a shabby denim jacket
and reeking of cigarette smoke, I saw her face fall. It wasn't just
a little droop at the corners of her mouth. It was as if all the
blood had drained out of her face – her skin was ashen. And
though she remained totally charming towards Jay, serving him
plenty of food, even laughing at his impersonation of a Nigerian
businessman, I could see she was disappointed. She remained
slightly distracted throughout the evening, as if she was trying
to work out how – after everything she and my father had done
for me – I could choose to end up being with someone who
didn't have a penny. And, even worse, a man who was married
with children.

And now, sitting there with Naima, I finally understood just
what I had put my mother through by asking her to meet Jay;
someone of whom I knew she would disapprove. I suddenly felt
for her. All my life she had worked hard to keep up with who I
was, always trying to accept my British way of life. What had I
ever done to respect or understand hers?

'What about your friends. Any of them married?' Naima
asked.

I was about to shake my head, when I realised that it was no
longer true. At some point, while I had been busy travelling or
working, most of my friends had either got married or settled

down. How did that happen? It was somewhat akin to my plans to buy a house for my mother and me to live in together. I kept postponing it, always arguing that I was too busy. Until now, when everyone else owned a house and there I was, priced out of the market. But, hey, at least I could take consolation in the fact that I had an exciting job in TV!

Just then I heard my mobile phone ring. I had left my bag in the hallway. As I reached for my phone, it stopped. As I scrolled down to see who had rung, a text from my exec popped up. It said something along the lines of: 'Any progress on rads?!'

A shiver ran down me. I hastily threw the phone back into my bag. As I got up to return to the kitchen, I caught sight of Naima's husband and her sons sitting in the living room. I would have averted my eyes, but something about the scene compelled me to look. There they were, her sons. Archetypal British Muslim boys, dressed in designer tracksuits with shorn hair and the beginnings of beards on their pimply chins. But they weren't watching TV or banging around arguing, like I would have been doing at my mother's house. They were sitting dutifully around their father as he read the Urdu daily paper. It wasn't necessarily the serenity between them that moved me, but rather seeing – in this day and age, in this impoverished place – the ancient idea of respect for an elder being played out. How often did one see that these days?

As I left, I gave Naima a big hug. Yes, I resented the fact that she had to be so mindful of what her husband might say. But, on the other hand, look how far they had both come from the way things were done back home. No woman in her family had ever enjoyed such freedom before, being allowed to run a shop. In fact, in one generation she had made a massive leap and, more

310

amazingly, managed to keep her family totally intact. That was something to be applauded.

During my research trips I discovered a new, articulate generation of Muslims emerging who were not shy about engaging with uncomfortable media questions. Though when the list of questions was whittled down, it usually meant clarifying Muslim positions on terrorism, extremism, women's rights and dodgy mullahs. Still, in the current climate, where one only heard the skewed views of the Muslim radicals, it was heartening to hear intelligent British Muslim opinion. And yet not everyone shared my enthusiasm.

'But if it's tension you want in the film,' I said, trying to keep my voice steady, 'you've got it between the different Muslim voices.'

'No, no, no,' replied the exec. 'Isn't there anyone you've spoken to who says that nine-eleven was a good thing?'

'I grudgingly opened up my notebook. 'Bradford, Blackburn, Crawley,' I heard the exec say, hoping to jog my memory by citing the places I had visited. Despite his sing-song voice, I knew he was getting edgy. I continued scanning my notes. It would be so easy to turn this unpleasant situation around. I could look up at the exec, be my usual charming TV self, forward him my interviewees' names and everyone would love me again.

But I had had enough. Career or no career, this wasn't worth it. 'Umm, no,' I said, banging my notebook shut, startling the exec. 'No one jumps out at me.'

'I think we're going to have to rethink this story,' said the exec, put out by my diffident manner.

'Yeah, good idea,' I replied, nodding thoughtfully at him. 'I'll put my mind to it, too.'

Although I felt a massive burden lift from me as the meeting disbanded, I also felt sad. There was an urgent need to explain who British Muslims were and, similarly, for British Muslims to confront their issues. And the fact that I couldn't help facilitate the debate at work left me feeling disappointed.

22

Paul – the American

'Are you sure?' said Paul, staring at me sceptically.

'What do you mean, am I sure?' We were standing in the departure lounge about to board a plane home from Rome and my shrill voice was beginning to attract looks. 'Those Muslims who go round saying anti-Semitic things, well they're just politically unsophisticated. My dad always used to tell us how Jews were our role models.'

Paul didn't reply but I could see he wasn't too convinced.

'You know,' he said finally, as we handed in our boarding cards at the check-in desk. 'I really think you should write an article about this.'

'Don't be silly,' I replied, rolling my eyes. Though deep down I felt flattered that Paul would think my views could be of interest to anyone.

Given half a chance, I would have loved to write an article that would offer some insight on Muslims – especially in these days and times. But the problem was I was terrified of putting my views down on paper. Was writing an article that would put

British Muslims under more scrutiny the sensible thing to do? Even if it was, was I the right person to be doing it? I mean, even though I identified with being a Muslim more than ever, there would be many of my co-religionists who would say I wasn't a proper Muslim. No, I decided, it was better to steer clear of the issue – and leave it to a 'real' Muslim to put the record straight about the community.

The problem was Paul. He wouldn't let the matter go.

'I really wish you would write,' he said again, as we boarded the plane. 'I don't think people out there really know what Muslims are like. Or at least what you're saying they're like.'

I sighed, but a nagging feeling of frustration lingered. That – and a terrible sense of guilt.

I had only known Paul for a month and he was already turning my life upside down. I had met him a few minutes after I had left Jay's flat. And by left, I mean walked out of our relationship for good, with all my belongings squeezed into a black bin-liner.

It wasn't an easy decision. But the relationship was no longer working. So, one morning, with a heavy heart, I got up and left. As I closed his front door behind me, panic gripped me. I had never felt this insecure when my other relationships had ended. But Jay was the closest I had come to finding a perfect match. What was the likelihood of ever meeting anyone as suitable again? I hadn't got far from Jay's flat when I heard someone shout my name. The familiar face sitting at the far table outside a café off Inverness Street in Camden Town was Nick, a friend of a friend of a friend dating back to my schooldays, sitting with another man. I was tempted to just nod and walk off. But some desire to prove that I was invincible made me stop.

'Last time I saw you, you were heading off to work,' Nick said as I drew near him. 'At the BBC, wasn't it?'

I nodded. I felt tongue-tied, unable to answer. Maybe I wasn't so invincible after all.

'My friend here has just finished a film,' Nick said quickly to cover the embarrassing pause. He turned to his acquaintance. With the sun in my eyes, I was only aware of a huge man wearing a suit.

'Yeah, it's about . . .' I heard an American voice drawl.

I made an effort to listen, but it was difficult. These days any conversation about the media made me switch off. I nodded politely, even when the American cringingly dropped in the words 'asylum seekers' and 'immigration'. I must have made a witty retort, because Nick's acquaintance laughed out very loud and then asked if he could have my number. He said he was desperate to pick the brains of someone who worked in British television.

I was taken aback by this American's forwardness and I think Nick was too – I later found out that it was the first and last time they'd ever met – but we both pretended that, in the spirit of networking, it was the most normal thing to ask for my number like that.

'Twat,' I muttered to myself, walking away. Banging on about asylum seekers. How predictable could one get? But I had given him my number.

A few weeks later found me making my way up Charlotte Street to meet the American to discuss TV. I was riddled with doubts. First off, being from New York, he was bound to have dodgy views about Muslims. Next, he could be some weirdo for all I knew. I hastily wiped off my lipgloss.

Paul certainly didn't fit into any familiar box. I wasn't sure I liked him. I had decided that he had been too forceful on the phone when asking me for advice about his impending meeting at some production company. I tried to put him in his place,

315

telling him how crap TV was. It was a wonder we were meeting at all. 'We're only meeting to discuss work,' I told myself as I walked into the bar. 'One drink and out,' I decided, as I spotted him sitting by the window in an armchair. He was rather good-looking – how come I hadn't noticed that before?

We launched into an immediate conversation about work.

'Oh, so you're Muslim?' Paul said, when I finished telling him about some of the programmes I had recently worked on.

'Yes,' I replied, defiantly. That'll throw him, I thought. Make him keep his distance. He really did look far too straight for me, reclining there in an armchair in that smart John Smedley jumper. But he didn't appear one bit put out by my response. In fact, he seemed genuinely interested in my back-ground and what I had to say about it, which flattered me no end. Who listened to me these days? Let alone laughed so hard at my jokes?

'It's funny, I don't think I've ever met a Muslim,' he said when we decided to order more drinks. Just one more, I said to myself.

'Well, I'm not a religious Muslim.' Now that I decided I kind of liked him, I thought it best to put the record straight. 'To be honest, my father was an atheist,' I explained wondering why I had brought my father up. 'Actually, he was a hard-core Communist.'

'Really?' said Paul. 'So was my grandfather.'

I looked at Paul with new interest. Suddenly he felt less alien. In fact, his jumper looked really nice on him. And that was the beginning. When I sheepishly admitted that I was the only Muslim I knew who hadn't read the Koran – thinking that the significance of my confession would be totally lost on him – he had replied that he was the only Jew he knew who hadn't been bar mitzvahed.

316

As for his film about immigrants and asylum seekers – the one that I had been so dismissive about the day we first met – that proved to be riveting. It was about a mysterious, stateless man called Alfred who had been living in bureaucratic limbo on a bench in Charles de Gaulle Airport for the last decade or so. Wow! What an original take on the subject of belonging!

It wasn't long before we became inseparable. And yet, I didn't totally trust the relationship. For a start, I had never been one to rush from one relationship to another. Could you really find another soulmate so quickly – and accidentally? And secondly, even though Paul felt very familiar to me, he was also very different. I had spent my life being fascinated by ethnic differences and what being the 'other' meant, but when it came to Paul – who truly was the 'other' in my eyes – I wasn't always prepared to accept the differences between us. The post-9/11 times we were living in made me edgy.

I might have appeared to be cheery, but inside I was a mass of anger, ready to combust at any minute. If I hadn't spent the day raging over what some media pundit had said about Muslim suicide bombers or Arab 'limb-amputators' (Kilroy-Silk); or what some Western feminist declared on the oppressed state of Muslim women; or how another schoolboy called Osama had just had his fingers broken in the playground; or hearing another politician bang on about Muslim segregation and Islamic head-dress; or the impact of the government's latest security initiative, I found myself spending much of my day-to-day life explaining to non-Muslims who Muslims were. In the past, I would have relished a passionate debate on the subject. But now I shied away from it.

That is why in my private life I sought solace and familiarity. I didn't want to be with someone to whom I would have to explain the fundamentals of my life. And with Paul, a white,

317

middle-class American male, I found myself having a lot of explaining to do.

My sister's wedding, an extravagant Wembley affair that my mother was organising at Ealing Town Hall for three hundred guests, was almost too much for me and our relationship.

Much to my sister's alarm, my mother had reinvented herself as a professional wedding planner. She had hired a DJ outfit – Soundz of Vemblee – to proudly play their eclectic mix of bhangra, hip-hop and Bollywood tunes, which would be amplified ten-fold by their gigantic speakers, more commonly found at Glastonbury. She had already hired an Indian video firm – Romantique – to capture the entire event on their state-of-the-art Dixon's home-video camera. And she had booked Mr Sidiqui and Mr Rehman to do the catering: on polystyrene plates, with plastic cutlery and bottles of Coca-Cola. But, most importantly, she had put down a massive deposit on a pair of gold and purple Rajasthani thrones on which the bride and groom were to sit on stage.

'No way am I sitting on that!' Farah cried in despair when my mother showed her a picture of the thrones. But my mother wasn't having any of it. She had waited long enough to see one of us get married, and she wasn't about to settle for some modest affair – she was going for all the trimmings. Then, suddenly, a few days before the wedding, she was rushed to hospital. We suggested postponing the wedding, but my mother wouldn't hear of it.

'You stay put and get your health back. Better to be alive so you can see your future grandchildren,' said Mrs Jobson while visiting my mother. Over the years they had become the closest of friends. 'The Lord has a reasoning for everything.'

My mother, ever susceptible to such fatalism, thought these to be very wise words.

Paul had taken pity on me and in his idiosyncratic, bulldozing way, had invited himself to the wedding. I did have to suppress a little giggle when I saw him turn up at Ealing Town Hall. He looked so monumentally out of place, walking up the would-be grand municipal staircase in his blue Savile Row suit, trailing behind Aunt Feroz's four-generation family, dressed in their shiniest outfits from Ealing Road.

'Nice dress,' he had said, staring at my orange-sequinned sari.

'It's called a sari,' I replied tersely.

'Doesn't anyone mingle?' Paul had said, peering into the main hall. His eyes skirted the rows of Asian families, piously refraining from small talk as they waited for the bride to arrive. Over the years, while Sikh and Hindu weddings had become more 'exotic' events, Wembley Muslim weddings had become increasingly dreary, something the ladies of the *mahalla* were very proud of.

'We never allowed any music at Munir's wedding,' Aunt Bilquis once proclaimed, showing off her Islamic credentials. 'Not even a tape recorder.'

'We didn't either,' Mrs Khan had quickly responded, not one to be outdone. 'In fact, when Afshan got married, it was simple-pimple. No biriyani, only rice and dhal.' Hence the dour ambience at my sister's wedding. Even the Jobsons and Mrs McGuinness, sitting at the far end of the room, were staring into blank space.

From the corner of my eye I saw Perveen and Shazia motion towards Paul and mouth to me, 'Cor, he's fit.' I don't think they had ever imagined that I could go out with someone who was, well, fit. I think in their minds they saw me being with some weedy intellectual guy.

Spurred on by the Bhajis' approval, I was softening my attitude when I noticed Paul's body had tensed up. He was staring uncomfortably at the *hijab* posse. What was he thinking, I wondered. Was he feeling his Americanness and Jewishness? I felt Paul cast his eyes over me. My heart jumped. Was he wondering, what am I doing with her? That's when I remember thinking: What am I doing with him?

It was a thought that would frequently cross my mind over the next few months, especially when political conversations between us felt more like Paul cross-examining me on Islam, race, weapons of mass destruction, Afghanistan, etc. Why couldn't he leave me alone? Couldn't he see how exposed I felt talking about such issues in the current climate?

What made the situation even worse was that it was precisely the times we were living in that made our relationship so fascinating to others, prompting even more questions. 'So is it a problem that he's Jewish and you're Muslim?' our friends would frequently ask us. 'What about your parents? Do they approve?'

'Of course they do,' I would answer. And I suppose that was kind of true. As Peter, Paul's father told me, he had never given Muslims a second thought – that is, until 9/11. And now he had met me, well he didn't think any differently either.

'As far as I am concerned,' he said, patting my knee affectionately. 'You are just an English girl who happens to have brown skin.'

My mother had other concerns. I had brought Paul round for dinner, confident that my mother would finally approve of my choice of boyfriend. But she wasn't impressed; the facts were just not adding up. 'But how can you be both American and Austrian?' my mother asked Paul, her voice full of suspicion. She had commandeered the main sofa in the room and was firing her questions from there. The way my mother saw it, people fell into two categories. Those who had a British passport and those who did not. And as far as she was concerned, those who did not have British citizenship would do anything to get it. Paul with his two citizenships and homes in different countries was sounding too complicated, if not dodgy.

'Ahh, well,' said Paul, oblivious to the subtext in my mother's question, 'it dates back to the Second World War when the Nazis . . .'

'Oh, shame,' said my mother, shaking her head. 'So bad what happened to the Jews.'

'Yeah, well, my family lived in Austria and they had to flee. In fact, they fled to France where my father lives now. I lived there too, for a while.'

'France?' said my mother, sitting up with a start. 'Why are Americans living in France?'

I rarely saw Afshan these days. I tried to tell myself this was because she was busy with family. But deep down, I knew Afshan disapproved of my lifestyle and, if I was honest, I wasn't exactly keen on hers, either. In fact, every time I rang her home, her four-year-old daughter would pick up the phone and, before you had a chance to say hello, she would say, 'Hello, are you a Muslim?'

'What does it matter?' I would want to scream.

But, despite our differences, I felt nostalgic for the old times. So, when Afshan invited me around to her house and told me that Perveen would be coming too, I happily said yes. As I approached Afshan's flat, from Kilburn High Road, I saw her waving at me from her balcony. Who could miss the black scarf? I waved back, warmed by her friendliness. But it was only when I was halfway across the road that it hit me: the woman I was waving to wasn't Afshan. It was Perveen.

'Surprised eh?' she said, as she ran down to meet me in the courtyard.

'No. Why should I be?' I said, smiling brightly, as if it was the most normal thing for Perveen, lifestyle queen, to be wearing a headscarf.

'What does Asif say?' I asked, trying not to stare. Asif was her husband.

'Well, he's scared for me, isn't he?' she sighed. 'But that's more reason why I've got to do it. Why should I run away from being Muslim?'

Even though Afshan and Perveen stuffed me with samosas and then gave me a detailed rundown of what was going on in the *mahalla*, I couldn't help feeling that they were behaving rather guardedly. Not once did they slag anyone off. That was a first. The one time Perveen nearly called Aunt Ruhksanah's newly arrived Pakistani daughter-in-law a bitch, Afshan hastily intervened and said, 'It's not for us to judge, only Allah can.'

Perveen was feeling vexed because Aunt Ruhksanah's ultra-modern daughter-in-law from Pakistan had said to Perveen, in a posh Bollywood accent, after looking her up and down in obvious horror: '*Urreh yaar*, why you wearing that scarf on your head? This is England.'

'I tell you, right, if Allah hadn't been on my side, I'd have smacked her across the face,' said Perveen.

It might not have been the respite I was looking for, but at least I felt better for laughing.

'So, how's things?' asked Afshan, turning to me.

I sighed. Finding myself in sympathetic company, I began telling them about how, since 9/11, all my old insecurities about fitting in, about being British had returned. What made it worse was that there were so few people around me who I could talk to about how I felt.

'You know,' Afshan said, smiling sympathetically. 'Once upon

322

a time, I would have probably felt the same. But since I became a proper Muslim, I no longer feel those insecurities.'

'Really?' I said, unsure of the direction the conversation was going in.

Afshan nodded. 'When we were growing up, we used to go out, have a laugh, do all the things that English people do, but you know what?' she said, her voice hardening. 'I never knew who I was.' Afshan stopped. She didn't need to elaborate, for both Perveen and I knew what she was getting at. 'You don't realise how unhappy and insecure you are at the time. It only hits you when you're older. And by then it's too late.'

Something about Afshan's candour made me sit up. When was the last time I had heard her speak from her heart? Speak without peppering her language with Islamic citations.

'Same with me,' nodded Perveen. 'This will always be my country for good or for bad. But the main thing is that I no longer feel insecure. Allah's changed my life. Yours could change too.'

I looked at them and felt this deep desire to be persuaded. They both looked at me, willing me to join them. How incredible it would be to be at peace with myself.

'We were so lost before, look at the madness we got up to,' I heard Afshan say.

And in that instant, I hurtled back to reality. 'It wasn't that bad,' I said, annoyed. I'm sure I had been here with Afshan before. How dare she belittle our – my – past? I didn't want to run away from it. I spent some of the best years of my life growing up in Wembley. In fact, that era of multiculturalism, so unpopular these days, was the best thing that had ever happened to me. Why should I throw away my memories – why should I rewrite them? I suddenly wanted to leave, return to my life with Paul, where experience, argument and debate were cherished, not stultified.

'You know what?' Afshan said, knowingly. 'I think you will come round one day. I really do.'

I shrugged.

It was raining when I left Afshan's house and my mood was similarly grey. Part of me wondered if I had just turned my back on something that could have changed my life for the better. I envied Afshan and Perveen for their conviction. They were as convinced about their own view of the world as most English people I knew were about theirs. Why couldn't I have certainty in my own life?

But one thing I did know: how little of Afshan's and Perveen's embrace of Islam had anything to do with the Koran. The experts might blame the Koran and segregation for Islamacising Muslim youth. But, speaking to Afshan and Perveen, it was obvious to me that their life struggle was about something closer to home, something more human. It was about belonging. All their lives, they had been outsiders. Outsiders in Britain. Outsiders in a community which they often held in contempt. But in Islam they had found respect, purpose and, most importantly, belonging. Not that Afshan and Perveen or even Amir would ever agree with me, so desperate were they to erase their ungodly past as British children in the seventies.

I was sick of the self-deception and crudeness of the debate. I had to reclaim my history before it became conveniently forgotten. Suddenly Paul's idea of writing an article that might give an insight into a British Muslim community – albeit through its attitudes to anti-Semitism – began to appeal to me. But how to approach the story? I wanted to explore why attitudes towards Jews, amongst those I knew, had hardened in recent years. It hadn't been like that when I was growing up. I knew my views on the subject could end up offending everyone. Jewish people could think I was minimising anti-Semitism and Muslims could say I was betraying the community by bringing the subject up. But I thought it was an important issue to raise — anti-Semitism was leaving the Muslim community morally bankrupt.

I had to start with my father, who had first introduced me to Jews and the concept of anti-Semitism. But I found myself shying away from writing about him. It felt strange celebrating his views on Muslim–Jewish relationships when I felt so ambivalent about his other political ideas, especially his stance on Britishness.

Is that all you're going to say about your dad?' said Paul who, irritatingly, had been trying to read my article over my shoulder.

'What do you mean?' I said, covering my work with my hands.

'Well, you could expand upon what kind of man he was, his ideas and . . .' continued Paul, refusing to be brushed off.

'Why?' I said, looking at my article. I had succinctly described what my father had told me about Jews; what else was there to say?

'Wouldn't he have disapproved of the way your community has turned to Islam?'

'Yes, but he wouldn't have been necessarily right,' I cut in sharply.

'I don't know what your problem is,' Paul said sceptically. 'But I think you've got a block about your father somewhere.'

'Don't be silly,' I said, forgetting the doubts and anger that had erupted towards my father a few years back. No, Paul had obviously misread the situation. After all, being an Asian, I could only have the highest respect for my elders. I dared not think about it any further. This was taboo material. But I put my head down and wrote. I did manage to cobble an article together. And, luckily for me, it was well received. The biggest thrill in seeing my article in the *Guardian*, my words in print, was that it felt like the most honest piece of work I had ever done.

But that wasn't what pleased my mother. A few months later, much to her relief, Paul and I got married.

My mother might have had her doubts about Paul and be wary of 'love marriages', but after the wedding ceremony – a tear-soaked, emotional affair climaxing in a big passionate kiss for the bride from the groom, causing my mother to lower her eyes with embarrassment – she seemed to have revised her position.

'You know,' she said solemnly, steering Paul and I aside. There was obviously something on her mind, an important realisation. In her role as elder wise woman, it was something she felt duty-bound to share with us. 'I think that you will both be very happy.'

23

Mr Hai's Daughter

There is something eerie about breastfeeding your child, giving him sustenance, while images of death and carnage play out on the television screen.

Our son, Nico, was born a few days before the 7 July 2005 terror attacks. The baby-advice books for new parents advised that a child be breastfed in a stress-free environment – as if that was possible in the world we now lived in. Several times I had to turn the television off so as not to transfer negative hormones to the baby during feeding. Or that is how I explained it to my mother, who was fast coming to the conclusion that I was odder than ever. She was finding my whole approach to baby-rearing, complete with routines and strictly timed naps, totally perplexing.

'Why is the baby sitting in front of the washing machine?' she asked me another time, while I watched a police press conference on the Stockwell shooting in 7/7's aftermath.

'Babies find the sound of the washing machine soothing,' I said, impatiently. 'The book says it reminds them of the womb.'

'Womb,' my mother replied. 'But he's baby — how he remember womb?'

'OK, Mum,' I sighed. The last thing I wanted was a lecture from my mother on how to bring my son up. 'Look, I need to watch this.'

'Oh, that,' she said contemptuously, looking at the screen. 'Idiots. These mad Muslims — heads grown too big.'

During the coverage I would often catch Paul looking at me, wondering what I thought, especially when it was discovered that the bombers were British-born. But I refused to answer him. Since 9/11, I had spent a lot of time explaining British Muslims. And yet, when it came to discussing the extremists, exploring who they were, I always held back, arguing that they were just misguided youth, all talk and no action who would only revel in media attention.

I was wrong. So wrong. The extremists hadn't been all talk and no action. Some of them had been sufficiently evil, indoctrinated, alienated, angry, driven — whatever adjective one may care to use — to do the unthinkable: perpetrate terror attacks on British soil, murder their fellow citizens. I felt humiliated and consumed with anger. How dare the bombers try to speak on every British Muslim's behalf?

But as the coverage of the attacks continued to unfold, revealing more details on the suicide bombers, other questions arose. The bombers might blame Blair's foreign policy for their terrorist attacks, but I remained convinced that factors closer to home might offer better explanation. What had alienated them from their fellow British citizens in the first place to attract them to an interpretation of Islam that favoured murder as a vehicle of protest?

These are the questions I hoped the politicians and pundits would ask. But instead it wasn't long before the journalists were gallivanting around Pakistan in their field jackets, searching out *madrassas*, Islamic schools, as if they might hold the answers to the terrorists' motives.

'But the bombers are British,' said a bemused President Musharraf in a BBC radio interview. Britain refused to see the Muslim extremists in their country as their story. Instead, much to my dismay, hostile criticism of Muslims and multiculturalism resumed, in tandem with a predictable debate over Britishness. As ever, the real story was soon lost.

Ever since 9/11 I had anguished over the Muslim part of my identity. But I now realised that my Britishness was just as troublesome. I had always been proud of being British, but the way politicians and the media were now forcing their phoney definitions down our throats – superficially evoking the principles of the Enlightenment along the way – left me feeling less British than I had ever felt in my entire life.

Could I have ever imagined, a few years back, that we would return to such dark times, when 'being different' would incite such hostility? But then, as a child would I have ever imagined a time when we would even discuss our immigrant selves in the same context as our Muslim selves? If my father was alive today, he would have certainly been horrified. He would have probably blamed multiculturalism.

It was Paul who suggested that I should visit my father's grave.

'Are you mad?' I had cried at Paul when he mentioned the idea. Soon hot tears were streaming down my face. Paul looked at me in alarm. I don't think he had realised the emotions his suggestion would open up in me. Neither did I. Was I feeling guilty? My father had been dead for some twenty years. I am ashamed to say that in that whole time, I had never visited his burial site. The thought of seeing his final resting place had always terrified me so much that I had gladly hidden behind the excuse provided by the aunties: Muslim women don't visit cemeteries.

Courtesy of Afshan, I now knew that this was not true. 'Course you can visit,' she once told me. 'You know the aunts. They practise culture, not Islam.'

The June morning sun is intense, but a tranquil peace rests over the cemetery. We've parked by the chapel, under a shady oak tree and are searching the cemetery grounds, looking for the Muslim section where my father is buried. Names from all over the world are engraved in the headstones. Chavez, Mohammed, Smith, Bari, McGovern, but so far no Hai. Looking at the well-tended sites adorned with wreaths and pretty potted plants, I worry about the state of my father's gravestone. I fear the worst. His grave unkempt, desolate, a weed-ridden bit of earth – the Hai family's ultimate shame.

'Are you OK?' Paul asks. He's trailing a few steps behind, carrying our son.

I nod, stoically. But I don't feel that way. Ever since I made the decision to visit, it's as if I've left myself open to an invasion from my past, legions of uncomfortable truths that I find difficult to acknowledge. I do have a block about my father. It seems that I have spent a good deal of my life feeling very conflicted about him. At times, ashamed. The shame, I suppose, I can account for. Growing up in England, hadn't I been taught from an early age that immigrants, especially 'Pakis', were an embarrassment? But my feelings had been even more intense because my father had also been the epitome of an English gentleman – something which, as I grew older, I had come to resent far more. For to me the English were a group of people who I could never belong to. They were responsible for inculcating me with feelings of self-doubt and silent rage.

To my relief, I find my father's gravestone has been well maintained. A handsome red rosebush grows over it, flowers in the breeze gently caressing the top of Syed Samsamul Hai's headstone.

Beloved Husband
and
Father

I try to recall some of the anger I have felt for so long, hoping to provoke cathartic tears. But none come. Instead, confronted with his humble resting place, in this most serene of spots, all I feel is a deep peace descending upon me.

Who was this man, my father? Why, he was just an ordinary Indian man who came to this country and worked hard to support his family and raise his three children to be good British citizens. Anyone who might care to look at my brother, my sister and me would say that my father had achieved his ambitions. Operation Children had been a success, after all. And Operation Wife, come to that. So how could I have allowed my memories of him to become so clouded?

That evening, I return home to my mother's house to dig out my father's articles. There are six of them, commentary pieces published in a Pakistani political magazine. The last time I looked at them was when earnest Graham from the SWP visited our house. But in my now calmer and sanguine state, I feel I am finally ready to look at them again. As I open the magazine, the corners musty and brown from age, all my old wariness returns. What if I uncover some half-baked political opinion? What if my father really does turn out to be an apologist for Stalin? Or an anti-Semite, for that matter? Or an Uncle Tom who rejected Islam because he saw it as being a product of the East?

331

I skim the sentences and slowly I get drawn into Mr Hai's thoughts on Pakistan's nascent democracy, Islam, the China–USSR fallout and other urgent topics of his times. I can't help being impressed by the thoughtfulness of his arguments and the clarity of his writing style.

There is one article that seems especially powerful and prophetic. Even though his subject was Pakistan in the 1950s, his argument has a resonance today:

> . . . unless we remove the blinker of 'religion' from our eyes, we cannot take an enlightened and correct view of our predicament. Religion may act as a channel between an individual and his creator, but it has no place in state ideology or politics. Religion always encourages dogma and it has always been an irrational force. It has always denied the validity of human reason. It has tried to understand the world by intuition rather than experience. It has always stood for authority against the individual.

I put down the article, confused. Of course, I agree with my father. Religion doesn't have a role to play in politics or in our public lives. And yet, I don't feel entirely comfortable with his conclusions. My father's disapproval of religion extended to a disapproval of our old culture and ethnic loyalties. He couldn't accept such ideas having any bearing on our modern British selves. And yet, that was what provided me with an invaluable sense of who I was in later life.

My father never understood why, in the England I had grown up in – complete with Union Jacks, swamping speeches by Thatcher, Paki beatings and later calls for loyalty test – embracing my 'other' self was so important. And wasn't it the case that

332

being close to my cultural heritage also allowed me to reconnect with my mother after my father's death. I had lost one parent, I couldn't bear losing another.

At first, it had been painful to accept the vast gulf between us, which first opened on that afternoon many years ago when my father, Uncle Aslam and Aunt Hilda decreed that it would be best if my mother no longer spoke to us children in Urdu. But, slowly, I had found a way to get to know and respect her again. In fact, during those difficult years following my father's death, my mother's no-nonsense, pragmatic attitude to life had been an inspiration. And today, even though my mother and I rarely agree on much, we've found a way of accommodating each other. Though with three grandchildren and two son-in-laws to look after and feed, my mother doesn't have time to dwell on the faultlines of our relationship.

But these days, I wonder whether the price one pays to belong can be too high. I lament how some of my old friends in the *mahalla* have compromised their individuality, ready to go along with every diktat or folly of tribal politics in their desperate need to belong. But I think about what my father did in order to belong. Here, I suppose, I must be thankful to him. Yes, he put me on a path towards assimilation, but he also gave me the tools to take control of my life and to resist the easy answers – so alluring in these confusing days. What better gift could a father pass on to a child?

My father hadn't brought me up to cower behind tradition or look to others to speak on my behalf. Even though I am a girl, he had always encouraged me to speak up for myself. Time to reclaim his legacy, find my true voice – which lives between various worlds – and work out the making of Mr Hai's daughter.

But there is one problem.

'Mum, I'm writing this book about Dad and being British . . .'

'No politics,' my mother cuts in.

For a second I flinch, my usual reticence instantly flooding back. How can I be both a good daughter and the writer of a book that will divulge personal material about our family on such a sensitive subject? And then, I think, if I don't write and others don't either, how will we Asian Muslims ever contribute to the debate – mostly being conducted by others – about our Britishness?

After all, this is our country too.

www.virago.co.uk

virago

To find out more about Yasmin Hai and
other Virago authors, visit:
www.virago.co.uk

Visit the Virago website for:

- Exclusive features and interviews with authors, including Margaret Atwood, Maya Angelou, Sarah Waters and Nina Bawden

- News of author events and forthcoming titles

- Competitions

- Exclusive signed copies

- Discounts on new publications

- Book-group guides

- Free extracts from a wide range of titles

PLUS: subscribe to our free monthly newsletter